Pe(
and Nursing
Intervention

Pediatric Drugs and Nursing Intervention

Helen Russell, R.N., M.A., M.Ed.

Professor of Nursing
Queensborough Community College
of the City University of New York

McGraw-Hill Book Company

New York St. Louis San Francisco Auckland Bogotá Düsseldorf
Johannesburg London Madrid Mexico Montreal New Delhi
Panama Paris São Paulo Singapore Sydney Tokyo Toronto

PEDIATRIC DRUGS AND
NURSING INTERVENTION

Copyright © 1980 by McGraw-Hill, Inc. All rights reserved. Printed in the United States of America. No part of this publication may be reproduced, stored in a retrieval system, or transmitted, in any form or by any means, electronic, mechanical, photocopying, recording, or otherwise, without the prior written permission of the publisher.

2 3 4 5 6 7 8 9 0   SMSM   8 3 2 1 0

This book was set in Caledonia by Bi-Comp, Incorporated. The editors were Laura A. Dysart and Timothy Armstrong; the designer was Elliot Epstein; the production supervisor was Milton J. Heiberg.
Semline, Inc., was printer and binder.

Library of Congress Cataloging in Publication Data

Russell, Helen, date
    Pediatric drugs and nursing intervention.

    Includes index.
    1. Pediatric pharmacology.   2.   Children—
Diseases—Chemotherapy.   3.   Pediatric nursing.
I. Title.
RJ560.R85   618.9′2′0061   79-13320
ISBN 0-07-054298-8

To the memory of my parents
and also to Saul

True believer
A long ways from home

("Sometimes I Feel like
a Motherless Child")

Contents

Preface

Pediatric pharmacology, a dynamic new discipline, studies the unique relationship of growth and developmental processes to both therapeutic and adverse drug responses in infants and children.

Although there has been a decrease in the number of new drugs reaching the market, several interacting trends have increased nursing responsibilities associated with pediatric drug administration.

It has long been recognized that infants and children respond to drug therapy differently than adults, and laboratory analytic techniques which confirm these differences are now in common use. Laboratory studies of pediatric response to antibiotics, anticonvulsants, and digoxin indicate that individual variation in drug response among children of the same age and size is not uncommon. These variations make it clear that laboratory results must be interpreted in light of the individual child's clinical response to the drug. While use of laboratory techniques does provide insights into the prediction and prevention of some adverse drug reactions, it does not replace careful nursing assessment of clinical drug response.

Survival of many high-risk newborn infants and extension of pediatric practice to include adolescent medicine requires the pediatric nurse to understand the growth and developmental characteristics of a patient population which includes small infants and large adolescents.

The rise in expectations and the increased sophistication of health care consumers have produced a demand for accurate, current drug information for children, their parents, and interested community-based groups. As parents and other concerned adults voice growing alarm over use of central nervous system stimulants in school-age children and use of pediatric patients in clinical drug trials, nurses must be prepared to provide the information on which these adults make decisions.

Increasing drug costs make it imperative that nurses avoid unwarranted expenditures by utilizing nursing measures which promote optimal therapeutic effectiveness of each drug which they administer.

While adverse effects produced by some drugs are known and are readily identifiable, a significant number of adverse drug reactions might remain undetected. Such "hidden" reactions are best identified by the nurse, the most consistently available health professional.

The recent changes in several nurse practice acts and the growing numbers of pediatric nurse associates has resulted in many nurses assuming roles formerly filled by physicians.

These trends make it clear that nursing responsibility for pediatric drug administration goes far beyond the manipulative, technical tasks of preparation and administration. While safe, effective drug administration to infants and children requires utilization of these tasks, it also requires knowledge and appreciation of pediatric pharmacology, growth, and development and of the relation of growth and development to drug response.

The goal of this book is to provide a concise, accurate work which summarizes current practical and theoretical information on pediatric pharmacology. It is hoped that the work will increase nursing contributions to the field by stimulating interest in seminars, writing, adverse drug reaction reporting, and other activities. Such participation by nurses will ultimately promote effectiveness of pediatric drug therapy as well as reduce the incidence of adverse drug reactions.

Content presented is not only selective but also concise; consequently, no attempt was made to present comprehensive discussions of growth and development, anatomy and physiology, or fundamentals of nursing. While it was not feasible to include all the drugs prescribed for infants and children, the book does present the more frequently prescribed drugs. Since the mathematical operations of dosage calculation are well presented in other works, no dosage calculation is included. Readers who desire in-depth information on those topics are directed to the many excellent texts available in these areas.

Chapter 1, "Developmental Aspects of Drug Response," addresses drug response and its relationship to the growth and developmental process. Laboratory and clinical methods of assessing both therapeutic and adverse drug response, nursing measures to promote optimal therapeutic response, and nursing interventions to prevent or identify adverse responses are also discussed. The challenges of pediatric dosage and methods of determining appropriate dosage for infants and children are explored. Tables which clarify and summarize adverse drug reactions during gestation, labor, and delivery and after birth are included in this chapter.

Chapter 2, "Administering Drugs to Infants and Children," utilizes text, numerous tables, and selected line drawings which present appropriate nursing interventions associated with drug administration to infants and children of various age groups. Pediatric dosage forms and appropriate administration strategies for all pediatric age groups are presented in depth. Tables detailing the critical steps in the administration of parenteral (subcutaneous, intramuscular, and intravenous) and topical (eye, ear, rectal, and vaginal) drugs are an integral part of the chapter.

In the remainder of the book, drugs are divided into

categories (e.g., topical agents, antineoplastic drugs, etc.), and common properties of each drug category are discussed in text. Unique properties of individual drugs in each category are presented in convenient table format. These tables include official and proprietary names, usual pediatric doses, and pertinent information on administration. Unless otherwise noted, doses cited in this work are those of the *United States Pharmacopeia XIX*.

This book can be used by nursing students and nursing practitioners in the classroom and the clinical setting. As a work which summarizes relevant concepts from several disciplines, the book lends itself to classroom use as a complement to pediatric nursing or pharmacology texts. In the clinical situation it is suitable as a quick reference source for drug information and administration techniques.

I should like to express sincere thanks to consultants Marguerite Luizzo, R.N., Head Nurse, Pediatrics, Queens General Hospital, Jamaica, New York, and to Arturo J. Alballi, M.D., Chairman of Pediatrics, International Hospital, Miami, Florida.

Appreciation is acknowledged for the encouragement and suggestions given by colleagues Elizabeth J. Dickason, R.N., Venus Flowers, R.N., and Katie Mannix, R.N.

Gratitude is expressed for support and assistance received from Mr. Jimmy Calvin, Mrs. Eileen Cohen, Mrs. Ethelin Doman, and Mr. Edward Hinds.

My family is thanked for its understanding, encouragement, and forbearance during the long months of completing this project.

Very special gratitude is extended to Mr. Saul H. Bethay, whose patience, encouragement, assistance, and advice made this book possible.

Helen Russell

Pediatric Drugs and Nursing Intervention

Developmental Aspects of Drug Response

AGE-DEPENDENT FACTORS OF DRUG RESPONSE

The changes which occur as the developing human being progresses from birth to adolescence have profound influence on drug action and effect. The unique differences in neonatal (as opposed to adolescent) drug response are more obvious, but subtle changes in the response to drugs occur throughout the growth and developmental cycle.

Drug Response and Growth-Developmental Level

Neonate The clear-cut variations in drug effects on neonates are the result of the infants' small body mass, low body fat content, high body water volume, and enhanced membrane (i.e., skin, blood-brain barrier) permeability. In the period immediately after birth, lack of gastric acid, absence of intestinal flora and enzyme function, and increased gastrointestinal transit time have significant effects on absorption of oral drugs. Immaturity of drug inactivation systems and incomplete development of renal excretion also contribute to modification of drug effects in neonates.

Older Infant and Young Child In the older infant and young child, the decrease in total body water, increase in body mass, decrease in membrane permeability, and changes in body fat produce less obvious alterations in drug response. The infant has a high metabolic rate and a rapid turnover of body water, which results in a proportionately higher fluid, calorie, and drug dosage requirement per kilogram of body weight than that of the adolescent. Maturation of drug metabolizing systems and the development of urinary elimination mechanisms also result in changes of drug response.

Preschool- and School-Age Child Rapid maturation of systems (central nervous, cardiovascular, gastrointestinal, lymphatic, etc.) and of biochemical functions continues to modify drug response in the preschool-age and school-age child.

Pubescent Child and Adolescent The growth spurt, increase in adrenal steroids, and rise in sex hormones (i.e., estrogen in girls, androgens in both sexes) which precede puberty affect drug response in this age group. Increase in male muscle mass, increase in female body fat, and stabilization of basal body temperature in both sexes also affect adolescent drug response.

DRUG ACTION AND EFFECT

Drugs Acting at Receptor Sites

Drugs generally produce their effects by combining with an enzyme, cell membrane, or other cellular component. The cellular component with which the drug combines to produce its effect is termed a *receptor* or *receptive* substance. It is believed that drug receptors have a chemical or structural attraction for a highly specific drug. A drug gains access to the receptor after it reaches the bloodstream and travels to the location of the receptor.

The combining of a drug with its receptor starts a series of events which are characteristic of the drug. The initial event of the series is the drug's action; subsequent events of the series are the drug's effects. Drug action is not observable; drug effects, on the other hand, may be observable or measurable. Most drugs produce several effects; however, the effect which is characteristic of the drug is more readily elicited.

Drugs Not Acting at Receptor Sites

Drugs which do not act at receptor sites produce their effects by replacing deficiencies, by chemical antagonism, and by nonspecific actions. Treatment of diabetes with insulin and treatment of iron-deficiency anemia with iron are examples of replacement therapy. Chemical antagonism is used to neutralize excessive gastric acid with antacids. The volatile general anesthetics depress membrane excitability by virtue of their high lipid solubility.

Age and Receptor Function

Several investigators have reported on the relation of receptor site function and level of maturity. Jusko suggests that in senescence, decline in receptor sites, decrease in transmitter content of affected tissues, and rigidity of responsive tissues may affect drug action (Jusko, 1976, p. 6).

A controlled study revealed that adrenergic receptors are present and functioning in premature and full-term infants (Yaffee and Stern, 1976, pp. 385–386). In this study, the degree of receptor response appeared to correlate with birth weight.

Infants and children require a total daily digoxin dose that is approximately twice that of an adult on a basis of the ratio of drug to dose (Mirkin, 1976, p. 557). This increased requirement of digoxin has been attributed to a greater affinity of the child's developing myocardial digoxin receptors for digitalis derivatives (Singh, 1976, p. 579).

The increased sensitivity of neonates to curare and atropine as well as their resistance to succinylcholine

(Anectine) may be secondary to immature development of the receptors for these drugs (Walson and Bressler, 1976, pp. 32, 39).

METHODS OF ASSESSING PEDIATRIC DRUG RESPONSE

Drug response in infants and children can be assessed by observable, measurable clinical manifestations (e.g., blood pressure, temperature) and by laboratory determination of drug concentration in body fluids (i.e., plasma, serum). Neither of these methods of assessing drug response can be relied upon alone to prevent adverse drug effects and to promote maximal therapeutic effects.

Assessing Drug Response by Laboratory Methods

Clinical Pharmacokinetics　Determination of drug concentrations in body fluids is utilized to characterize the time course of drug absorption, distribution, metabolism, and excretion. These laboratory values are also used to determine relationships between these four processes and therapeutic and adverse drug responses. The discipline in which one studies and characterizes drug response is known as *clinical pharmacokinetics.*

Dynamic Processes Studied　Drug *absorption* is the process by which the drug molecules move from the administration site into the bloodstream. The movement of the drug from the bloodstream into other body fluids and tissues is termed *distribution. Metabolism*, the complex chemical process which modifies the drug and facilitates its removal from the body, is also known as *biotransformation.* The process by which the drug or its metabolites are removed from the body is termed *excretion.*

It is generally accepted that these four dynamic processes affect plasma concentrations of drugs. There is also a direct relationship between plasma drug concentration and therapeutic and adverse drug effects.

Laboratory Techniques While pharmacokinetics generally monitors drug concentration in serum or plasma, saliva can be used to monitor theophylline concentrations (Gibaldi and Levy, 1976, p. 1991). Recent developments in sensitive analytical techniques make it feasible to use capillary blood (e.g., finger or heel stick). This prevents the blood loss and discomfort of venipuncture. Since pharmacokinetics involves study of the time course of the four dynamic processes, it might be necessary to obtain specimens at regular intervals.

Indications Pharmacokinetic studies are particularly important in neonates, in children with poor liver or renal function, for drugs that have a narrow margin between therapeutic and toxic dose (e.g., digoxin), and for drugs given prophylactically [e.g., phenytoin (Dilantin) to prevent seizures]. These laboratory studies are also important for drugs which produce few observable, measurable clinical responses.

Drugs Studied Many antibiotics, anticonvulsants, and other drugs have been studied and characterized in pediatric populations. Penicillins, aminoglycosides (streptomycin, etc.), chloramphenicol (Chloromycetin), digoxin, phenobarbital, phenytoin, furosemide (Lasix), and diazepam (Valium) have been characterized in the various pediatric age groups.

These preparations represent the drugs most frequently prescribed for infants and children. This pharmacokinetic information documents many age-related differences in drug response which previously were poorly understood. Knowledge of these age-related differences in drug absorption, distribution, metabolism, and excretion have reduced the incidence of adverse drug effects in pediatric patients.

Useful Pharmacokinetic Data Although numerous pharmacokinetic characteristics of a drug are determined, only the average half-life, usual therapeutic plasma concentration, and metabolic fate are of concern to nurses.

Average half-life is the average time required for drug concentration to decrease by 50 percent after absorption and distribution (Gibaldi and Levy, 1976, p. 1866). This characteristic correlates with duration of drug action and determines the frequency of administration: e.g., the average serum half-life of methicillin (Staphcillin) in infants 3 to 6 weeks of age was found to be 1.1 h (Sarff et al., 1977, p. 1006).

The usual therapeutic plasma concentration represents the concentration which produces beneficial effects in the average child of a given age group. Individual variations in plasma concentrations due to genetic, physiological, and maturational factors have been identified. One hour after administration of amikacin (Amikin) to 12 children (3 to 12 years of age), the average serum concentration was 17 μg/ml (Kahn et al., 1976, p. 873).

Metabolic fate is used to determine the routes by which given percentages of a drug are inactivated and removed (Gibaldi and Levy, 1976, p. 1867).

Clinical Uses of Data   Interpretation of these characteristics is unique for each pediatric age group and has several uses. Assessing patient compliance in ambulatory children, adjusting dosage, and monitoring for drug toxicity are the most common applications of pharmacokinetic characteristics.

INTRODUCTION TO DRUG ABSORPTION, DISTRIBUTION, METABOLISM, AND EXCRETION

The four processes of drug absorption, distribution, metabolism (biotransformation), and excretion involve drug movement across several types of biological membranes. Gastrointestinal epithelium, capillary endothelium, and other membranes which drugs traverse differ; however, the mechanisms by which drugs cross these membranes are similar. Drug molecules cross membranes by diffusion or by active transport mechanisms. Highly lipid soluble drugs are primarily nonionized [e.g., diazepam (Valium)] and, as such, cross all membranes much more rapidly and effectively than poorly lipid soluble, ionized drugs (e.g., penicillin G).

Drug Absorption

Absorption is fundamental to the three subsequent processes and is subject to numerous variations. Since absorption consists of movement of drug molecules into the bloodstream, the administration route is crucial to this process.

Blood Flow   Blood flow to the site of administration is the major factor in the rate of drug absorption. Absorption from vascular administration sites is more rapid than that from sites which offer limited blood flow.

Pathological states which reduce circulation (i.e., shock, hypotension, local edema, and congestive heart failure) reduce drug absorption. Heat, exercise, and other measures which increase blood flow enhance drug absorption.

Absorbing Surface   The area of absorbing surface of the site of administration is also an important determinant of drug absorption. Absorption from sites which offer an extensive absorbing area (e.g., small intestine) is more rapid than from those with a small absorbing surface area (e.g., stomach). Measures which increase the absorbing surface area of an administration site (e.g., massage after an intramuscular injection) enhance absorption (Greenblatt and Koch-Weser, 1975, p. 543).

Dosage Form   Drug absorption is also affected by the concentration of drug administered and the solubility of the dosage form. Diffusion is a basic mechanism of drug absorption; thus, high drug concentrations are rapidly absorbed. Liquid dosage forms and drugs in aqueous vehicles are absorbed faster than solid dosage forms (i.e., tablets, capsules, suspensions, etc.) or preparations in poorly soluble vehicles.

Enteral Absorption

Oral Absorption   Oral absorption is erratic and therefore unreliable; however, a wide variety of liquid and solid dosage forms are available for administration by this route.

Gastric Absorption   Variations in oral drug absorption are due to physiological, maturational, and pharmaceutical factors. Movement of drug molecules across the gastrointestinal epithelium does not differ from that across other body membranes. The gastric pH does affect absorption; barbiturates, penicillins, and other weak acids remain nonionized in the gastric acid and are absorbed well in the stomach. Weak bases (e.g., quinidine) are ionized in the gastric pH and thus are better absorbed in the more alkaline intestinal pH.

   Antacids or other drugs which decrease gastric acidity may promote ionization of weak acids, thereby decreasing their absorption in the stomach. Basic drugs, on the other hand, are less ionized by decreased gastric acidity and may be more rapidly absorbed.

Intestinal Absorption   Most drug absorption occurs in the small intestine, where the rich blood supply and extensive absorbing area are most favorable.

Physiological Factors Which Reduce Oral Drug Absorption

First Pass Drug Destruction   After a drug crosses the gastrointestinal membrane, it enters the portal circulation and passes directly through the liver before entering the systemic circulation (Goldstein, 1974, p. 143). This movement through the liver is known as the *first pass*. Drugs which are partially metabolized during the first pass [e.g., hydralazine (Apresoline), isoproterenol (Isuprel), and propranolol (Inderal)] require oral doses sufficient to allow for this effect (Greenblatt and Koch-Weser, 1975, p. 968). Lidocaine (Xylocaine) is well absorbed from the intestine; however, it is completely inactivated during the first pass and therefore is not administered orally (Goldstein, 1974, p. 143).

Drug Destruction by Gastric and Intestinal Constituents   Erythromycin base and penicillin G are examples of drugs which are degraded in the gastric acid. Dosage forms with enteric coatings (the coating resists dissolution in the stomach but is dissolved in intestinal fluid) or which are buffered presumably resist gastric destruction.

Insulin, epinephrine, and histamine are among the drugs which are completely destroyed by intestinal enzymes and thus are not suitable for oral administration.

Alterations of Gastric Emptying Time   The time required for the drug to reach the intestine (i.e., *gastric emptying time*) is an important determinant of gastric absorption. Prolongation of gastric emptying time increases exposure to gastric acid, thereby increasing the risk of destruction of unstable drugs [e.g., acetominophen (Tylenol)]. Such an increase in gastric emptying time delays absorption of stable drugs (e.g., sulfonamides) but does not affect the total amount ultimately absorbed. Atropine and other anticholinergics may decrease drug absorption by delaying gastric emptying time. The presence of food decreases drug absorption by delaying gastric emptying and by preventing drug contact with the absorbing surface of the stomach. Food may also form insoluble complexes with drugs (e.g., tetracyclines) and thus reduce absorption. The rate of aspirin and sulfonamide absorption is slower when food is present; however, the total amount of both drugs absorbed is not decreased.

Shortening of gastric emptying time, on the other hand, reduces drug exposure to gastric acid and tends to increase absorption. Intestinal absorption is increased due to longer contact with the extensive lower tract absorbing surface.

Alterations of Intestinal Motility   Diarrhea, cathartics, and other factors which increase intestinal motility decrease drug exposure to the intestinal membrane. This might be expected to decrease absorption of some drugs; however, antibiotics and digoxin can be well absorbed in the presence of diarrhea (Mirkin, 1976, p. 549).

Oral Absorption in the Newborn   In the immediate newborn period, the lack of gastric acid, short gastric emptying time, and enhanced gastrointestinal membrane permeability promote absorption of most oral drugs. The absence of intestinal flora and lack of intestinal enzymes might decrease absorption of certain drugs. It has been suggested that mechanisms which transport some drugs across the neonatal intestinal membrane might be deficient (Mirkin, 1976, p. 550).

Pharmaceutical Factors Affecting Oral Absorption

Oral drugs in soluble solutions are readily absorbed from the gastrointestinal tract. Solid oral dosage forms (i.e., tablets, capsules, powders, etc.) cannot cross the gastrointestinal membrane until they have been dissolved in the gastrointestinal fluids. If dissolution is extremely slow, a portion of the drug will be lost in the feces (Gibaldi and Levy, 1976, p. 1865). A slow dissolution rate increases drug exposure to gastric acid, thereby increasing the risk of degradation.

Hetacillin (Versapen), erythromycin estolate (Ilosone), and chloramphenicol palmitate (Chloromycetin) are esters which cannot be absorbed until they have been converted by intestinal enzymes. Infants with immature intestinal enzyme function may be unable to convert these drugs; thus, they may be lost in the feces.

Bioavailability of Oral Drugs   The rate and extent to which a drug is absorbed from its dosage form is termed the *bioavailability* of the product (drug) (Gibaldi and Levy, 1976, p. 1865). Some oral dosage forms of digoxin, tetracycline, phenytoin (Dilantin), and chloramphenicol

(Chloromycetin) are incompletely absorbed. These variations in bioavailability have been attributed to particular characteristics of the drug and to the circumstances of its production (Goodman and Gilman, 1975, p. 8).

Timed-Release Oral Drugs   Timed-release drugs are specially formulated to promote slow absorption over a period of several hours. They are used when a prolonged duration of action is desirable and are considered more convenient than other dosage forms. Ekko Capsules Junior (Dilantin) and Dimetane Extentabs (antihistamine combination) are timed-released drugs used in pediatrics. There is evidence that these products are often erratically absorbed and may be more susceptible to changes in gastric pH and gastrointestinal motility.

Buccal and Sublingual Absorption

Buccal and sublingual drugs cross the oral mucosa rapidly, and administration by these routes avoids drug destruction by gastrointestinal fluids and the liver.

The effectiveness of buccal and sublingual absorption in children is dependent upon whether a child is old enough to keep the drug in contact with the absorbing membrane (i.e., between cheek and gingiva, beneath tongue) and to refrain from swallowing until the tablet is completely dissolved. Since these routes may produce unpleasant taste and mild irritation, even older children may not be able to cooperate.

Rectal Absorption

Rectal absorption of tapered pediatric suppositories and rectal solutions is very slow, highly unreliable, and may produce irritation. It is also difficult to control the dosage actually absorbed; however, this route avoids destruction by gastrointestinal constituents and the liver. Rectal absorption in the neonate apparently occurs quite readily.

The presence of feces in the rectal ampulla decreases

absorption, presumably by limiting drug access to the absorbing membrane. Nowak and associates reported that the efficiency of aspirin suppository absorption correlated with the time between suppository insertion and first defecation, i.e., retention time (Nowak et al., 1974, p. 25).

Inflammation of the colon increases the amount absorbed of a hydrocortisone retention enema (AMA Department of Drugs, 1977, p. 1065). Administration of an aminophylline retention enema apparently permits better dosage control than administration of the same drug as a rectal suppository (AMA Department of Drugs, 1977, p. 628).

Pulmonary Absorption

Gases (e.g., nitrous oxide), volatile liquids [e.g., halothane (Fluothane)], and aerosol preparations [epinephrine (Adrenalin) and isoproterenol (Isuprel)] are rapidly absorbed across the pulmonary epithelium and respiratory tract mucosa. The rich blood supply, extensive absorbing surface area, and high permeability of the respiratory tract account for the large amounts of drug absorbed. Pulmonary dosage is difficult to regulate, and some drugs irritate the respiratory tract mucosa.

Absorption of aerosol drugs can be increased by administering small particles and by instructing the child to hold the breath momentarily after inhalation (Goldstein, 1974, p. 141).

Topical Absorption

Most drugs do not penetrate intact skin; however, cutaneous absorption can be increased by rubbing the drug into the skin, incorporating the drug in an oily vehicle, and using a moist dressing. Cutaneous absorption is also increased by direct application of the drug to denuded areas or wounds.

Neonate   The skin of the newborn does not present a barrier to the absorption of topical drugs. Neonates bathed with hexachlorophene absorbed significant amounts of this drug, and the severity and incidence of adverse reactions correlated with gestational age, drug concentration of the bath, and thoroughness of rinsing (Shulman et al., 1974, p. 689). The amount of boric acid absorbed and the adverse reactions increased when the drug was applied to excoriated diaper areas in infants.

Ophthalmic Absorption

Sterile solutions placed into the conjunctival sac enter the aqueous humor by crossing the conjunctival epithelium. Ocular inflammation or injury decreases the blood–aqueous humor barrier, thereby increasing absorption of gentamicin (Garamycin) and many other drugs (AMA Department of Drugs, 1977, p. 955).

Ophthalmic absorption is promoted by measures which increase the amount of drug the eye can retain and which increase the length of time the drug is in contact with the absorbing membrane. Instructing the child to hold the head back during instillation, to close the eye, and to refrain from blinking promotes absorption by these methods ("Research Leads to More Effective Way," 1976, p. 2371).

Neonate   Enhanced ophthalmic absorption in the newborn apparently resulted in systemic toxicity after instillation of an eye preparation in premature twins (Hill, 1976*a*, p. 576).

Nasal Absorption

Nasal solutions are often well absorbed across the nasal and sinus mucosa. Solutions which trickle into the throat may be swallowed and absorbed from the gastrointestinal tract. Infants and young children are more likely to swallow these preparations. Swallowing of nasal solutions can be avoided by instilling the preparation with the child's head in the lateral head low position (AMA Department of Drugs, 1977, p. 645; also, see Table 2-3).

Absorption of Parenteral Drugs

Parenteral administration routes include intravenous, intramuscular, subcutaneous, intradermal, and, rarely, intrathecal.

Drugs injected into the bloodstream or spinal fluid do not require absorption. Intradermal drugs are injected between layers of the skin to assess local response, and absorption is not the objective of the route.

Intramuscular Absorption

Drugs administered by intramuscular route are not always absorbed rapidly and completely (Greenblatt and Koch-Weser, 1976, p. 544). Intramuscular absorption is related to several physiological and drug factors.

Physiological Determinants of Intramuscular Absorption   Blood flow to the intramuscular administration site is the major determinant of the rate of drug absorption. Absorption is more rapid from the deltoid muscle than from the vastus lateralis muscle and is slowest from the gluteal muscles (Greenblatt and Koch-Weser, 1976, p. 544). These variations in absorption rate are due to differences in blood flow to these muscle groups. The particularly slow gluteal absorption seen in adult females is presumably explained by accidental injection into poorly vascular fat tissues.

Conditions which decrease blood flow (e.g., shock, congestive heart failure, myxedema) reduce intramuscular drug absorption. In the event that an adverse reaction occurs after intramuscular administration, it is not possible to prevent further absorption of the drug (Greenblatt and Koch-Weser, 1976, p. 545).

Nursing Measures Which Promote Absorption   Exercise (active and passive), application of heat, and other measures which increase blood flow also promote intramuscular drug absorption. Massage of the injection site spreads the drug over a larger absorbing surface area, thereby promoting absorption (Greenblatt and Koch-Weser, 1976, p. 543).

Age and Intramuscular Drug Absorption   The small muscle mass of the newborn, particularly the premature, is often inadequate for all but the least irritating drugs. It has been suggested that the thermal instability common in newborns is also a deterrent to absorption of intramuscular drugs. Premature and full-term infants do absorb intramuscular penicillin, oxacillin, ampicillin, and other antibiotics adequately (Yaffee and Stern, 1976, p. 386).

Drug Determinants of Intramuscular Absorption   While drugs in aqueous vehicles are rapidly absorbed from the muscle, digoxin, diazepam (Valium), phenytoin (Dilantin), and other drugs in poorly soluble vehicles are incompletely absorbed. These drugs often precipitate at the injection site and are either gradually redissolved or removed by phagocytosis. Other poorly absorbed drugs include ampicillin, cephradine (Velosef), and dicloxacillin (Dynapen) (Greenblatt and Koch-Weser, 1976, p. 544).

LONG-ACTING   INTRAMUSCULAR   DRUGS Procaine penicillin, Depo-Testosterone, and repository corticotropin are examples of intramuscular drugs which have been combined with poorly soluble substances to provide slow absorption over a period of several hours. These preparations are often absorbed erratically and incompletely.

Subcutaneous Absorption of Drugs

Drugs in aqueous vehicles are promptly absorbed from the subcutaneous tissues; however, the limited blood flow to these tissues limits absorption of many other preparations. Incorporation of a vasoconstrictor with the drug (e.g., Novocain with epinephrine) slows absorption by decreasing circulation to the injection site. Insoluble substances added to the drug (e.g., Protamine Zinc Insulin) also promote slow absorption from subcutaneous tissues.

Immobilization of the injection site or application of cold decrease subcutaneous absorption by virtue of effects on local blood flow.

Drug Distribution

During distribution drugs move from the bloodstream into the cellular, interstitial, and transcellular fluids. It is during the distribution process that drugs gain access to their receptor sites.

Drug distribution is dependent primarily on the lipid solubility of the drug, the regional blood flow of the tissues, the maturity of physiological membranes, and the extent to which the drug is stored in body tissues. Highly lipid soluble drugs (e.g., sulfonamides) are widely and rapidly disseminated to the brain, liver, and other vascular tissues. Less vascular tissues (e.g., muscle, fat) are penetrated later.

Age and Drug Distribution   Drugs are distributed in body fluids; thus, alterations of fluid compartments might affect the distribution process. The newborn has a comparatively high total body water volume, and water constitutes 85 percent of the small premature infant's weight as compared with 70 percent of the full-term infant's weight (Yaffee and Stern, 1976, p. 387). The extracellular fluid volume is also larger in the newborn, representing 39 percent of the body weight as compared with 15 to 20 percent of an older child's weight. This large extracellular fluid compartment apparently affects neonatal response to succinylcholine (Anectine). Succinylcholine is widely distributed throughout the extracellular fluid compartment, and newborn resistance to the drug may be explained by the drug's distribution in a larger pool, i.e., the proportionately large extracellular fluid compartment (Goudsouzian and Ryan, 1976, p. 349).

Drug Distribution to the Central Nervous System In spite of the brain's rich blood supply, drug distribution to the central nervous system is unique. Movement of drugs from the bloodstream across the capillary endothelium is restricted by the close approximation of the glial cells (astrocytes) with the capillary endothelium. Drug access to the cerebrospinal fluid is limited by the epithelium of the choroid plexus. This limitation of access is termed the *blood-brain barrier*. It is important to point out that since certain drugs penetrate the central nervous system readily, there is no absolute barrier.

Highly lipid soluble drugs (e.g., tetracyclines, diazepam) penetrate the blood-brain barrier rapidly. Poorly lipid soluble drugs [e.g., gentamicin (Garamycin), penicillins] penetrate slowly and inefficiently under normal circumstances.

AGE AND DRUG DISTRIBUTION TO THE CENTRAL NERVOUS SYSTEM The incomplete glial development of neonates, particularly the premature, enhances permeability of the blood-brain barrier and permits drugs and bilirubin to enter the central nervous system. Penicillins cross the neonatal blood-brain barrier when these drugs are administered in large doses, when they are administered by rapid intravenous infusion, or when they are administered to neonates with renal failure (Rolewicz, 1976, p. 561).

ABNORMAL STATES WHICH INCREASE PERMEABILITY OF THE BLOOD-BRAIN BARRIER Meningitis, brain tumors, and cranial trauma increase the permeability of the blood-brain barrier in infants and children of all ages. In the presence of these conditions drugs which do not ordinarily enter the central nervous system may do so without difficulty.

Plasma Protein Binding of Drugs Some drugs are reversibly bound to plasma proteins (usually albumin), fat, bone, or other tissues. Drugs bound to these tissues are not free to gain access to receptor sites and thus are pharmacologically inactive. Some tissue-bound drugs are released from binding tissues when plasma concentrations fall; thus, these tissues are said to act as *drug storage depots.*

Digitoxin (Purodigin), furosemide (Lasix), warfarin, and diazepam (Valium) are examples of drugs which are extensively bound to plasma albumin. The individual variations of albumin binding in these drugs may be due to genetic factors (Gibaldi and Levy, 1976, p. 1991).

DRUG DISPLACEMENT FROM ALBUMIN BINDING SITES Two extensively bound drugs may compete for albumin binding sites, and the drug with the higher affinity for the site may displace the drug with lower affinity. While the displaced drug may be redistributed, this will usually produce only a slight increase in drug effect (Goodman and Gilman, 1975, p. 10).

ABNORMAL STATES WHICH AFFECT ALBUMIN BINDING OF DRUGS The increased numbers of fatty acids associated with renal impairment may also displace drugs from protein binding sites (Jusko, 1976, p. 4). The decrease in plasma albumin which accompanies the nephrotic syndrome reduces the number of available binding sites; consequently extensively bound drugs would achieve higher plasma concentrations (Gugler and Azarnoff, 1976, p. 3).

Plasma Protein Binding and Age Plasma protein binding is comparatively low in the newborn infant; consequently, plasma concentrations of extensively protein bound drugs are higher.

There is a comparatively low concentration of plasma proteins in the newborn period, and existing plasma proteins have fewer binding sites than in older children. In the neonate, available binding sites are usually occupied by bilirubin, maternal hormones, and other endogenous substances.

DISPLACEMENT OF DRUGS FROM ALBUMIN BINDING SITES IN THE NEONATE   An extensively albumin bound drug administered to a newborn can displace bilirubin from albumin binding sites, thereby producing hyper-bilirubinemia. In susceptible infants (e.g., premature), this excessive bilirubin might penetrate the brain and produce permanent cerebral damage (kernicterus). Sul-fonamides, furosemide (Lasix), large doses of vitamin K, and sodium benzoate (contained in caffeine and Valium) have produced this interaction in newborn infants. Ad-ministration of these drugs to the mother during labor and delivery and during breast feeding have also been implicated in this interaction.

Acidosis, cold stress, and hypoglycemia in the neonatal period result in production of free fatty acids, which may also displace drugs from albumin binding sites.

Drug Storage in Body Fat   Thiopental (Pentothal) is an example of a highly lipid soluble drug which has a high affinity for fat. Upon administration, such drugs enter the brain rapidly, and as cerebral tissues quickly achieve maximal concentration, the drug is redistributed to body fat. Al-though fat is less vascular than the brain, the drug has a higher affinity for the adipose tissue. Low thiopental concentrations persist in body fat for as long as 3 h after initial administration. While this redistribution of the drug to fat terminates drug action, it produces cumula-tive effects if the drug is repeated.

FAT STORAGE AND AGE   The body fat content of the newborn infant is relatively low, comprising 1 percent of body weight in premature and 15 percent in normal full-term infants (Yaffee and Stern, 1976, p. 387). It has been suggested that the central nervous system of the neonate contains a higher proportion of the total body fat than the central nervous system of the older child (Yaffee and Stern, 1976, p. 382).

One could theorize that this decrease in total lipid

mass and increase in central nervous system fat would affect distribution of highly lipid soluble drugs [e.g., thiopental (Pentothal)].

FAT STORAGE IN THE OBESE AND EMACIATED CHILD In older children the alterations of body fat associated with obesity and extreme emaciation obviously affect fat storage of drugs.

Drug Storage in Other Tissues   The tetracyclines have a high affinity for the rapidly growing teeth and bones of infants and young children. These drugs chelate with the calcium of these structures to form a fluorescent complex.

Drug Metabolism

Metabolism, or biotransformation, involves chemical reactions which convert a drug to an inactive or less active compound. Metabolic reactions usually yield a less lipid soluble metabolite, which is more readily eliminated than a highly lipid soluble one.

Not all metabolites are pharmacologically inactive. Allopurinol (Zyloprim) and prednisone (Deltasone) are examples of drugs which are metabolized into pharmacologically active compounds. Active metabolites are either excreted unchanged or undergo further metabolic reactions.

Poorly lipid soluble drugs (e.g., penicillins and many other antibiotics) are not metabolized, but are excreted unchanged. Some drugs are partially metabolized (e.g., digoxin) or extensively metabolized [chloramphenicol (Chloromycetin)] before excretion.

Most drug metabolic reactions occur in the liver; however, the gastrointestinal tract, kidney, and plasma may also biotransform drugs.

Hepatic Drug Metabolizing Systems   Within the liver drugs are metabolized by microsomal and nonmicrosomal enzyme systems, both of which carry out several types of biotransformation. Most drugs undergo several metabolic reactions; thus, a drug is converted to several different metabolites.

Microsomal Drug Metabolism   The microsomal enzymes not only biotransform the majority of drugs but they also participate in metabolism of fatty acids, bilirubin, steroid hormones, and other endogenous substances. These microsomal enzymes are under genetic control, and the wide individual variations in rate of drug metabolism by these enzymes [e.g., of isoniazid (INH), phenytoin (Dilantin), hydralazine (Apresoline)] are attributed to genetic differences.

Induction and Inhibition of Microsomal Enzymes   Microsomal enzyme function can be induced or inhibited by numerous drugs and environmental chemicals. Susceptibility of microsomes to induction and inhibition is also genetically determined. Induction of microsomal enzymes is extremely complex; however, cigarette smoking, phenobarbital, chemical insecticides, and chronic alcohol abuse are documented inducers. Acute alcohol abuse, chloramphenicol, and phenytoin inhibit microsomal enzymes.

Nonmicrosomal Drug Metabolism   The nonmicrosomal enzyme systems metabolize fewer drugs, and while there are variations in the rate at which they biotransform drugs, none of these systems is known to be inducible (Goodman and Gilman, 1975, p. 18).

Hepatic Impairment and Drug Metabolism   Hepatitis, obstructive jaundice, and other conditions which impair liver function or decrease liver blood flow also decrease drug metabolism. In the presence of these conditions, drugs biotransformed in the liver must be administered in reduced dosage.

Age and Drug Metabolism

At birth hepatic drug metabolizing systems are immature and consequently function inefficiently, particularly in the premature. In addition, neonates have significant concentrations of fatty acids and bilirubin which compete with drugs for metabolizing systems (Rolewicz, 1976, p. 563). This deficiency in drug metabolism results in prolonged, excessive drug concentration and is the basis for increased risk of drug toxicity in the newborn. The inability of the newborn to metabolize drugs efficiently necessitates special drug dosage adjustments for this age group.

Microsomal enzymes which metabolize chloramphenicol are particularly inefficient in the first 2 weeks of life. Administration of this drug to premature infants in a dosage based on body weight produced prolonged, excessive drug concentrations in 60 percent of these infants. The half-life of the drug in neonates was 26 hs as compared with 4 h in older children. Chloramphenicol toxicity (gray syndrome) which occurred in these newborns, has also occurred after administration of this drug to mothers during labor and delivery and during breast feeding (Yaffee and Stern, 1976, p. 391).

Maturation of Hepatic Metabolizing Systems Although drug metabolizing systems become somewhat more efficient in the later neonatal period, they do not reach adult levels for many months.

Microsomal Induction in the Newborn The microsomal inducing effects of phenobarbital have been successfully utilized in the neonate. Administration of phenobarbital to mothers before delivery or to the newborn after birth apparently induces microsomal systems which conjugate bilirubin. Infants exposed to phenobarbital in this manner have demonstrated appreciably lower serum bilirubin concentrations (Mirkin, 1976, p. 55; Yaffee and Stern, 1976, p. 393).

Excretion of Drugs

Most drugs or their metabolites are excreted by the kidney; however, the biliary system, intestinal tract, and lung are also drug excretory routes. Some drugs are excreted into the breast milk.

Renal Excretion of Drugs   Drugs are excreted by the kidney as metabolites and in the unchanged form; thus, renal impairment may prolong a drug's effects and produce adverse reactions. In the presence of renal impairment, drugs normally excreted by the kidney (e.g., penicillin, gentamicin, and many other antibiotics) accumulate in the bloodstream. Reduction of dosage under these circumstances prevents drug toxicity.

Urinary pH and Drug Excretion   Changes in urinary pH may affect the rate at which a drug is excreted. Ingestion of ammonium chloride, ascorbic acid, or other drugs which *acidify* the urine increases the rate at which pseudoephedrine (Sudafed), meperidine (Demerol), quinidine, and other weak bases are excreted. Sodium bicarbonate and other drugs which *alkalinize* the urine increase the rate at which phenobarbital, aspirin, nitrofurantoin (Furadantin), and other weak acids are excreted.

While increasing the rate at which a drug is excreted shortens its effect, decreasing urinary excretion increases the drug's duration of action.

Age and Drug Excretion   Neonatal renal mechanisms are incompletely developed, and their function is inefficient. Glomerular filtration and renal blood flow in the newborn are 30 to 40 percent below those of the adult (Rolewicz, 1976, p. 564). Renal excretion of drugs in the newborn is significantly lower than that in older infants. Elimination of penicillin G in premature infants was reported as 17 percent of that in older children when values were corrected for surface area (Yaffee and Stern,

1976, p. 394). At 5 days of age, the glomerular filtration rate and renal plasma flow have increased by 50 percent; by the seventh day of life, glomerular filtration is approximately 50 percent of the adult value; and at 1 year, it equals that of the adult (Mirkin, 1976, p. 556).

NEONATAL DOSAGE AND URINARY EXCRETION OF DRUGS Poor renal excretion of antibiotics and other drugs increases the risk of prolonged, excessive concentrations in neonates. Maturation of renal function during this period results in variable drug plasma concentrations, and dose adjustment by pharmacokinetic methods is often necessary.

Biliary Excretion of Drugs Some drugs [e.g., digitoxin, nafcillin (Unipen)] are secreted into the bile, pass into the intestine where they are partially reabsorbed across the intestinal membrane, and then undergo a cycle of biliary secretion and intestinal reabsorption that is termed *enterohepatic recirculation*. These drugs are eventually excreted in the urine; however, they may undergo a long period of secretion and reabsorption, and a major portion of the drug may be trapped in this circulation, thereby prolonging drug action.

Intestinal Excretion of Drugs After biliary secretion into the intestine, drugs such as erythromycin and doxycycline (Vibramycin) are excreted into the feces.

Drugs Excreted into Breast Milk Many drugs or their metabolites cross the mammary gland epithelium and are excreted into the breast milk. Diuretics, barbiturates, sulfonamides, and other weak acids generally achieve lower concentrations in breast milk than in plasma. Erythromycin, quinidine, antihistamines, and other weak bases reach higher concentrations in milk than those in plasma.

Savage suggests that the administration route and integrity of maternal renal function may affect drug concentrations in breast milk. Up to 1 g of streptomycin daily poses no problem to a nursing infant in the presence of normal maternal renal function. Renal failure in the mother, however, increases streptomycin milk concentrations 25-fold. After administration of oral erythromycin to a lactating woman, small amounts of the drug appear in the milk. The erythromycin concentration increases tenfold, however, when the drug is administered by the intravenous route (Savage, 1976, p. 212).

ADVERSE DRUG REACTIONS IN CHILDREN

Definition

An adverse drug reaction is defined as "any drug response which is noxious and unintended and which occurs at doses used in man for prophylaxis, diagnosis, or therapy" (Karch and Lasagna, 1976, p. 204). This definition does not include poisoning, drug abuse, therapeutic failures, or failure to comply.

Risk

Any drug which produces an adverse reaction in an adult can produce a similar reaction in an infant or child. The mechanisms of many adverse drug reactions are unclear; however, reactions are associated with excessive drug concentrations. Immaturity of drug metabolism and excretion pathways, genetic variations in drug metabolism, and large doses apparently increase the risk of adverse drug reactions in children.

Severity

Adverse drug reactions vary from mild nausea (e.g., with iron preparations) to life-threatening anaphylactic shock (e.g., with penicillin). A study of adverse drug reactions in six hospitals throughout the world revealed that nausea, drowsiness, allergic skin reactions, electrolyte disturbances, and arrhythmias were the most common adverse events (Goldstein et al., 1974, p. 815). Adverse reactions in children may be dramatic (e.g., convulsions immediately after intravenous infusion of aminophylline) or less obvious (e.g., peripheral neuritis after prolonged administration of isoniazid).

Prevention

Much knowledge of adverse reactions in infants and children is retrospective and was acquired after drugs were used and tragedies occurred; e.g., chloramphenicol (Chloromycetin) has been linked with gray syndrome, and hexachlorophene with induced neurotoxicity in infants. Pharmacokinetic characterization of numerous drugs in infants and children makes it possible to predict and prevent many adverse drug reactions.

Hill identifies the three ways by which a child can be exposed to an adverse drug reaction: transplacentally, when the drug is administered to the mother during pregnancy and delivery; by ingestion of the drug in breast milk after administration of the drug to a nursing mother; and by direct administration of the drug to the child (Hill, 1976a, p. 566).

Incidence

The true incidence of pediatric adverse drug reactions is not known; however, one study found adverse reactions equal to those in adults. In adults, 4.8 percent of drug orders administered were associated with adverse reactions, compared to 5.8 percent drug orders administered to children. In hospitalized adults, 4.7 percent of drug orders administered were associated with life-threatening adverse reactions as compared to 3.6 percent in children. Total drug reactions in adults were reported in 0.44 percent of adults and 0.55 percent of children (Bleyer, 1975, p. 309).

Adverse Reactions Associated with Transplacentally Acquired Drugs

Drugs administered to the gravid female generally reach the infant. Most pregnant women receive several drugs during pregnancy and delivery. A study of 168 pregnant women cited an average intake of 11 drugs during pregnancy and an average of 7 drugs during labor and delivery (Doering and Stewart, 1978, pp. 843–846). Frequent ingestion of laxatives, antacids, and other over-the-counter drugs by pregnant women increases drug intake considerably.

Teratogens

In early pregnancy (first 8 to 12 weeks), drugs may produce structural malformations of the embryo (e.g., thalidomide), while in later pregnancy they affect the growth of an intact fetus (e.g., iodine). Drugs which cause structural malformations and alterations of growth are known as *teratogens*. Many drugs have been positively identified to have, or are suspected of having, teratogenic potential. A drug's teratogenic potential is apparently related to the time of administration, (i.e., early or late pregnancy), the dose administered, and genetic "makeup" of the mother. (See Table 1-1.)

Identifying Teratogens Identification of drugs which cause adverse reactions during gestation can be very difficult. Many women do not remember the prescription drugs taken during their pregnancy, and over-the-counter drugs and the effects of environmental chemicals (e.g., pesticides) complicate the picture. Adverse reactions might not be evident until several years after birth (e.g., vaginal cancer in female offspring years after administration of diethylstilbestrol to mothers).

Transplacental exposure to narcotics of abuse (i.e., heroin, morphine) does not produce structural malformations; however, the long-term effects on the child's behavior, intelligence, and social adjustment might be significant.

Table 1-1   Transplacentally Acquired Teratogens

Drugs	Adverse Effect
STEROID HORMONES	
Testosterone	Masculinization of female offspring
Progesterone	Masculinization of female offspring
Diethylstilbestrol:	Masculinization of female offspring
Seventh to eighth week	Genitourinary tract abnormalities in male offspring
After eighth week	Vaginal cancer in preadolescent or adolescent female offspring
ADRENOCORTICOSTEROIDS	
Cortisone (prednisone)	Cleft palate (suspected)
Dexamethasone (Decadron)	Cleft palate (suspected)
ANTIMICROBIALS	
Kanamycin (Kantrex)	Deafness (suspected)
Streptomycin	Deafness
Tetracyclines	Discoloration and hypoplasia of teeth
	Retardation of bone growth
	Cataracts (suspected)
	Structural malformations (suspected)
ANTICANCER DRUGS	
Chlorambucil (Leukeran)	Gross malformations
ANTITHYROID DRUGS	
Potassium iodide	Goiter
Propylthiouracil	Goiter
Radioactive iodine	Destruction of thyroid
ANTICONVULSANTS	
Phenytoin (Dilantin)	Mental retardation
Barbiturates	Developmental retardation
Paramethadione (Paradione)	Malformation of cranial-facial structures
Trimethadione (Tridione)	Limb malformations
	Deafness (suspected)

Table 1-1   Transplacentally Acquired Teratogens (*Continued*)

Drugs	Adverse Effect
ORAL ANTICOAGULANTS	
Warfarin (Coumadin)	Deformity of nasal structures
	Mental retardation
	Hemorrhage
PSYCHOTROPIC DRUGS	
Imipramine (Tofranil)	Limb reduction anomalies
Diazepam (Valium)	Congenital malformations (suspected)
Phenothiazines (Thorazine, etc.)	Retinal damage (suspected)
Meprobamate (Miltown)	Congenital malformations (suspected)
Thalidomide	Shortened or absent limbs
	Other malformations
ANTIDIABETIC DRUGS	
Tolbutamide (Orinase)	Congenital malformations (suspected)
DRUGS OF ABUSE	
LSD	Chromosomal breakage (suspected)
	Skeletal malformations (suspected)
Alcohol, in excess	Mental retardation
	Developmental retardation
	Limb malformations
	Craniofacial malformations
	Congenital heart disease
Heroin	Withdrawal syndrome
Methadone (Dolophine)	Long-term effects unknown
Morphine	

Adverse Reactions Associated with Labor and Delivery Drugs   The effects of drugs administered during labor and delivery are usually readily identified and short-lived. Analgesics and anesthetics produce central nervous system depression in the infant. Excess intravenous fluids may cause convulsions or electrolyte disturbances, while excess uterine stimulants are associated with anoxic encephalopathy (Hill, 1976*b*, p. 25).

Adverse Reactions of Drugs Administered Directly to the Infant   During the neonatal period immaturity of liver and kidney function may increase the risk of adverse reactions particularly in premature infants. The persistence of maternal hormones and drugs in the newborn's bloodstream also increases the risk of such reactions. (See Table 1-2.)

Adverse Reactions Associated with Drugs Ingested in Breast Milk

Since most drugs administered to the nursing mother enter the breast milk, the increase in breast feeding may represent a source of increasing significant adverse drug reactions in infants (see Table 1-3).

Some drugs are excreted into breast milk as inactive metabolites. Insulin and epinephrine (Adrenalin) are destroyed by the infant's gastrointestinal tract and do not present a problem. Heparin is not excreted into breast milk; thus, its administration does not affect the nursing infant.

Drugs cross the mammary epithelium by diffusion, and since breast milk is more acidic than plasma, weak bases [(i.e., antihistamines, erythromycin, theophylline, and isoniazid (INH)] attain breast milk concentrations similar to or higher than those in plasma. Weak acids (i.e., sulfonamides, penicillins, barbiturates, and diuretics) attain lower concentrations in milk than in plasma (Savage, 1976, p. 212; also, see Table 1-4).

Breast milk concentrations also are affected by the dose, route, and maternal excretion rates. Large doses and administration by the intravenous route produce higher concentrations in milk. Maternal renal impairment increases breast milk concentrations of drugs excreted in the urine (Savage, 1976, p. 212).

There is much controversy regarding drug concentra-

3

Table 1-2   Drugs with High Potential for Adverse Reactions in the Neonatal Period

Drugs	Adverse Effect
Chloramphenicol (Chloromycetin)	Circulatory collapse (gray syndrome)
Hexachlorophene	Cerebral damage Respiratory arrest Cardiovascular disturbances
Boric acid (topical)	Rash Gastrointestinal disturbances Renal damage Circulatory failure
Digitalis preparations	Arrhythmias Neurological and gastrointestinal disturbances
X-ray contrast media (Cardiografin)	Renal shutdown Renal hemorrhage
Tetracyclines	Increased intracranial pressure Temporary suppression of bone growth Discoloration and hypoplasia of teeth

Anticholinergic agents:
  Atropine
  Cyclopentolate (Cyclogyl)
	Dilated pupils
	Urinary retention
	Fever
	Tachycardia
	Erythema

tions in breast milk. These disagreements are the basis for the conflicting reports on drugs contraindicated during breast feeding and drugs which warrant monitoring of the nursing infant (O'Brien, 1975, p. 24).

Table 1-3   **Drugs Contraindicated During Breast Feeding***

Atropine
Anticancer drugs
Anticoagulants
Antimicrobials:
   Chloramphenicol (Chloromycetin)
   Metronidazole (Flagyl)
   Nalidixic acid (NegGram)
   Streptomycin
   Sulfonamides
   Tetracyclines
Central nervous system drugs:
   Bromides
   Diazepam (Valium)
   Narcotics
   Phenobarbital
   Primidone (Mysoline)
   Lithium
   Phenothiazines (e.g., Thorazine)
Carisoprodol (Soma)
Dihydrotachysterol (Hytakerol)
Ergot (e.g., Sansert)
Radioactive materials

* During short-term maternal therapy with these drugs the infant is fed formula or frozen breast milk obtained before the mother starts taking the drug. Breast feeding is not resumed for a period appropriate to the drug's term of excretion (Hill, 1976a, pp. 572–573).

Adverse Reactions Associated with Drugs Administered Directly to the Child

In the older infant and child, adverse reaction may be confused with the underlying illness (e.g., excessive epinephrine inhalation for treatment of asthma attack may prolong the attack) (AMA Department of Drugs, 1977, p. 631). The infant and young child are unable to describe such adverse reactions as the ringing in the ear and dizziness associated with gentamicin or the blurred vision associated with atropine. Antihistamines and adrenergic drugs contained in over-the-counter cold

Table 1-4   Drugs Requiring Monitoring of the Infant During Breast Feeding

Drugs	Adverse Effect
Analgesics	Lethargy, poor feeding, drowsiness
Aspirin	Bleeding
Anticonvulsants	Drowsiness
Cathartics	Gastrointestinal hypermotility
Ampicillin	Rash, diarrhea, sensitization, candidiasis
Penicillin G	Sensitization, candidiasis
Psychotropics	Lethargy, poor feeding, drowsiness
Oral contraceptives	Effects unknown
Isoniazid (INH)	Peripheral neuritis
Oral hypoglycemics	Hypoglycemia
Propranolol (Inderal)	Arrhythmias
Salicylates	Bleeding

remedies, cough syrups, and nose drops may also cause adverse reactions in pediatric patients.

Adverse reactions in children are manifested by many signs and symptoms, including hypersensitivity (allergic) phenomena, alteration of growth, damage of anatomic or physiological systems, and numerous others (see Table 1-5).

DRUG INTERACTIONS IN INFANTS AND CHILDREN

General Considerations

Drugs administered simultaneously or sequentially may interact to increase or decrease the therapeutic effect of each other (Table 1-6). These drug interactions may be beneficial [e.g., probenecid (Benemid) prolongs the action of penicillins] or adverse (e.g., aspirin increases the action of anticoagulants). Children who receive drugs over a long period of time (e.g., anticonvulsants, bronchodilators) are at risk of such drug interactions. Many over-the-counter drugs (antacids, laxatives, nose

(*Text continued on page 40.*)

Table 1-5 **Drugs with High Potential for Adverse Reactions When Administered Directly to the Infant and Child**

Adverse Effect	Drugs
Suppression of growth	Anabolic steroids: nandrolone decanoate (Deca-Durabolin), nandrolone phenproprionate (Durabolin)
	Adrenocorticosteroids: hydrocortisone (Cortef), prednisone (Meticorten)
	Psychotropic drugs: haloperidol (Haldol), phenothiazines (e.g., Thorazine)
	Central nervous system stimulants: dextroamphetamine (Dexedrine), methylphenidate (Ritalin)
	Vitamins in excess: vitamin A, vitamin D
Temporary suppression of bone growth	Tetracyclines (children under 8 years)
Hallucinations	Antihistamines (contained in many over-the-counter nose drops and cough and cold remedies)
	Atropine and other anticholinergic agents: Cyclogyl, Mydriacyl
Restlessness, agitation, insomnia, excessive crying	Antihistamines Nasal decongestants Bronchodilators Central nervous system stimulants
Increased intracranial pressure (in infants)	Tetracyclines (in infants) Adrenocorticosteroids Vitamin A (in excess)
Ataxia	Barbiturates Minocycline (Minocin) Phenytoin (Dilantin) Amikacin (Amikin), streptomycin
Damage to the eighth cranial nerve (auditory and vestibular)	Furosemide (Lasix) Aspirin and other salicylates Viomycin (Viocin) Gentamicin (Garamycin)

Adverse Effect	Drugs
	Kanamycin (Kantrex)
	Neomycin
Peripheral neuritis	Isoniazid (INH)
	Vincristine (Oncovin)
	Hydralazine (Apresoline)
	Ethambutol (Myambutol)
Eye damage	Topical corticosteroids
	Ethambutol (Myambutol)
	Thorazine
	Chloroquine (Aralen)
Renal damage	Penicillins
	Lead
	Salicylates
	Outdated tetracyclines
	Cephaloridine (Loridine)
	Anticonvulsants
	Gentamicin, streptomycin, amikacin
	Neomycin, kanamycin
Nephrotic syndrome	Penicillinamine (Cuprimine)
	Trimethadione (Tridione)
	Probenecid (Benemid)
Acne	Iodides
	Corticosteroids
Cutaneous eruptions	Penicillins (particularly ampicillin)
	Allopurinol (Zyloprim)
	Anticonvulsants
	Nitrofurantoin (Furadantin)
	Sulfonamides
	Phenobarbital
	Anticancer drugs
Exaggerated sunburn	Tetracyclines
	Hexachlorophene
	Phenothiazines
Asthma attack	Aspirin
	Bethanechol (Urecholine)
	Acetylcysteine (Mucomyst inhalation)
	Epinephrine inhalation

Table 1-5   Drugs with High Potential for Adverse Reactions When Administered Directly to the Infant and Child (*Continued*)

Adverse Effect	Drugs
Anaphylaxis	Penicillins Heparin Aspirin Parenteral iron Dextran preparations
Unpleasant taste, altered taste sensation	Carbenicillin (Geopen) Clindamycin (Cleocin) Clofibrate (Atromid-S) Gold preparations Griseofulvin (Grisactin) Iron
Liver damage	Isoniazid (INH) Rifampin (Rimactane) Erythromycin estolate (Ilosone) Acetaminophen (Tylenol) Sulfonamides Methyldopa (Aldomet) Chlorpromazine (Thorazine)
Blood dyscrasias	Chloramphenicol (Chloromycetin) Anticonvulsants Penicillins Hydralazine (Apresoline) Sulfonamides Anticancer drugs
Ileus, intestinal obstruction	Atropine Bulk-forming laxatives Diphenoxylate (Lomotil)
Electrolyte disturbances	Sodium and potassium penicillin salts Diuretics Salicylates Ammonium chloride Sodium bicarbonate Potassium chloride

Table 1-6   Drug Interactions*

Drug(s)	Interaction and Effect	Relevant Nursing Action

Cholestyramine (Questran) with:
   Thyroid hormone
   Digitalis derivative
   Warfarin
   (Coumadin)
	Decrease in effect of thyroid, digitalis, and warfarin due to binding in intestine.	Administer thyroid and cholestyramine 5 h apart (*Evaluations of Drug Interactions,* 1976, p. 234).
		Administer digitalis 1½ h before cholestyramine (*Evaluations of Drug Interactions,* 1976, p. 62).
		Administer warfarin and cholestyramine at least 3 h apart (*Evaluations of Drug Interactions,* 1976, p. 278).

Oral antacids with:
   Isoniazid (INH)
   Digitalis
   derivatives
   Pseudoephedrine
   (Sudafed)
	Oral antacids with aluminum ions (e.g., Amphojel, Robalate) decrease effect of isoniazid and pseudoephedrine by complexing with these drugs.
	Antacids generally decrease digitalis effect by complex action.
		Administer isoniazid, digitalis derivative, and pseudoephedrine 1 h after antacids (*Evaluations of Drug Interactions,* 1976, p. 16).

Nitrofurantoin (Furadantin) with food	Increased nitrofurantoin effect secondary to delayed gastrointestinal transit time (prolonged exposure to intestinal absorbing membrane) (AMA Department of Drugs, 1977, p. 830).	Administer nitrofurantoin shortly before or after meals.

Tetracyclines with:
   Oral antacids
   Laxatives
   Sodium
   bicarbonate
   Antidiarrheals
   Iron preparations
   Food (particularly
   dairy products)
	Decreased tetracycline effect due to complexation with these drugs and food. [Doxycycline (Vibramycin) and minocycline (Minocin) are not significantly affected by food and antacids.]	Administer tetracyclines 2 to 3 h before food and the drugs listed.

*Drug interactions are extremely complex, and whether or not such an interaction actually occurs is dependent on several interrelated factors. Dosage, genetic variation in microsomal susceptibility to induction, and the sequence in which drugs are administered are examples of such factors.

Table 1-6   Drug Interactions* *(Continued)*

Drug(s)	Interaction and Effect	Relevant Nursing Action
Lincomycin (Lincocin) with Kaopectate	Decreased lincomycin effect due to complexation with Kaopectate.	Administer Kaopectate 2 h before lincomycin.
Methotrexate with salicylates	Increased methotrexate effect due to displacement from binding sites.	Monitor for toxicity. Discuss methotrexate dosage adjustment with prescriber.
Oral anticoagulants with: Sulfonamides Nalidixic acid (NegGram) Clofibrate (Atromid-S) Chloramphenicol (Chloromycetin)	Increased anticoagulant effect due to displacement from binding sites.	Monitor for toxicity (bleeding tendency, interpret laboratory reports). Discuss anticoagulant dosage adjustment with prescriber.
Barbiturates with: Corticosteroids (Prednisone, etc.) Quinidine Doxycycline (Vibramycin)	Decreased corticosteroid, quinidine, and doxycycline effect due to increase in rate of their metabolism.	Discuss dosage adjustment with prescriber to assure therapeutic concentrations.
Rifampin (Rimactane) with: Oral anticoagulants Corticosteroids	Decreased anticoagulant and corticosteroid effect due to increase in rate of their metabolism.	Discuss dosage adjustment with prescriber to assure therapeutic concentrations.
Allopurinol (Zyloprim) with: Cyclophosphamide (Cytoxan) Mercaptopurine (Purinethol)	Increased cyclophosphamide and mercaptopurine effect due to decrease in rate of their metabolism.	Monitor for toxicity. Discuss dosage adjustment with prescriber.
Phenytoin (Dilantin) with: Isoniazid (INH) Oral anticoagulants	Increased phenytoin effect due to decrease in rate of its metabolism.	Monitor for toxicity. Discuss dosage adjustment with prescriber.

Table 1-6   Drug Interactions* (*Continued*)

Drug(s)	Interaction and Effect	Relevant Nursing Action
Furazolidone (Furoxone) with: Aged cheese (e.g., cheddar) Chianti, sherry Fermented sausage (pepperoni) Dried fish Pickled herring Epinephrine (Adrenalin) and related drugs	Hypertensive crisis due to increased release of norepinephrine at adrenergic neurons.	Teach parents and older children to avoid these foods and drugs during furazolidone therapy.
Probenecid (Benemid) with: Penicillins Cephalosporins (e.g., Keflin)	Increased penicillin and cephalosporin effect due to decrease in their urinary excretion.	Monitor for toxicity.
Sodium bicarbonate and excessive antacids with: Meperidine (Demerol) Quinidine Gentamicin (Garamycin) Pseudoephedrine (Sudafed)	Increased meperidine, quinidine, gentamicin, and pseudoephedrine effect due to decrease in their urinary excretion.	Monitor for toxicity. Teach patients dangers of excessive urinary tract alkalinization.
Ammonium chloride with: Aspirin Phenobarbital Nalidixic acid (NegGram) Nitrofurantoin (Furadantin) Acetazolamide (Diamox)	Increased aspirin, nalidixic acid, phenobarbital, nitrofurantoin, and acetazolamide effect due to decrease in their urinary excretion.	Monitor for toxicity.

drops, cold remedies, and cough syrups) complicate the identification of drug interactions.

Drugs also interact with some foods which decrease their absorption (e.g., tetracyclines and dairy foods) or affect their urinary excretion (e.g., acid-ash, alkaline-ash diets).

The literature contains long lists of actual and potential drug interactions; however, there is not always agreement on the clinical significance of reported interactions.

Mechanisms

The mechanisms of many drug interactions are complex, and an unknown number of interactions are diagnosed as manifestations of the underlying health problem. Some interactions occur at large drug doses or in children who metabolize one or more drugs unusually slowly. Interactions involving drug distribution occur most often in the neonate.

Additive interactions (e.g., increased central nervous system depression produced by sedatives combined with general anesthetics) and antagonistic drug interactions (central nervous system stimulants counteract phenobarbital sedation) are readily identified.

Interactions involving drugs whose effects can be measured by laboratory or other means have been well investigated, e.g., the reaction between oral anticoagulants (prothrombin time) and anticonvulsants (drug serum concentration).

Drug interactions which involve alterations of drug absorption, distribution, metabolism, and excretion, and interactions affecting adrenergic mechanisms have also been investigated.

BIBLIOGRAPHY

AMA Department of Drugs: *AMA Drug Evaluations*, 3d ed., Publishing Sciences Group, Littleton, Mass., 1977.

Bleyer, W. A.: "Surveillance of Pediatric Adverse Drug Reactions: A Neglected Health Care Problem," *Pediatrics*, vol. 55, no. 2, 1975, pp. 308–310.

Doering, P. L., and R. B. Stewart: "The Extent and Character of Drug Consumption During Pregnancy," *Journal of the American Medical Association*, vol. 239, no. 9, 1978, pp. 843–846.

Evaluations of Drug Interactions, 2d ed., American Pharmaceutical Association, Washington, D.C., 1976.

Gibaldi, M., and G. Levy: "Pharmacokinetics In Clinical Practice, I," *Journal of the American Medical Association*, vol. 235, no. 17, 1976, pp. 1864–1867.

_____ and _____: "Pharmacokinetics In Clinical Practice, II," *Journal of the American Medical Association*, vol. 235, no. 18, 1976, pp. 1987–1992.

Goldstein, A., et al.: *Principles of Drug Action: The Basis of Therapeutics*, 2d ed., Wiley, New York, 1974.

Goodman, L. S., and A. Gilman: *The Pharmacological Basis of Therapeutics*, 5th ed., Macmillan, New York, 1975.

Goudsouzian, N., and J. Ryan: "Recent Advances in Pediatric Anesthesia," *Pediatric Clinics of North America*, vol. 23, no. 2, 1976, pp. 345–359.

Greenblatt, D. J., and J. Koch-Weser: "Clinical Pharmacokinetics, II," *New England Journal of Medicine*, vol. 293, no. 19, 1975, pp. 964–969.

_____ and _____: "Intramuscular Injection of Drugs," *New England Journal of Medicine*, vol. 295, no. 10, 1976, pp. 542–546.

Gugler, R., and D. L. Azarnoff: "The Clinical Use of Plasma Drug Concentrations," *Rational Drug Therapy*, vol. 10, no. 11, 1976, pp. 1–7.

Hill, R. M.: "Adverse Drug Reactions In Children," *Pediatric Annals*, vol. 5, no. 9, 1976a, pp. 566–577.

———: "Iatrogenic Problems in Neonatal Intensive Care," in *Report of the Sixty-ninth Ross Conference on Pediatric Research,* Ross Laboratories, Columbus, Ohio, 1976*b*, pp. 22–26.

Jusko, W. J.: "Drug Dosage Adjustments In Diseased Patients," *Rational Drug Therapy,* vol. 10, no. 6, 1976, pp. 1–8.

Kahn, A., et al.: "Amikacin Pharmacokinetics in the Therapy of Childhood Urinary Tract Infection," *Pediatrics,* vol. 58, no. 6, 1976, pp. 873–876.

Karch, F. E., and L. Lasagna: "Evaluating Adverse Drug Reactions," *Adverse Drug Reaction Bulletin,* no. 59, 1976, pp. 204–207.

Mirkin, B. L.: "Drug Disposition and Therapy in the Developing Human Being," *Pediatric Annals,* vol. 5, no. 9, 1976, pp. 542–557.

Nowak, M., et al.: "Rectal Absorption from Aspirin Suppositories in Children and Adults," *Pediatrics,* vol. 54, 1974, pp. 23–26.

O'Brien, T. E.: "Excretion of Drugs in Human Milk," *Nursing Digest,* vol. 3, no. 4, 1975, pp. 23–31.

"Research Leads to More Effective Way of Administering Eyedrops," *Journal of the American Medical Association,* vol. 236, no. 21, 1976, p. 2371.

Rolewicz, T. F.: "A Rational Approach to Antibiotic Therapy in Infants and Children," *Pediatric Annals,* vol. 5, no. 9, 1976, pp. 558–565.

Sarff, L., et al.: "Clinical Pharmacology of Methicillin in Neonates," *The Journal of Pediatrics,* vol. 90, no. 6, 1977, pp. 1005–1008.

Savage, R. L.: "Drugs in Breast Milk," *Adverse Drug Reaction Bulletin,* no. 61, 1976, pp. 212–214.

Shulman, R. M., et al.: "Neurotoxicity of Hexachlorophene in the Human: 1. A Clinicopathology Study of 248 Children," *Pediatrics,* vol. 54, no. 6, 1974, p. 689.

Singh, S.: "Clinical Pharmacology of Digitalis Glycosides," *Pediatric Annals,* vol. 5, no. 9, 1976, pp. 578–584.

Walson, P. D., and R. Bressler: "Drugs and Age," in *Drugs of Choice 1976–1977,* Mosby, St. Louis, 1976, pp. 30–42.

Yaffee, S., and L. Stern: "Clinical Implications of Perinatal Pharmacology," in *Perinatal Pharmacology and Therapeutics,* Academic, New York, 1976, pp. 371–401.

2
Administering Drugs to Infants and Children

ILLNESS AND RESPONSE TO DRUG ADMINISTRATION

Illness, parental separations, and hospitalization may produce unmanageable anxiety levels in infants and children. Some children respond to the crises by regressing to a previous level of growth and development and may refuse medication. The child's response to illness and to drug administration is determined by his or her level of growth and development, previous experiences with drug administration, and cultural conditioning. It is important to point out that each child is a unique individual; two children of the same growth and developmental level with similar experiences do not necessarily exhibit similar responses to illness or to drug administration. There may also be variations in response to drug administration in the same child as the child progresses along the illness-to-health continuum.

Individualizing Drug Administration

While adults accept drugs from a preoccupied stranger, infants and children are more selective, not only in which drugs they accept but also about the behavior of the adult offering the drug. Children generally accept drugs from adults they know and trust and who provide support and comfort in a loving, unhurried manner. Drug administration techniques must be individualized for the child's growth and development, the dosage form, and the child's health problem.

Parental Involvement

Children generally accept oral drugs from parents and other nurturing adults, and, when feasible, these adults should be permitted to administer oral drugs with a nurse's guidance. Parents can also be invaluable sources of information about the child's favorite feeding or medication ritual, food and beverage likes, personal jargon, etc.

Safe Drug Administration

Drug administration to infants and children requires knowledge of appropriate dosage forms, proper storage of drugs, knowledge of pediatric pharmacology, and knowledge of growth and development.

PEDIATRIC DOSAGE

An appropriate dose produces beneficial therapeutic responses with minimal adverse effects. A therapeutic response requires adequate drug absorption from administration sites and distribution to sites of action (receptors). Adequate metabolism and excretion of the drug or its metabolites prevents adverse drug effects.

Individualizing Pediatric Dosage

Determination of appropriate dosages for infants and children is an ongoing challenge for pediatric researchers and prescribers. Pediatric dosages must be individualized for patients of varying sizes and levels of maturity. The small premature newborn and the large, well-developed adolescent obviously present different dosage requirements. Pediatric dosage is further complicated by the growth and developmental alterations which occur during infancy, childhood, and adolescence. Changes in lean body mass, fluid volume, fat content, plasma protein concentration, and membrane permeability warrant appropriate changes in dosage. Maturation of liver and renal function as well as development of biochemical systems also contributes to the complexity of pediatric dosage determination.

Illness and Pediatric Dosage

Many abnormal states affect drug response in infants and children. The increased metabolic rate and alterations of fluid and electrolyte status associated with pediatric infections alter dosage requirements. Intestinal malabsorption as seen in cystic fibrosis and celiac sprue obviously affect drug absorption.

Genetic variations in drug metabolism, concurrent use of multiple drugs, and poor absorption of a particular dosage form also have implications for pediatric dosage.

Neonatal Dosage

Neonatal dosage presents special challenges, particularly in the small premature infant. Immaturity of drug metabolizing and excreting systems, decrease in drug tissue binding, and numerous other physiological characteristics make dosage requirements for the newborn unique.

Prior to present knowledge of drug absorption, distribution, metabolism, and excretion in pediatric patients, dosage for infants and children was determined by fixed rules.

DETERMINING PEDIATRIC DOSAGE

Fixed Dosage Rules

Fixed dosage rules assumed that since a child's dose is smaller than an adult's dose, the appropriate dose for a child is a fixed portion of the adult dose. The adult dose used by these rules was described as an "average" for a 150-lb adult. Pharmacokinetic studies have revealed wide individual variations in adult dosage requirements for many drugs; hence, the concept of an "average" adult dose is untenable, and basing pediatric dosage on a portion of this average adult dosage is obviously not advisable.

Most such fixed rules used either the age or weight of the child as the common denominator for calculating drug dosage. Since there were no provisions for individualizing dosages, our interest in these rules is primarily historical. During the neonatal period, dosage rules are particularly unreliable; however Shirkey suggests that from 6 months to 2 years of age, they might begin to be relatively reliable or safe (Shirkey, 1973, p. 6).

Pediatric Dosage Rules Based on Age   Fried's rule for a child under 1 year of age:

$$\frac{\text{Child's age (in months)}}{150} \times \text{adult dose} = \text{child's dose}$$

Young's rule for a child 2 years old or older:

$$\frac{\text{Child's age (in years)}}{\text{Child's age (in years)} + 12} \times \text{adult dose} = \text{child's dose}$$

These age rules would provide identical doses for all children of the same age, and they are particularly unreliable for children who are much smaller or larger than the norms for a given age.

Pediatric Dosage Rules Based on Weight   Clark's weight rule for a child 2 years old or under:

$$\frac{\text{Child's weight (in pounds)}}{150} \times \text{adult dose} = \text{child's dose}$$

Using a child's weight as a basis for calculating drug dosage is not unreliable per se; however, administering identical doses to children of the same weight is not reliable. Use of fixed weight rules also presents problems in dosing infants and large adolescents. If only the adult dose is known, calculating the infant's dose on the basis of the infant's weight as compared with the adult's weight underdoses the infant. On the other hand, if only the infant dose is known, increasing the infant dose on the basis of the adolescent's weight would overdose the adolescent (Crawford et al., 1950, p. 788).

Dosage Based on Body Surface Area

Drug dosage can also be determined by using a unit of body surface area as the common factor. Supporters of this method state that it is superior to those which use body weight and that it can be used to determine dosage in patients of all ages.

Regardless of body size, there is a constant ratio between basal metabolic rate and body surface area. Body surface area also correlates closely with blood volume, cardiac output, glomerular filtration, and organ growth and development (Shirkey, 1973, p. 7). Proponents of the body surface area method state that it can also be used to determine fluid, electrolyte, and calorie requirements in individuals of all ages.

Dosage based on this method is expressed in terms of unit dosage per square meter of body surface. If the dosage of a drug is 25 mg per square meter of body surface in 24 h, this dosage is usually expressed as 25 mg/m² per 24 h.

Estimating Body Surface Area The surface area can be estimated by use of a nomogram or by complex mathematical calculations. Several nomograms which estimate surface area from height and weight are in common use. The reliability of the surface area method rests on the accuracy with which the body surface area is estimated or calculated. Critics of the method maintain that the errors inherent in determining body surface area make this method less reliable than dosage based on accurate weights.

Evaluation of Method Use of body surface area to determine dosage provides a consistent method of expressing dosage for patients of all sizes. Shirkey states that using body surface area allows expediency and accuracy satisfactory for clinical use; however, he cautions that this method does not guarantee the accuracy of individual dosage (Shirkey, 1973, p. 9).

SOURCES OF PEDIATRIC DOSAGE SCHEDULES

Present sources of pediatric dosage schedules include the official compendium (*United States Pharmacopeia XIX*, 1975) and manufacturers' recommendations. Both are based on pharmacokinetic data obtained during clinical drug trials in pediatric patients of various age groups. These official and nonofficial schedules are not inflexible recommendations; they represent a starting point from which to individualize dosage for children of all age groups (e.g., neonate, older infant). Unless otherwise noted, the pediatric dosage schedules cited in this book are those listed in the official compendium (*United States Pharmacopeia XIX*, 1975).

Official Pediatric Doses

Many pediatric doses listed in the *United States Pharmacopeia* are expressed in terms of both body weight and body surface area (e.g., 5 mg per kilogram of body weight or 150 mg per square meter of body surface). When appropriate, dosage for the newborn infant is listed separately [e.g., for chloramphenicol (Chloromycetin) and digoxin].

Nonofficial Pediatric Doses

Manufacturers' dosage recommendations are included in the package insert of each prescription drug. This package insert which is approved by the Food and Drug Administration may restrict use of the drug in infants and children. The package insert of drugs which have not been pharmacokinetically characterized in infants and children includes a statement to the effect that these drugs are not recommended for use in pediatric patients. This qualification has moved Shirkey to describe children deprived of such drugs as "therapeutic orphans." Drugs that lack sponsorship for use in children are also referred to as "therapeutic orphans" (Shirkey, 1975, p. 284).

Therapeutic Orphans

Many of these "orphaned" drugs are commonly used in pediatric practice (Asnes and Grebin, 1974, p. 91). The legality of using such drugs is not clear. It is generally accepted that a drug that is reasonably safe in adults should not be withheld from a sick child merely because it has not been characterized in children. The American Medical Association Department of Drugs suggests that drug labelings (i.e., dosage recommendations of the package insert) in themselves do not set the standard for what is good medical practice (*AMA Department of Drugs*, 1977, p. xxxix).

Table 2-1   Growth and Development Principles of Pediatric Drug Administration

Infant: 0 to 1 Year	
PSYCHOSOCIAL CRISIS	RESOLUTION OF PSYCHOSOCIAL CRISIS THROUGH DRUG ADMINISTRATION
Trust versus mistrust.	
Oral sensory period.	Holding, stroking, and caring for infant before, during, and after drug administration promotes development of trust.
Governed by pleasure-pain principle.	

Table 2-1   Growth and Development Principles of Pediatric Drug Administration (*Continued*)

CHARACTERISTICS	Encouraging parents to participate in drug administration involves them in resolution of this psychosocial crisis.
Dependent.	
Gains satisfactions through bodily contacts, e.g., being held, dressed, fed.	Speaking softly and supporting securely (while holding, lifting, etc.) during drug administration also help develop trust.
ANXIETIES	
Fears loud noises and falling.	TYPICAL RESPONSE TO DRUGS
	Does not fear oral or parenteral drug administration.

Neonate

RELEVANT REFLEXES, BEHAVIOR	TYPICAL RESPONSE TO DRUGS
Gagging, sucking, and swallowing are present.	Aimless motor activity, flexion of body.
Little conscious awareness.	DRUG ADMINISTRATION TECHNIQUES
Does not distinguish self from others.	Administer liquid oral dosage forms with dropper, oral syringe, or other appropriate device.
	Place small amounts of drug inside of mouth and permit infant to suck and swallow slowly.
	Do not force infant to swallow oral drugs.
	Immobilize securely for parenteral administration.

1 to 3 Months

RELEVANT MOTOR DEVELOPMENT	TYPICAL RESPONSE TO DRUGS
Motor activity more purposeful.	Turns head away from oral drugs.
Sucking reflex begins to fade.	Cries immediately after parenteral administration.
Focuses eyes on bright objects.	

Table 2-1   Growth and Development Principles of Pediatric Drug Administration
        (*Continued*)

---

3 to 6 Months

RELEVANT MOTOR DEVELOPMENT	TYPICAL RESPONSE TO DRUGS
Responds to verbalization.	Reaches for and grasps medication dropper, cup, etc.
Distinguishes mother from other adults.	Prefers to take oral drugs in feeding position.
Follows objects with eyes.	
Deciduous teeth begin to erupt.	

---

6 to 9 Months

MOTOR AND SOCIAL DEVELOPMENT	TYPICAL RESPONSE TO DRUGS
Smiles and verbalizes (coos).	Grasps and explores medication cup with mouth.
Fears maternal separation and strangers.	Accepts liquids, powders, etc., from teaspoon.
Enjoys simple games (peek-a-boo).	
Rolls and moves constantly.	DRUG ADMINISTRATION TECHNIQUES
	Encourage mother to administer oral drugs with guidance.
	Play peek-a-boo or other games before and after administering drugs.

---

9 to 12 Months

MOTOR AND SOCIAL DEVELOPMENT	TYPICAL RESPONSE TO DRUGS
Responds to smiles, conversation, and games.	Shows displeasure with medication by whimpering, moving away, etc.
Fears maternal separation.	Accepts liquid drugs from cup.
	Grasps and returns empty medication cup.

Table 2-1   Growth and Development Principles of Pedriatric Drug Administration
(Continued)

Toddler: 1 to 3 Years

PSYCHOSOCIAL CRISIS

Autonomy versus shame and doubt.

Muscular anal period.

Body image concepts developing.

Superego develops from limits set by nurse and other caring adults.

Accepts toilet training and moves toward reality principle.

CHARACTERISTICS

Negativistic, ritualistic, ambivalent, does not know right from wrong.

Moves about constantly, exploring his or her expanding world.

Temper tantrums common.

ANXIETIES

Fears maternal separation, unknown adults, and strange experiences.

RESOLUTION OF PSYCHOSOCIAL CRISIS THROUGH DRUG ADMINISTRATION

Providing warmth, physical contact, and discipline before, during, and after medication administration promotes development of autonomy.

Setting limits provides security and safety.

Allowing child to reduce anxiety by familiar rituals (e.g., using favorite spoon, cup, etc.) provides security and reduces frustrations.

Avoid impatient facial expressions, gestures, or other behavior which conveys irritation with toddler's slowness.

During tantrums remove child from cause and provide love and safety.

Avoid giving too many drugs at one time.

Do not force toddler to swallow oral drugs.

---

1 to 2 Years

MOTOR AND SOCIAL DEVELOPMENT

Very responsive to surroundings (people, objects, etc.).

Moves constantly.

Short attention span.

Feeds self with spoon.

Drinks with straw.

TYPICAL RESPONSE TO DRUGS

If drug administration interrupts activities, may have tantrum.

Offers physical and verbal resistance to drug administration.

Says no when means yes.

Explores medication cart or tray when given the opportunity.

Delays accepting drugs.

Does not fear oral drugs.

Table 2-1 **Growth and Development Principles of Pediatric Drug Administration**
(*Continued*)

Cries at sight of syringe, intravenous equipment, etc.

2 to 3 Years

SOCIAL DEVELOPMENT

Knows name, age, and gender.

Identifies eyes, ears, and nose.

Some awareness of owning toys, books, and other objects.

TYPICAL RESPONSE TO DRUGS

Offers physical resistance to parenteral drugs.

DRUG ADMINISTRATION TECHNIQUES

Use colorful cups, straws, and balloons to decorate medication cart.

Administer liquid drugs with cup or spoon.

Allow child to choose color of spoon, straw, or cup.

Permit child to hold cup while drinking medication.

Set limits on which objects child can explore (e.g., cup, balloon).

Immobilize firmly for parenteral medications.

Encourage child to cope by holding favorite stuffed animal, toy, etc., during parenteral administration.

Permit release of aggression by encouraging child to throw a ball or pound clay after injection is administered.

Preschool Age: 3 to 6 Years

PSYCHOSOCIAL CRISIS

Initiative versus guilt.

Locomotor genital period.

Superego is crystallized by resolution of the oedipal conflict, and the child is ready for school at 5 or 6.

RESOLUTION OF PSYCHOSOCIAL CRISIS THROUGH DRUG ADMINISTRATION

Providing a secure environment in which the child can seek answers to questions regarding medications promotes development of initiative.

Table 2-1   Growth and Development Principles of Pediatric Drug Administration
(Continued)

CHARACTERISTICS

Creative, curious about the environment.

Asks questions continually.

Interested in sexual differences.

Knows right from wrong.

Forms attachments outside the home.

ANXIETIES

Monsters, bodily harm, loss of blood, pain, deformity, death, and loss of parents.

Nightmares are common.

MOTOR AND SOCIAL DEVELOPMENT: 3 TO 4 YEARS

Likes to please adults.

Verbalizes needs and wishes.

Attention span increases.

MOTOR AND SOCIAL DEVELOPMENT: 4 TO 5 YEARS

Begins to understand past, present, and future.

Has an imaginary playmate, who is blamed for child's shortcomings.

Likes to do things by self.

MOTOR AND SOCIAL DEVELOPMENT: 5 TO 6 YEARS

Verbalizes constantly.

Begins to lose deciduous teeth.

Exerts some self-control.

Physically capable of swallowing solid oral dosage forms (tablets, capsules,

Setting limits provides safety and develops self-control.

DRUG ADMINISTRATION TECHNIQUES

Encourage questions regarding medication; answer truthfully at a level appropriate to child's understanding.

TYPICAL RESPONSE TO DRUGS

Feels that medications are punishment for wrongs committed and that excessive blood loss and pain will result.

Offers formidable resistance to parenteral administration.

Accepts oral drugs; drinks medication with minimal assistance.

Curious about drugs administered to other children.

Worries about drugs which will be administered at a future time.

DRUG ADMINISTRATION TECHNIQUES

Permit imaginary playmate to sample oral drugs if so requested.

Do not force child to swallow oral drugs.

Prepare child for parenteral administration by permitting child to administer injection to a doll (Brandt et al., 1972, pp. 1403–1404).

Explain that injections are not punishment but to help him or her "get well."

Immobilize firmly during injection.

Permit child to visualize injection site after drug is administered to validate that there is no deformity, hemorrhage, etc.

Table 2-1   Growth and Development Principles of Pediatric Drug Administration
(Continued)

etc.); however, may be unable to do so during illness.	Apply small dressing to injection site.
	Provide security and love.
	Encourage release of aggression, as by throwing a ball, spanking a doll, etc.

School-age: 6 to 10 Years

PSYCHOSOCIAL CRISIS

Sense of industry versus inferiority.

Period of latency.

Superego aids in controlling and directing instinctual drives.

Discovers parents are not infallible.

May turn to other adults for guidance.

Learns fair play and cooperation necessary for reality adaptation and participation in environment.

CHARACTERISTICS

Strong sense of duty and responsibility.

Enjoys useful tasks.

Likes recognition from adults and peers for accomplishment.

Starts collections (e.g., shells, stamps).

Forms close relationships with peers of same sex, may join clubs.

Tolerates maternal separation without excessive anxiety.

RESOLUTION OF PSYCHOSOCIAL CRISIS THROUGH DRUG ADMINISTRATION

Assisting child to solve problems associated with drug administration and to participate in the administration process gives child a sense of accomplishment and promotes development of industry.

Nurse's behavior may influence child's self-image (e.g., "good child" accepts, "bad child" refuses medications).

TYPICAL RESPONSE TO DRUGS

Likes to be told what is expected of him or her.

Wants to cooperate.

Desires recognition for accepting medication.

DRUG ADMINISTRATION TECHNIQUES

Explain purposes of medication.

Provide opportunity to ventilate feeling regarding medication administration.

Permit choice of oral liquid or solid dosage form when possible.

Permit child to perform useful tasks from which she or he gains a sense of accomplishment (e.g., filling drinking cup from water fountain, discarding empty medication cup in waste paper can).

Table 2-1   Growth and Development Principles of Pediatric Drug Administration
(*Continued*)

Reward child with praise, gold star, or other means of approval.

SOCIAL DEVELOPMENT:
6 TO 7 YEARS

DRUG ADMINISTRATION
TECHNIQUES

May be rude and act up in the presence of adults.

Set limits of behavior during drug administration.

Movements often clumsy.

First permanent teeth erupt.

SOCIAL DEVELOPMENT:
7 TO 8 YEARS

DRUG ADMINISTRATION
TECHNIQUES

Points out what he or she perceives as inconsistencies in nurse's administration of drugs to children of varying ages and illness.

Provide structure by explaining what is expected at drug administration time.

TYPICAL RESPONSE TO DRUGS

May be cruel to younger or different children.

Tattles on another child who "spits up" oral medication or removes intravenous infusion.

SOCIAL DEVELOPMENT:
8 TO 9 YEARS

TYPICAL RESPONSE TO DRUGS

Can understand that medications "make one well."

Looks upon nurse with hero worship.

Wishes to cooperate with parenteral administration; however, moves or cries out involuntarily during the injection.

DRUG ADMINISTRATION
TECHNIQUES

Prepare child by explaining purposes of parenteral administration.

Allow child to visualize and/or handle administration equipment, if feasible (Brandt et al., 1972, p. 1404).

Assist child to remain motionless by gentle immobilization.

After administration encourage release of aggression, as by dribbling basketball.

Table 2-1   Growth and Development Principles of Pediatric Drug Administration
(Continued)

SOCIAL DEVELOPMENT:
9 TO 10 YEARS

Understands causes and effects.

Strives for independence.

Adolescence: 10 to 18(?) Years

PSYCHOSOCIAL CRISIS:
EARLY ADOLESCENCE,
10 TO 14(?) YEARS

Sense of identity versus identity confusion.

Period of puberty and adolescence.

PSYCHOSOCIAL CRISIS:
LATE ADOLESCENCE,
14 TO 18(?) YEARS

Intimacy versus isolation.

Period of young adulthood.

The preadolescent growth spurt results in dramatic physical and physiological changes. Revision of body-image concepts are necessary if the child is to cope with changes in size and contours which occur at puberty.

Development of identity requires the child to discover him or herself (i.e., feelings, goals) and to prepare for adult roles.

CHARACTERISTICS

Stress, conflict, impulsiveness, and moodiness are common in these age groups. The child is unpredictable and fluctuates between acting childishly and grown-up.

Peer group becomes very important. "Crushes" on an adult figure common.

RESOLUTION OF PSYCHOSOCIAL CRISIS THROUGH DRUG ADMINISTRATION

Placing adolescents in close proximity with each other permits them to gain identity and intimacy by sharing feelings, goals, and commitments.

Music, activities, and behavior peculiar to their age group may isolate them from younger patients and nurses.

TYPICAL RESPONSE TO DRUGS

Concerned about effects drugs have on skin (e.g., iodides cause acne), on body weight (e.g., corticosteroids cause fluid retention), etc.

Girls worry about permanent scars (e.g., vaccination marks), staining (e.g., Imferon produces permanent brown stain), etc.

Both sexes dread appearing "uncool."

Both sexes may be critical of nurse, hospital, and other health workers.

May alternate negativism and cooperation.

Boys may be awkward holding medication cup, turning over in bed, and other motions.

Changing male voices may be unreliable at embarassing times.

Table 2-1   Growth and Development Principles of Pediatric Drug Administration
(Continued)

ANXIETIES

Failure in social, career, and academic endeavors. Feelings of inadequacy about future.

Concern with body appearance (skin, weight, clothing) and functions (heavy perspiration, menstruation, maturing body).

PHYSICAL DEVELOPMENT

Girls reach puberty 1 to 2 years before boys.

PSYCHOSOCIAL DEVELOPMENT

The late adolescent develops intimacy by making a commitment to others of both sexes.

The child must prepare for emancipation from parents and a role in the adult world.

Girls generally dexterous, poised, and self-assured.

DRUG ADMINISTRATION TECHNIQUES

Explain purposes and objectives of medication administration.

Encourage questions and expression of feelings.

Answer questions truthfully.

After administration of parenteral drugs encourage release of aggression by physical activity (e.g., dancing vigorously).

PEDIATRIC DOSAGE FORMS AND THEIR STORAGE

Drug Stability

Drug stability refers to the extent to which a dosage form retains its potency. Conditions of storage, i.e., temperature, humidity, light, etc., are major factors in the stability of some drugs. In institutions which utilize unit dosage systems or satellite pharmacies, drug storage is obviously not a major concern. Institutions which use the stock system of drug administration require proper drug storage as an integral part of nursing responsibility. Most hospital pharmacies indicate recommended storage conditions on drug containers. Manufacturers' package inserts are also vital sources for specific drug storage information. Drugs should never be stored near sources of heat, fluorescent light, or in humid environments.

Loss of potency may be characterized by changes in color, loss of clarity, or odor. Drugs which have undergone such changes should not be administered without consultation with a pharmacist. Administration of an unstable drug results in subtherapeutic doses, exposes the child to the drug without achieving benefits from the exposure, and represents an unwarranted expense. Drugs which are not used frequently should be discarded before or on their expiration dates. Ingestion of outdated drugs has caused serious adverse reactions (e.g., outdated tetracyclines have produced renal damage) (AMA Department of Drugs, 1977, p. 743).

Preparation of Drugs for Administration

Sterile preparations for parenteral administration are supplied as dry powers, ready-to-inject solutions, and ready-to-inject suspensions. Sterile dry powders must be reconstituted according to the recommendations of the package insert. Use of the recommended diluent, use of the recommended volume, and administration according to directions assure that the drug will retain its potency. Storage of the reconstituted drug must also be according to the manufacturers' package insert.

Selection of an Appropriate Dosage Form

While the pediatric prescriber generally indicates the dosage form to be administered, the child may be unable to accept the prescribed dosage form. In this event the nurse should suggest an alternate dosage form or a route appropriate to the child's level of development and condition.

ORAL DOSAGE FORMS

Since the oral route of administration is the one most frequently used, a wide variety of oral drugs are available for use in infants and children. Solid and liquid dosage forms especially prepared for children are usually well accepted by pediatric patients.

Solid Oral Dosage Forms

Pediatric solid oral dosage forms are smaller in size and contain smaller doses than do those for adult patients. They are generally tasteless and are quite conveniently swallowed by children of 5 to 6 years and over. Children 5 to 6 years old are physically able to swallow solids; however, during illness the child may be unable or unwilling to do so.

Storage of Solid Oral Dosage Forms Solid oral dosage forms should be stored in closed containers away from radiators, moisture, and strong light.

Solid Oral Dosage Forms Used in Pediatrics

Tablets Coated tablets [e.g., allopurinol (Zylorim) tablets] are intended for ingestion, while uncoated tablets may be administered by buccal and sublingual routes. Special coatings for tablets mask unpleasant tastes or odors, resist destruction in the gastric acid, or provide prolonged drug effects. Vitamins, analgesics, and antibiotics are available as pleasantly flavored chewable tablets. Discoloration, mottling, and swelling are indications of tablet instability.

Capsules Capsules [e.g., penicillamine (Cuprimine) capsules] consist of a soluble gelatin shell which contains the active drug in powder, granule, or oily form. These dosage forms are tasteless and easily swallowed. Hardening or softening of the shell and distension of the shell are manifestations of instability.

Powders Powders are solid dosage forms which consist of dry, finely divided drug. Availability of pediatric liquid dosage forms has decreased the use of dry powders; however, some drugs are dispensed as dry powders to be mixed with water to form a liquid suspension. Dry powders can be administered by mixing them with food or appropriate beverage. Caking or changes in color indicate instability.

Liquid Oral Dosage Forms

Pediatric liquid oral dosage forms are pleasantly flavored and scented preparations which are well accepted by children. Storage conditions and shelf life for these oral liquids vary greatly; thus, it is important to verify this information with the pharmacist.

Suspensions Suspensions [e.g., dicloxacillin (Dynapen) suspension] are finely divided, undissolved drugs which are suspended in a liquid vehicle. Since the undissolved drug tends to settle from the liquid, suspensions must be well shaken before administration to assure proper dispersion. Many suspensions are stable for 10 to 14 days under refrigeration. Caking of the undissolved drug or presence of large crystals is evidence of instability.

Elixirs Elixirs (e.g., digoxin elixir) are clear, sweetened liquids which consist of an active drug in a solvent of alcohol and water. They are often used for cough syrups and expectorants. Cloudiness, gas formation, or odor indicate instability.

Syrups Syrups [e.g., isoniazid (INH) syrup] are liquid preparations of drugs in a concentrated, sweetened aqueous solution. Sugar-free syrups are available for diabetic children. Precipitation, cloudiness, or gas formations are signs of instability.

Solutions Solutions [e.g., nafcillin (Unipen) sodium solution] are liquid dosage forms which contain a drug dissolved in water or other vehicle.

Tinctures   Tinctures (e.g., belladonna tincture) are alcoholic solutions prepared from vegetable drugs or chemical substances.

Critical Points in Oral Drug Administration to Infants and Children[1]

1. Validate drug dispensed and medication ticket by comparing both with original prescription.

2. Use a dosage form appropriate to child's growth and development and health problem. (Discuss inappropriate dosage form with prescriber.)

3. Measure liquid dosage form with accurate, standardized measuring devices only (oral syringe, standardized medication cups, etc.) (American Academy of Pediatrics, 1975, p. 327).

4. Use medical asepsis in all preparation and administration activities, i.e., wash hands before pouring, maintain cleanliness of all drugs and medication cups.

5. Mix powders with an appropriate and compatible solid or liquid which the child will accept.

6. Utilize a drug administration technique (i.e., dropper or teaspoon, etc.; position of administration) appropriate to child's growth and development and health problem.

7. Prevent aspiration of oral drugs by refraining from forcing children to swallow these preparations.

8. Promote development of psychosocial crises by use of appropriate drug administration techniques, provision for safety, encouragement of release of aggression, and provision for support and comfort before, during, and after drug administration.

---

[1] The technical, manipulative aspects of drug administration are discussed in other works. No attempt has been made to repeat these aspects, however; only points critical to pediatric administration have been listed.

9. Return drug to recommended storage area to maintain stability of the product.

10. In the event that vomiting occurs within 2 to 3 h of oral administration, discuss feasibility of repeating dose or use of an alternate administration route.

RECTAL ADMINISTRATION OF DRUGS

The rectal administration route is used occasionally for bronchodilators, antipyretics, and analgesics. Tapered pediatric rectal suppositories are available for administration by this route.

Critical Points in Rectal Suppository Administration

1. Place child in comfortable position (infant and toddler on back with knees flexed, older child on side).

2. Explore rectum gently with well-lubricated gloved finger. Do not administer drug if feces is present in rectal ampulla.

3. Remove suppository wrapper, lubricate tapered end, and instruct child to relax internal rectal sphincter by breathing through opened mouth.

4. Gently insert tapered end of suppository beyond internal sphincter. (*Note:* The presence of the suppository stimulates peristalsis and produces expulsion and defecation in some infants and young children. Holding the buttocks together for a short time prevents expulsion of the drug.)

5. Record time between suppository insertion and first defecation (retention time); communicate retention time to the physician.

Administration of Rectal Solutions

Hydrocortisone solution and aminophylline solution are administered as small-volume retention enemas by rectal catheter of appropriate size.

ADMINISTRATION OF VAGINAL DRUGS

Special vaginal preparations include tablets [e.g., Nilstat (nystatin)]; creams (e.g., AVC); and suppositories (e.g., Vagisec Plus). Vaginal tablets and creams are inserted with special applicators, which are dispensed with the drug and are used only for the individual child. These special insertion devices deposit the drug high into the vaginal vault, and are used for the duration of drug therapy. Suppositories, on the other hand, are inserted manually; i.e., without the use of special insertion devices.

Since the vagina is not a sterile cavity, surgical asepsis is not ordinarily used for administration of vaginal drugs. Cleanliness of drug and applicator and proper hand-washing are essentials of the process. Use of gloves, while optional with special insertion devices, is important for insertion of vaginal suppositories. Some older adolescents can be taught to insert vaginal preparations, with adult guidance.

Vaginal tablets, creams, and suppositories usually melt at room temperatures; thus, these preparations are stored under refrigeration. The package insert should be consulted for the specifics of product storage.

Since many pediatric services provide care for adolescents up to 18 years of age or until their entry into college, administration of vaginal drugs is not rare. Moreover, a younger child who was exposed to diethylstilbestrol during gestation may also require such drugs. The importance of explaining the purposes and mechanics of insertion can not be overemphasized. When feasible, the child's mother should be involved in the teaching and administration of these preparations.

Critical Points in Administration of Vaginal Drugs

1. Explain the purposes and mechanics of vaginal administration to the child; provide time for expression of feelings, and time to assess child's knowledge of reproductive tract.

2. Instruct child to void before insertion.

3. Place child in a comfortable position which provides adequate access to area. *Assure privacy by appropriate screening and draping.*

4. Instruct child to exhale to relax vaginal musculature.

5. *Suppository insertion:* After removing wrapper, lubricate preparation and gloved index finger, and insert gently into the vaginal cavity. *Tablet and cream insertion:* Place drug into special insertion device and lubricate the entire assembly to facilitate administration. Insert gently, and push plunger or other mechanism forward. Wash insertion device before returning to bedside storage area.

6. Place perineal pad or other absorbing surface beneath hips, and leave child at bed rest after insertion. Adolescent may prefer to wear perineal pad with sanitary belt.

7. Remain at bedside to answer questions and provide support.

INSTILLATION OF EAR PREPARATIONS

Ear solutions and ointments are instilled into the ear canal to treat external ear inflammation and, when the tympanic membrane is perforated, to treat inflammations of the middle ear. These preparations may also be utilized to remove impacted cerumen and foreign bodies from the external ear. It is essential that all ear preparations be warmed to body temperature before instillation to avoid unpleasant sensation and discomfort.

Most ear preparations are combinations of several drugs in a single dosage form; antibiotics, local anesthetics, anti-inflammatory agents, and analgesics are often incorporated into these preparations.

Adverse Reactions to Ear Preparations

Ear preparations may cause pruritus, erythema, and other cutaneous reactions; in the presence of tympanic membrane perforation systemic reactions may occur [e.g., ear damage after gentamicin (Garamycin) instillation].

Although the external ear is not sterile, perforation of the tympanic membrane permits the drug to gain access to the sterile environment of the middle ear. The typical response of the infant and young child to ear instillation is a source of trauma. These children usually move their head and extremities vigorously, and attempt to grasp the dropper. While the soft plastic droppers of common use are safer than glass droppers, accidents are still possible.

Methods to Increase Effectiveness of Ear Preparations

Ear preparations are effective only if the ear canal is kept clean and dry; moisture, secretions, or residual drugs provide media for bacterial growth and prevent contact of drug with inflamed surfaces. Before instillation, all residual drug and other debris should be removed gently with suction or a sterile small cotton applicator (AMA Department of Drugs, 1977, p. 998). Measures to prevent trauma must be employed; older children should be cautioned against placing fingers or other objects into the ear; infants and young children might require gentle elbow restraints to prevent self-inflicted ear trauma. Shampoo, bath water, and other substances must not be allowed to gain entry into the ear.

Critical Steps in Instillation of Ear Preparations (See Fig. 2-1)

1. Instill ear solutions in treatment room or other area away from distractions and individuals who increase the risk of trauma.

2. Explain objectives and methods of instillation to older child.

3. Prevent trauma in infant, young child, or uncooperative

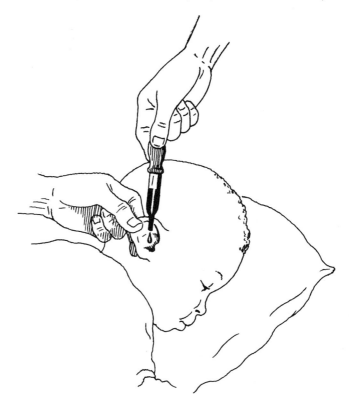

Figure 2-1 Instillation of an ear preparation for a child under 3 years of age. The arms have been immobilized and the pinna has been pulled down and back.

child by methods appropriate to child's growth and developmental level (e.g., mummy restraint for infant; placing the hand of the nurse which holds the dropper on the side of the child's head so that the dropper moves with the child's head, etc.).

4. Wash hands thoroughly.

5. Gently remove crusts, secretions, and residual drug from external canal with sterile cotton ball.

6. Place child on side with ear to be medicated uppermost.

7. Straighten ear canal: in children under 3 years old pull the pinna *down* and back; in children over 3 years old pull pinna *upward* and back.

8. Instill prescribed number of drops or prescribed amount of ointment into the ear canal without permitting the dropper or ointment tip to touch any part of the ear.

9. Keep child in this position for approximately 5 min after instillation to maximize contact of drug with the ear. [*Note:* If the eardrum is perforated, gentle pressure over the tragus or insertion of a saturated cotton wick will move the drug along the ear canal and enhance its penetration into the middle ear (AMA Department of Drugs, 1977, p. 99).]

10. Return medication to proper storage area.

NASAL INSTILLATION OF DRUGS

Methods of Instilling Nasal Drugs

Two methods of nasal instillations are commonly used for infants and children: the lateral head-low method (Parkinson's method) and the recumbent neck-extended method (see "Critical Steps in Instillation of Pediatric Nasal Solutions" later in this chapter). Drugs instilled into the nasal cavity often trickle into the hypopharynx and are swallowed by infants and young children. An appreciable amount of drug can be swallowed.

The lateral head-low method may prevent swallowing of nasal solutions; however, it may not open the sinus ostia (AMA Department of Drugs, 1977, p. 645). Instillation of solutions in the recumbent neck-extended method places the solution in contact with the sinus ostia; however, the child is more likely to swallow the drug.

Nasal Drugs

Nasal drops and sprays are administered to shrink engorged nasal and sinus mucosa. Many of these decongestants contain adrenergic drugs which open obstructed nasal passages and facilitate sinus drainage by restricting blood flow to edematous, engorged mucosa. Since the eustachian tube opens into the nasopharynx, nasal decongestants are used to promote drainage in middle ear infections.

Adverse Reactions to Nasal Solutions

Swallowing of nasal solutions which contain adrenergic decongestants may produce nervousness, hypertension, and central nervous system stimulation, particularly in infants and young children.

Administration of oily nasal preparations causes lipid pulmonary inflammatory conditions; thus, only aqueous nasal preparations are suitable for pediatric use.

While the nasal cavity is not sterile, the sinuses are easily infected by contaminated solutions. Therefore when possible each child should have an individual dropper-container or spray pack which is not shared with others. Sterility of stock nasal solutions can be maintained by use of sterile disposable droppers. The dropper, spray, or spray pack tip should never touch any part of the child's body or any other unsterile surface. Rinsing the individual reusable dropper or spray tip with hot water after each use decreases the risk of contaminating the solution (AMA Department of Drugs, 1977, p. 647).

The typical response of the infant and young child to nasal instillation can be a source of trauma. These children usually move their heads and extremities vigorously and attempt to grasp the dropper.

Stability of Nasal Solutions

Some nasal solutions are highly unstable in the presence of heat and light; consequently, these drugs must be stored under proper conditions and discarded at first evidence of instability.

Critical Steps in Instillation of Pediatric Nasal Solutions (See Fig. 2-2)

Nasal solutions are usually instilled 15 to 20 min before meals and at bedtime. Children with copious secretions should be gently suctioned before instillation.

1. Instill solution in treatment room or other area away

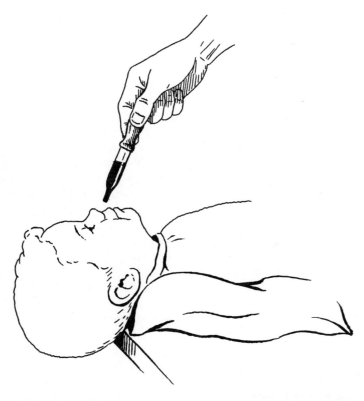

Figure 2-2   Instillation of a nasal solution for a young child using the recumbent neck-extended method. The arms have been immobilized and the child positioned on its back with a pillow beneath the shoulders.

from distractions and individuals who increase the risk of trauma.

2. Explain objectives and methods of instillation to older child.

3. Prevent trauma in infant, young child, or uncooperative child by methods appropriate to child's growth and developmental level (e.g., mummy restraint for infant, or placing the head of the nurse which holds the dropper on the child's forehead so that the dropper moves with the child's head).

4. Wash hands thoroughly.

5. Place child in correct position for instillation. *Lateral head-low instillation:* (*a*) Lay child on back with support (e.g., pillow, rolled sheet) under neck. (*b*) Instill prescribed number of drops into nasal cavity without touching child's body (touching dropper contaminates the device and stimulates sneezing). (*c*) Maintain child in this position for 5 min if possible to spread solution over mucosal surfaces. [*Note:* After completion of instillation, blowing one nostril at a time may expel secretions (Kendig, 1972, p. 996).]

    Recumbent neck-extended instillation: (*a*) Place child on back with pillow under shoulder and allow head to fall back over edge of a pillow (Leifer, 1977, p. 193). (*b*) Instill prescribed number of drops into nasal cavity without touching child's body (touching dropper contaminates the solution and stimulates sneezing). (*c*) Maintain child in this position for approximately 1 min (Scipien et al., 1975, p. 876).

6. Discard disposable dropper. Wash individual reusable dropper thoroughly with hot water before replacing into individual solution container.

7. Return solution to proper storage area.

8. Assess for adverse adrenergic reactions.

Administration of Nasal Sprays

Nasal sprays distribute fine, divided mists over a larger area than that reached by an equal volume of drops. This fine mist does not flow into the throat; consequently, there is minimal swallowing. It is difficult to control the dosage delivered by the spray; therefore, sprays are not recommended for use in children under 6 years old, and children old enough to use these preparations should do so only with adult supervision (AMA Department of Drugs, 1977, p. 646).

Critical Steps in Administration of Nasal Sprays

1. Place child in a sitting position with head bent forward.

2. Direct the spray tip into the nostril without touching nasal surfaces or occluding the airway.

3. Assist child to squeeze pack while he or she inhales briskly.

OPHTHALMIC INSTILLATION OF DRUGS

Sterile ophthalmic solutions are instilled into the conjunctival sac to treat infections and inflammations and for diagnostic purposes.

Adverse Reactions to Ophthalmic Instillation

Trauma and infections are serious complications of ophthalmic instillation, and an eye which has sustained injury (e.g., corneal abrasion) is highly vulnerable to infection. Only meticulous aseptic technique in ophthalmic instillation can prevent infection.

Measures to Prevent Infection

When possible, each child should have an individual dropper-solution pack or ointment tube which is not shared with others. In the event that a common stock solution is used, only sterile disposable droppers should come into contact with this solution. Ointment tips and droppers should never touch any part of child's body or any other unsterile surface.

Stability of Ophthalmic Solutions

Some ophthalmic solutions and ointments are unstable at high temperatures or in the presence of humidity. These preparations must be stored under the conditions recommended by the pharmacy or the package insert. Solutions stored under refrigeration should be warmed to room temperature before administration, and should be returned to refrigeration immediately after use. Ophthalmic solutions which have undergone changes in clarity or color or which contain particulate matter should be discarded. While crystals or particles on the outside dropper lip of an individual dropper-solution pack are not evidence of instability, they are a source of trauma. Before use of these solutions, crystals and particles should be carefully removed with sterile saline saturated sterile gauze squares.

Ophthalmic Instillation in Infants and Young Children (See Fig. 2-3)

The lacrimal ducts empty into the conjunctival sac, and eye solutions administered to infants and children often trickle into the nose and throat and are swallowed by the child. Anticholinergic diagnostic solutions (e.g., Cyclogyl) have caused systemic toxicity, possibly after excessive swallowing.

The typical response of the infant and young child to eye instillation is a source of trauma. These children usually move their head and extremities vigorously and attempt to grasp the dropper. While the soft plastic droppers of common use are safer than glass droppers, accidents are still possible.

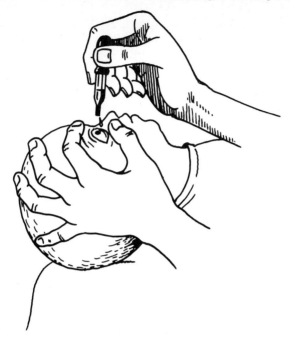

Figure 2-3   Instillation of an ophthalmic solution for an infant. Arms have been immobilized and, with the child positioned on its back, the drug is instilled into inner canthus.

Critical Steps in Instillation of Pediatric Ophthalmic Solutions

1. Instill drops in treatment room or other area away from distractions and individuals who increase risk of trauma.

2. Explain objectives and method of installation to older child.

3. Inspect solution for changes in color and clarity, particulate matter, and other evidence of instability. Discard solutions which manifest evidence of instability!

4. Wash hands thoroughly.

5. Remove crusts, unabsorbed drug, and other material

from lashes and lids, using sterile saline–saturated sterile gauze. Using a single motion, cleanse from inner canthus to outer canthus (Lewis, 1976, pp. 364–365).

6. Prevent trauma in infant, young child, and other uncooperative child by methods appropriate to child's growth and developmental level (e.g., mummy restraint for infant, or placing the hand of the nurse which holds the dropper on the child's forehead so that the dropper moves with the child's head).

7. Place child in correct position for instillation. *Instillation for cooperative or older child:* (*a*) Instruct child to sit with head tilted back and looking up. (*b*) Expose conjunctival sac by placing gentle pressure over bony prominence below lower lid, avoiding pressure on eyeball. (*c*) Instill prescribed number of drops into conjunctival sac. (*Note:* Dropping solution directly on cornea produces unpleasant sensation which frightens child and might injure cornea.) (*d*) Instruct child to close eye without squeezing, and to move eyeball around keeping eye closed.

   Instillation for infant, young child, and uncooperative child: (*a*) Attempt to reduce anxiety before instillation. [*Note:* Emotional reactions (e.g., crying, struggling) increase eye secretions and wash drug out of eye ("Research Leads to More Effective Way," 1976, p. 2371).] (*b*) With child lying on back solution can be instilled into the inner canthus (Scipien et al., 1975, p. 875). [*Note:* After instillation placing pressure at inner canthus minimizes amount of solution entering nose and throat, and reduces swallowing (AMA Department of Drugs, 1977, p. 942).]

8. Remove excess drug from lashes and lids with sterile gauze.

9. Offer child clean tissues.

10. Return solution to proper storage place.

Administration of Ophthalmic Ointments

Ointments are applied with the child in the same position as for administration of solutions. A thin ribbon of ointment is applied along the lower conjunctival sac, and as the child closes the eye and moves the eyeball around, the ointment is dispersed across the conjunctival area. The older child should be informed that vision may be blurred until the ointment is absorbed.

PARENTERAL DOSAGE FORMS

Sterile parenteral dosage forms include dry powders [e.g., cephalothin (Keflin)], solutions [e.g., gentamicin (Garamycin)], and suspensions (e.g., procaine penicillin G).

Parenteral Drug Administration

Parenteral administration introduces the drug beneath one or more layers of skin. The parenteral routes of most common usage in the pediatric setting include subcutaneous, intramuscular, and intravenous. Intradermal (intracutaneous) injection is utilized to assess response to minute doses of an allergenic extract, purified protein derivative (PPD), or other extract. Intrathecal injection, a method by which highly purified drugs are administered into the spinal subarachnoid space, is not utilized routinely. Local anesthetics [e.g., lidocaine (Xylocaine)] are injected intrathecally to produce spinal anesthesia, and antibiotics which do not normally penetrate the blood-brain barrier [e.g., polymyxin B (Aerosporin), amikacin (Amikin)] are also administered intrathecally to treat life-threatening gram-negative meningitis.

Advantages of Parenteral Administration

Since parenteral administration avoids drug destruction by gastrointestinal constituents and the liver, it not only produces prompter and higher drug concentrations but it also permits more precise control of dosage than does oral administration. In addition parenteral administration can be utilized for children who are unable to take drugs by the oral route.

Complications of Parenteral Drug Administration

Administration of parenteral drugs may be accompanied by microbial contamination, discomfort and inconvenience for the child, local tissue inflammation (i.e., muscle and vein inflammatory reactions), instability of drug solutions with loss of potency (efficacy), and particulate contamination of drug solutions.

Microbial Contamination   Parenteral administration of drugs requires use of meticulous aseptic technique to minimize the risk of infection. Use of sterile dosage forms, sterile equipment (i.e., syringes, needles, etc.), and preparation of the drug in a clean area of the nursing unit are essential. Although the skin can not be sterilized, careful cleansing can reduce microbial flora, thereby reducing the risk of contamination.

Discomfort and Inconvenience   While parenteral drug administration is seldom painful, it does produce varying degrees of anxiety, discomfort, and inconvenience for children of all age groups (see Table 2-1). These complications are best handled by adequate preparation of the child for the administration of the drug, and utilization of measures to reduce and/or relieve anxiety and physical discomfort (see Table 2-2).

Local Tissue Inflammation   Many parenteral drugs are highly irritating to muscular and venous tissues (e.g., cephalothin, diazepam) and cause a high incidence of local inflammatory reactions. Adequate dilution of these drugs according to recommendations of the package insert and deep administration into a large muscle mass or slow infusion into a large vein will minimize these complications.

Instability of Drug Solutions   After reconstitution, the stability of the drug in solution can be affected by the buffers or vehicles used in formulating the drug, by the concentration of the drug, the temperature and pH of the diluent, the presence of other drugs in the mixture, and the duration of the drug's exposure to light and air (Wood, 1977, p. 15).

Loss of stability may result not only in reduction of potency (efficacy) with inadequate dosing but also in adverse reactions. Since manufacturers make changes in buffering systems, vehicles, and preservatives, it is difficult to make authoritative statements on stability, solubility, and incompatibility of drugs (Poole, 1977, p. 218). The validity of existing drug compatibility lists is limited by the fact that such lists are often based on incomplete or conflicting information. Absence of precipitation following addition of a drug, rather than measured changes in drug activity, is often accepted as evidence of drug compatibility (Wood, 1977, p. 15). Since not all interactions between drug and solution or between drugs are characterized by changes of clarity or precipitate, the absence of such changes is not evidence of compatibility.

To reduce the risk of drug instability parenteral drugs must be prepared, administered, and stored according to the directions of the package insert. After preparation, drug solutions should be carefully assessed for changes in color, clarity, and precipitation. Any drug which undergoes changes not designated permissible by the package insert should not be administered.

Particulate Contamination   The prepared drug solution may be contaminated by fragments of rubber, glass, paper, and other undissolved matter. While small amounts of particles are introduced during manufacture of diluents, most such particles gain entry during preparation of the drug. During reconstitution of parenteral drugs care must be taken to dissolve all drug particles, and the solution must be inspected for undissolved matter of any type.

Critical Points in Parenteral Drug Administration to Infants and Children[2]

1. Validate the drug dispensed and the medication ticket by comparing both with original prescription.

2. Use a dosage form appropriate to the parenteral administration route (e.g., sterile suspensions are never administered intravenously; highly irritating drugs are never administered subcutaneously).

3. Utilize *meticulous aseptic technique* in all preparation and administration activities. Syringes, needles, drugs, antiseptic, etc., must be sterile. Careful hand-washing and cleansing of child's injection site reduce microbial population and risk of infection.

4. Administer only drug volumes appropriate to child's growth and development and the nature of the drug. Limited drug volumes (less than 0.5 ml intramuscularly in an infant) are administered by the intramuscular and subcutaneous routes. Larger volumes may be administered by the intravenous route.

5. Reconstitute and administer parenteral dosage forms according to the recommendations of the pharmacy or package insert. Use the recommended diluent, recommended volume, and administer at the recommended rate.

6. Do not mix more than one parenteral drug unless com-

---

[2] The technical, manipulative aspects of drug administration are discussed in other works. No attempt has been made to repeat these aspects, however; only points critical to pediatric administration have been listed.

patibility has been confirmed by the pharmacy or package insert.

7. Store all parenteral drugs under conditions recommended by the pharmacy or the package insert. Discard drugs at expiration of stability period.

8. Use two-needle technique to reduce discomfort of parenteral injection. Discard the sterile needle used to withdraw drug from vial, ampule, or other container. Replace this needle with another sterile needle which is sharper.

9. Use drug administration technique, provision for safety, and provision for support which are appropriate to child's growth and development and which promote development of his or her psychosocial crises.

10. Administer intramuscular injections into adequate muscle mass and rotate injection sites.

11. Assess injection site for local adverse reaction; assess child for systemic adverse reactions.

SUBCUTANEOUS ADMINISTRATION

Insulin, heparin, epinephrine, and several other drugs are injected into the subcutaneous tissues directly beneath the skin. The subcutaneous route is suitable only for nonirritating drugs and for small drug volumes. Long-acting insulins and several other insoluble suspensions are also administered by the subcutaneous route. (Many diabetic children and their parents are taught to administer insulin into the subcutaneous tissues.)

While accessible subcutaneous tissues are located beneath most of the skin surfaces, recommended subcutaneous injection sites include the thighs, upper arms, lower abdomen, and the intrascapular and subscapular areas. The amount of available subcutaneous tissue varies greatly with the child's size, state of hydration, and the amount of adipose tissue present. A neonate or small dehydrated child may have a very thin layer of subcutaneous tissue, while in an obese preadolescent these tissues may extend quite far beneath skin surfaces.

Adverse Reactions

Subcutaneous injection of irritating drugs, injection of large drug volumes, and repeated use of the same injection site produces pain, atrophy, and hypertrophy of tissue. Induration, necrosis, and tissue sloughing may also occur after administration of drugs into the subcutaneous tissues. Thoughtful selection of drugs to be administered by this route, limitation of drug volumes administered, and careful rotation of injection sites will minimize and/or avoid these adverse reactions. Meticulous aseptic technique to prevent infection is an essential part of the subcutaneous injection process.

Administration of Subcutaneous Injections (See Fig. 2-4)

Subcutaneous injections are administered with a small-gauge needle, (i.e., 23- or 25-gauge); however,

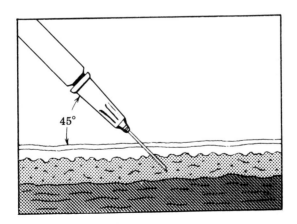

Figure 2-4 Subcutaneous injection into sparse subcutaneous tissues demonstrating a skin-needle penetration angle of 45°. The short needle does not reach deeper muscular tissues.

proper placement of the drug requires a needle of a length adequate to reach the child's subcutaneous tissues and to avoid injection into the deeper muscular tissues. During the injection process the angle at which the skin is penetrated is a factor in proper administration; e.g., an infant or child with sparse subcutaneous tissues obviously requires a shorter needle and a skin-needle penetration angle of 45° or less to place the drug in subcutaneous tissues (Fig. 2-4), but a large or obese adolescent will require a longer needle and may require a skin-needle penetration angle of 90°.

INTRAMUSCULAR ADMINISTRATION

While the intramuscular route can be used for a wide variety of drugs, highly irritating drugs and large drug volumes are not suitable for this route. Infants and young children generally lack adequate muscle mass for multiple intramuscular injections.

Intramuscular Injection Sites (See Fig. 2-5)

Recommended intramuscular injection sites for pediatric patients include ventrogluteal (gluteus medius and gluteus minimus muscles), laterofemoral (vastus lateralis muscle), anterofemoral (rectus femoris muscle), and middeltoid (deltoid muscle). Selection of one site over the other is dependent on the child's age, size, and development of muscular bodies and the nature of the drug (see Table 2-2).

Adverse Reactions

The intramuscular injection is associated with a comparatively high incidence of adverse reactions, some of which result in malpractice suits. Nerve damage with paralysis, muscular fibrosis with contracture, cellulitis, abscess formation, and tissue necrosis with sloughing

(*Text continued on page 88.*)

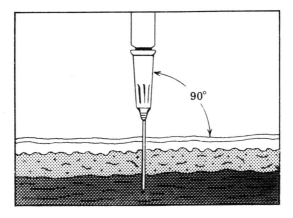

Figure 2-5 Intramuscular injection into muscle demonstrating a skin-needle penetration angle of 90°. The longer needle places the drug well into the muscle mass.

Table 2-2   Administration of Intramuscular Injection

Nursing Actions	Rationale
1. Explain objectives and methods of injection to older child (see Table 2-1 for growth and developmental implications).	Older children are capable of understanding the benefits of drug administration.
2. Use measures appropriate to infant and young child's growth and developmental level to reduce anxiety (see Table 2-1).	Anxiety reduction appropriate to developmental level promotes achievement of psychosocial crisis.
3. Consult site rotation record and select a tentative site which has not been recently used.	Minimizes inflammatory reaction, promotes absorption.
4. Use meticulous aseptic technique in preparing and administering drug.	Prevents infection.
Wash hands thoroughly.	Reduces microbial populations.
5. Select the smallest gauge needle which will deliver the drug readily.	Minimizes pain by decreasing muscle trauma.

Table 2-2   Administration of Intramuscular Injection (*Continued*)

Nursing Actions	Rationale
6. When feasible use neutralized preparations or those containing local anesthetic.	These preparations are less painful (Greenblatt and Koch-Weser, 1976, p. 545).
7. Discard needle used to draw up drug, and replace with sterile needle of same gauge and length for injection.	Needles are dulled by penetration of rubber stoppers and insertion into vials.
8. Leave 0.05 to 0.5 ml of air in syringe.	Air forces drug from needle, seals drug in muscle. (Geolot and McKinney, 1975, p. 788).
9. Remove any drug from outside needle shaft (use sterile wipe).	Leaves "track," irritates nerve endings.
10. At bedside screen child and expose site completely (remove underclothing, diaper, etc.).	Exposure of site permits adequate assessment.
11. Assess tentative site for adequacy of muscle, unabsorbed drug, local inflammatory reactions, etc.	Prevents injection into inappropriate sites.
12. Wash a soiled injection site with soap and warm water, then dry thoroughly. Wash hands thoroughly.	Minimizes risk of infection.
13. Place child in position of maximal muscle relaxation.	Penetration of a relaxed muscle is less painful (Lang et al., 1976, p. 800).
14. Immobilize in a manner appropriate to child's developmental level.	Reduces risk of trauma to child and nurse.
15. Palpate landmarks of site.	Reduces risk of accidental injection into bloodstream and joint spaces. Avoids nerve injury.

Note: Application of an ice cube or volatile spray to skin reduces cutaneous pain perception (Greenblatt and Koch-Weser, 1976, p. 544).

Table 2-2   Administration of Intramuscular Injection (*Continued*)

Nursing Actions	Rationale
16. Thoroughly cleanse skin with antiseptic (using circular motion start with center and work to periphery).	Cleansing the skin with an antiseptic reduces resident bacteria.
Allow skin to dry.	Penetration of dry skin is less painful (Pitel and Wemett, 1964, p. 107).
17. Compress and stretch skin over injection site.	Facilitates cutaneous penetration, and lessens pain (Pitel and Wemett, 1964, p. 107).
18. Penetrate skin and muscle in a single, deft motion. Use a skin-needle angle appropriate to the site and muscle depth (see discussion later in this chapter).	Decreases pain. Assures placement of drug into muscle body.
19. Do not introduce needle completely to its hub.	Leaving a margin of needle facilitates its removal should needle separate from syringe.
20. Aspirate gently, while withdrawing the needle slightly (*How to Give an Intramuscular Injection*, 1967, p. 52). Should blood appear in the syringe, withdraw needle a short distance and redirect into another area, then reaspirate (Pitel and Wemett, 1964, p. 107).	Avoids accidental injection into bloodstream. If the needle tip is pressing against the endothelial surface of a blood vessel, blood return is prevented.
21. Inject drug slowly.	Rapid distention of muscle by drug is more painful (Greenblatt and Koch-Weser, 1976, p. 545).
22. Apply pressure to skin with antiseptic wipe and remove needle.	Traction prevents skin adhering to needle as it is removed.
23. Apply gentle pressure with fresh antiseptic wipe should capillary bleeding occur.	Pressure promotes hemostasis.
Note: Massage of injection site promotes absorption (Greenblatt and Koch-Weser, 1976, p. 543).	Massage increases the area of muscular absorbing surface.

Table 2-2   Administration of Intramuscular Injection (*Continued*)

Nursing Actions	Rationale
Highly irritating drugs and those which discolor tissues may be forced into subcutaneous tissues by massage (Hays, 1974, p. 1071).	
Note: Warm soaks, passive range-of-motion exercises, and massage reduce muscular contractures of quadriceps muscles (McCloskey and Chang, 1977, p. 417).	These measures disrupt and stretch friable scar tissues.
24. Record use of site on the site rotation record.	Avoids too frequent use of any single site.
25. Assess child for pain, numbness, and limited use of extremity.	Identifies nerve damage and contracture.

are not uncommon. Accidental injection into the bloodstream and joint space, pain, infection and elevation of serum enzymes (e.g., creatinine phosphokinase) in infants and young children also occur. Multiple injections increase the risk of these adverse reactions; however, they do occur after a single injection. Disruption of the muscle tissue and the direct necrotizing effects of intramuscular antibiotics apparently contribute to contractures in children (McCloskey and Chang, 1977, p. 417). A decision of the Court of Civil Appeals of Texas in *Southwest Texas Hospital v. Mills* seems to suggest that complications of intramuscular injections are not always due to nursing negligence. In this case a female patient incurred severe left sciatic nerve injury after a preoperative medication was administered into the left buttock. The court held that there was no evidence that the nurse had failed to use ordinary or reasonable care or skill ("Injection Accidents," 1977).

Prevention of Adverse Reactions

Local inflammatory reactions (abscess formation, tissue slough, etc.) can be reduced by rotating injection sites and injection of the drug into a large muscle body. Administration of highly irritating drugs by the Z (zigzag) technique prevents leakage into subcutaneous tissues,

Table 2-3   Critical Points in Administration of Intramuscular Injection by Z Technique*

Nursing Actions	Rationale
1. After drawing up drug, leave from 0.1 to 0.5 ml of air in syringe.	Viscous drugs and older children require more air. This air pushes drug out of needle and seals the drug in the muscle.
2. Prior to penetrating the skin, retract skin and subcutaneous tissues approximately $\frac{1}{8}$ to $\frac{1}{4}$ in laterally and hold in this position.	Eliminates continuous needle path between subcutaneous tissues and muscle.
3. Aspirate after penetrating the skin.	
4. Inject drug slowly.	
5. Wait approximately 10 s.	Distributes drug within the muscle.
6. Remove needle and release retracted tissues immediately.	Seals drug in muscle.
7. Do not massage injection site.	May force drug out of muscle (Hays, 1974, p. 1071).
8. Discourage vigorous exercise and wearing of tight clothing.	May force drug out of muscle.
9. Encourage child to walk at a normal pace.	Promotes drug absorption.
10. Assess site for discoloration and local reactions.	Identifies adverse reactions.

* In addition to the nursing actions of ordinary intramuscular injection, these points are necessary for correct administration of the drug by the Z technique.

thereby avoiding inflammatory reactions and poor drug absorption.

Pain and poor drug absorption associated with intramuscular injection are increased by distension of muscle tissues with a large drug volume. Limiting drug volumes to 2 to 3 ml in an older child and less than 0.5 ml in the infant decreases these adverse reactions. Drugs with a pH far from physiological range are also more painful, and use of neutralized forms of these drugs reduces pain.

Z (ZIGZAG) TECHNIQUE (See Table 2-3)

The Z (zigzag) technique of intramuscular injection is a method by which discoloring (e.g., Imferon) and irritating (e.g., magnesium sulfate) drugs are injected into a muscle and sealed therein. In pediatric patients the Z technique is suitable only for the ventrogluteal site.

Hydroxyzine (Vistaril, Atarax) and diazepam (Valium) are commonly administered by the Z technique; however, Hays suggests that use of this method for all intramuscular injections will promote drug absorption (Hays, 1974, p. 1071). It would seem that the Z technique might reduce the incidence of local inflammatory reactions in pediatric patients.

INTRAMUSCULAR INJECTION SITES

The Ventrogluteal Site (Gluteus Medius and Gluteus Minimus Muscles) (See Table 2-4 and Fig. 2-6)

Gluteus medius arises at the outer surface of the ileum and inserts into the lateral surface of the greater trochanter. Gluteus minimus originates at the outer surface of the ileum and inserts into the anterior border of the trochanter. Both muscles abduct the thigh and rotate it medially.

At birth the gluteal muscles are small and consist primarily of fat. In children who have walked for 1 year

Table 2-4   **Location of the Ventrogluteal Site** (See Fig. 2-6)

1. With fingers pointing toward the child's head, place palm of the hand not being used for the injection on the greater trochanter of the femur.

2. Place the index finger of this hand on the anterior edge of the iliac crest.

3. Place the middle finger on the posterior edge of the iliac crest.

4. Draw an imaginary triangle between these three bony landmarks.

5. Administer injection in the lower half of this triangle, with the needle at a 90° angle to the skin and directed below the iliac crest (Pfizer, 1967, p. 53). (*Note:* Administer no more than 2 to 3 ml in older children and less than 1 ml in a toddler.)

(e.g., 2- to 3-year-olds) both muscles are well developed and their surfaces are extensive.

This site contains little subcutaneous tissue and the skin is quite insensitive; consequently, injections into this area are less painful than other sites. There are no major nerves or blood vessels, and multiple injections are generally well absorbed. However, the ventrogluteal site is contaminated by urine and feces in infants and young children. This site is recommended for

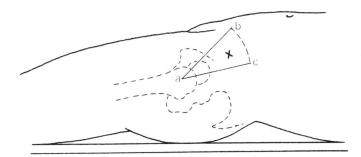

Figure 2-6   Ventrogluteal injection site (gluteus medius and gluteus minimus muscles) for a large adolescent: a, greater trochanter of the femur; b, anterior edge of the iliac crest; c, posterior edge of the iliac crest.

injection in children who have been walking for at least 1 year and in all older children. Injections can be administered with the child on the back, abdomen, side, or in the standing position.

The Laterofemoral Site (Vastus Lateralis Muscle)
(See Table 2-5 and Fig. 2-7)

Vastus lateralis, largest of the quadriceps group, is a broad, deep muscle in children of all ages. It arises at the greater trochanter and inserts into the patella; it extends the knee.

The site is removed from sources of urinary and fecal contamination; however, injection is quite painful. There are no major blood vessels and nerves deep in the area; however, the site is supplied by superficial blood vessels and nerves. Single injections are well absorbed; large volumes, irritating drugs, and multiple injections however, are poorly absorbed.

Laterofemoral is the preferred site for infants and young children, and it can be used for children of all

Table 2-5   **Location of the Laterofemoral Site** (See Fig. 2-7)

1. Palpate the greater trochanter of the femur.

2. Palpate the *lateral* aspect of the patella.

3. Draw an imaginary line between these two bony landmarks.

4. Divide this area on the lateral aspect of the thigh into three equal parts (the child's size will determine the measure used for this division). (*Note:* In an infant, measuring one finger's breadth above the patella and one finger's breadth below the trochanter will divide this area into three equal parts. For a large adolescent, a hand's breadth above the patella and below the trochanter usually divides the area into thirds.)

5. Administer the injection into the middle third of the site, with the needle parallel to the floor or directed slightly toward the anterior aspect of the thigh ("How to Give an Intramuscular Injection," 1967, p. 53).

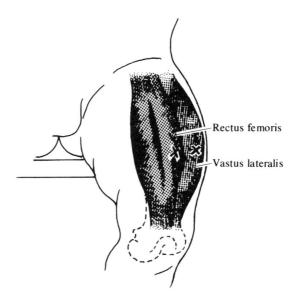

Figure 2-7   Anterolateral injection site (rectus femoris muscle)
and laterofemoral injection site (vastus lateralis) for an infant.

ages. Adverse reactions associated with use of this site
include muscular contracture and occlusion of the superficial femoral artery.

The Anterofemoral Site (Rectus Femoris Muscle)
(See Table 2-6 and Fig. 2-7)

Rectus femoris is a smaller muscle of the quadriceps
group which originates as two tendons at the anterior
inferior iliac spine and at the acetabulum and inserts
into the patella. The muscle extends the knee, and it
presents a limited muscular area for injections. This site
is considered an alternative injection site for infants and
children.

Located on the anterior, lateral aspect of the thigh,
the site is removed from sources of urinary and fecal

Table 2-6   **Location of Anterofemoral Site (Rectus Femoris Muscle)**
(See Fig. 2-7)

---

1. Palpate the greater trochanter of the femur.
2. Palpate the *middle* of the patella.
3. Draw an imaginary line between the two points.
4. Divide this area on the anterior aspect of the thigh into three equal parts (the child's size will determine the measure used for this division). (*Note:* In an infant, measuring one finger's breadth above the patella and one finger's breadth below the trochanter will divide this area into three equal parts. For a large adolescent, a hand's breadth above the patella and below the trochanter usually divides the area into thirds.)
5. Administer the injection into the middle third of the site with the needle on a front-to-back course perpendicular to the lateral plane of the body.

---

contamination. There are no deep major blood vessels or nerves in the area; however, it is supplied by superficial vessels and nerves.

Injections administered into the anterofemoral site are painful, and absorption of multiple injections is poor. Muscular contracture and superficial femoral artery occlusion may occur after injection into this site.

The Middeltoid Site (Deltoid Muscle) (See Table 2-7 and Fig. 2-8)

A thick, triangular muscle which arises from the clavicle and acromion process and inserts into the lateral humerus, the deltoid muscle flexes and assists in adduction of the arm. This area is an accessible alternate injection site which offers a limited muscle surface. The site can be used for single injections in children of all ages; however, limited volumes and nonirritating drugs are required. Injection into the area is painful; multiple injections are poorly absorbed and produce a high incidence of local inflammatory reaction. The area is

Table 2-7   **Location of the Middeltoid Site (Deltoid Muscle)** (See Fig. 2-8)

1. Palpate the axilla and locate the point on the lateral aspect of the arm which is in line with the axilla. This line is the inferior boundary of the middeltoid site.

2. Palpate the acromion process of the scapula. This process is the superior boundary of the site.

3. With one hand on the superior boundary and the other hand on the inferior boundary, move both hands laterally and locate two parallel points one-third and two-thirds of the way around the outer lateral aspect of the arm. These points are the medial and lateral boundaries of the site.

4. Administer the injection within this rectangular site, with the needle diverted slightly upward.

5. Do not inject more than 0.5 ml into an infant or young child or more than 1 ml into a large child.

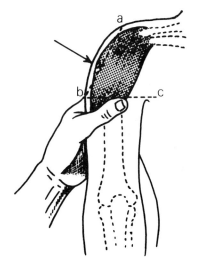

Figure 2-8 Middeltoid injection site (deltoid muscle) for a preadolescent: a, acromion process of the scapula; bc, inferior boundary of middeltoid injection site.

bounded by major nerves, blood vessels, and bony prominences, which must be avoided. Injury to the radial nerve, which occurs occasionally, is characterized by wrist drop. The area is, however, removed from sources of urinary and fecal contamination.

INTRAVENOUS ADMINISTRATION

Intravenous drug administration places the drug directly into the systemic circulation, thereby bypassing the process of absorption. Serum drug concentrations may increase rapidly after intravenous injection; however, careful adjustment of administration rate can control drug concentrations. In the event of an adverse reaction the drug cannot be removed from the bloodstream; however, immediate termination of administration will result in a decline of drug concentration. Most intravenous drugs are administered slowly, and the child must be under close nursing surveillance throughout the administration process.

Advantages of Intravenous Administration

The intravenous route can be used to administer large drug volumes and highly irritating drugs provided they are adequately diluted and administered slowly. It can be utilized for emergency situations (e.g., status asthmaticus, status epilepticus etc.), instances for which prompt response is crucial.

Complications of Intravenous Administration

Administration of drugs by the intravenous route is associated with a high incidence of complications, which include microbial contamination, particulate contamination, thrombophlebitis, and instability of the drug.

Microbial Contamination   Microbial contamination, the most frequent complication of intravenous drug administration, may occur during manufacture of the drug; however, this complication is most likely to occur when drugs are added to intravenous fluids. The risk of contamination is also increased by manipulation of the intravenous infusion set (e.g., changing bottles or bags, attachment of secondary infusion sets, changing infusion sets). Although preparation of intravenous drugs under a laminar flow hood reduces the risk of microbial contamination, one study reported a 17 percent contamination rate of drugs prepared under the laminar flow hood (Wood, 1977, p. 16).

Intravenous drugs and fluids may also be contaminated by microorganisms which migrate from the skin up through the administration set. Daily cleansing of the venipuncture site with alcohol followed by application of a disinfectant and/or antibiotic ointment and a dry, sterile dressing will decrease the risk of contamination by skin flora (Dison, 1975, p. 229).

Most bacteria which contaminate intravenous fluids and drugs require more than 24 h to reach numbers sufficient to cause infection ("IV Filters," 1975, p. 35). Changing the intravenous bottle or bag, primary and secondary administration set, and in-line burette (i.e., Soluset, Buretol) every 24 h reduces the risk of infection due to contaminated drugs and fluids.

Particulate Contamination   Glass, metal, rubber, and other particulate matter may enter intravenous drugs at time of manufacture; however, such contamination generally occurs when such drugs are prepared for injection (Wood, 1977, p. 16). The effects of particulate contamination are unknown; however, use of micropore filters (final filters or in-line filters) does remove particles, bacteria, and fungi from intravenous fluids ("IV Filters," 1975, p. 36).

Thrombophlebitis   Inflammation of the vascular endothelium may be due to irritative reactions to the drug, to the intravenous fluids in which the drug is dissolved, or to the plastic intravenous cannula. Venous irritative reactions can be minimized by adequate dilution of the drug, and by slow administration to decrease the amount of drug with which the vein comes into contact.

Drug Instability   Instability of intravenous drugs in solution can be prevented by reconstituting and storing drugs according to the recommendations of package inserts. Since the presence of two or more drugs in the same solution may decrease the stability of each one, it is not advisable to mix intravenous drugs unless their compatibility has first been confirmed by the pharmacy or package insert. Thus, each drug must be prepared in a separate syringe and administered with a separate in-line burette or other equipment.

Intravenous Dosage Forms

Aminophylline injection, epinephrine injection, and other water-soluble drugs are suitable for administration by the intravenous route. Phytonadione (AquaMephyton), an aqueous colloidal solution of vitamin K, is the only emulsion suitable for administration into the vein.

On the other hand, suspensions and drugs supplied in oily vehicles are never administered by the intravenous route. Intravenous injection of suspensions [e.g., penicillin benzathine suspension (Bicillin), isophane insulin suspension (NPH insulin)] is followed by deposition of insoluble particles in pulmonary vessels, where they produce multiple, small infarcts. Injection of epinephrine (Adrenalin) oil suspension or other drugs supplied in oily vehicles into the bloodstream results in formation of multiple fat emboli.

In the pediatric setting the drugs most frequently administered by the intravenous route include antibiotics (e.g., penicillin G), electrolytes (e.g., potassium chloride), antineoplastic agents [e.g., vincristine (Oncovin)], and aminophylline.

Methods of Administering Intravenous Drugs (See Table 2-8)

Intravenous drugs may be administered by direct injection, continuous infusion, or by intermittent infusion. The method utilized varies with the chemical-physical characteristics of the drug and the goals of drug therapy. Drugs such as diazepam (Valium) and phenytoin (Dilantin) are supplied in a nonaqueous vehicle; they should not be diluted or added to intravenous fluids, and thus are suitable only for direct intravenous injection. Cephalothin (Keflin) is irritating to the venous endothelium; however, pain and thrombophlebitis can be reduced by slow, intermittent infusion of well-diluted cephalothin. In emergency situations such as status asthmaticus, aminophylline or other appropriate drugs may be administered cautiously by continuous intravenous infusion.

Administration of intravenous drugs obviously requires access to a vein (1) by venipuncture, (2) through the injection site of an intravenous infusion administration set, or (3) through a heparin lock. While direct venipuncture may be necessary in emergency situations, repeated direct venipuncture for subsequent administration is technically difficult, uncomfortable, and tends to obliterate existing veins. Drugs administered by direct intravenous injection are usually injected into the injection site of an intravenous infusion set, while drugs for continuous intravenous administration are added to intravenous fluids and administered over a prolonged interval.

Direct Intravenous Injection of Drugs   Direct intravenous injection of drugs, usually considered a physician's responsibility, is indicated for emergency situations and for drugs which cannot be diluted. Since this method of administration produces rapid increases in serum drug concentrations, it carries a very high risk of adverse reactions. To reduce this risk, most drugs administered by direct intravenous injection are injected slowly. The

Table 2-8   Administration of Intravenous Drugs

Nursing Action	Rationale
1. Preparation of the drug:	
a. Observe meticulous asepsis in all drug preparations (i.e., use of sterile diluent and equipment, laminar flow hood, etc.)	Minimizes risk of microbial contamination.
b. Reconstitute drug with type and amount of diluent recommended by package insert.	Reduces risk of instability, thereby assuring retention of maximum potency and correct dosing.
c. Store drug under conditions recommended by package insert.	
d. Avoid mixing drugs unless their compatibility is verified first by literature or pharmacy (i.e., use separate equipment to prepare and administer drugs).	Prevents instability due to physical incompatibility.
e. Inspect prepared drug for particles (undissolved drug, glass, rubber, etc.).	Effects of particulate contamination are unknown.
f. Label unused drug with pertinent data before placing in appropriate storage area (i.e., date and time of preparation, concentration, date and time of expiration). Discard drug at end of stability period.	Promotes retention of maximum potency with correct dosing.
g. Drugs for continuous intravenous infusion should be added to infusion bottle or bag with the container in the "upright" (the opposite of infusion position) position.	Avoids "layering" of drug, thus promotes adequate mixing of drug with intravenous fluid.
h. Label bottle, bag, in-line burette, etc., with drug, dose, time started and time drug should have been completely administered, child's name, and other pertinent data.	Assures administration to correct child at the recommended rate.
2. Validate patency of the vein, assess vein for evidence of inflammation or infiltration.	Administration into subcutaneous tissues may cause severe tissue inflammation.

Table 2-8   Administration of Intravenous Drugs (*Continued*)

Nursing Action	Rationale
3. Use meticulous aseptic technique in administering the drug (cleanse injection site of primary tubing with antiseptic before piggybacking secondary set, change minibags or minibottles with utmost care, etc.).	Reduces the risk of microbial contamination.
4. Keep manipulations of primary infusion set to a minimum.	Reduces the risk of microbial contamination.
5. Administer drug at rate recommended by package insert.	Minimizes risk of local inflammatory reactions (i.e., pain, phlebitis).
6. During drug administration and after completion assess child closely for adverse reactions.	Early recognition permits immediate termination of drug and treatment of reaction.
7. Care of venipuncture site and intravenous infusion:	
a. Immobilize extremity in a manner appropriate to child's growth and developmental level. Permit minimal movement without opportunity to disrupt infusion.	Reduces risk of infiltration.
b. Protect scalp vein venipuncture site with commercial device or other appropriate protector.	Reduces risk of infiltration and accidents.
c. Assess venipuncture site frequently for evidence of infiltration, phlebitis, or other adverse reaction.	Permits early recognition and preventive measures.
d. Cleanse venipuncture site daily with antiseptic, followed by application of disinfectant and/or antibiotic ointment. Cover site with dry, sterile dressing.	Minimizes risk of microbial contamination.
e. Change all infusion equipment (infusion set, in-line burette, bottle or bag, etc.) at least once every 24 h.	Minimizes risk of microbial contamination.

child treated must always be carefully assessed for manifestations of adverse reactions.

Continuous Intravenous Infusion of Drugs Continuous intravenous infusion of drugs provides sustained serum drug concentrations over a prolonged interval. Incomplete mixing of the drug with the intravenous fluids into which it is dissolved may occur, particularly with plastic infusion bags. This inadequate mixing is more likely to occur if the drug is added to a plastic intravenous bag which is in the infusion (hanging) position (Wood, 1977, p. 17). Inadequate mixing of drug and intravenous solution occurs after addition of drugs to glass bottles in the infusion position only if the drug is added very slowly ("Plastic Containers," 1975, p. 44). After addition of the drug to the intravenous fluid, significant amounts of some drugs [e.g., vitamin A, warfarin (Coumadin)] may be attracted (adsorbed) to the surface of plastic intravenous infusion bags. The amount of drug adsorbed is determined by type of intravenous solution, its temperature, and the duration of time the mixture is stored (Wood, 1977, p. 16).

Intermittent Administration of Intravenous Drugs Intermittent administration is utilized when alternating increases and decreases in drug serum concentrations are indicated. This method of intravenous administration also decreases the time that irritating drugs are in contact with venous endothelium. Drugs for intermittent intravenous administration are usually administered with a secondary intravenous administration set (e.g., Soluset, Buretrol), which is attached (piggybacked) to the administration set of a primary intravenous infusion. Although the goal of intermittent intravenous administration does not change, the many types of administration sets available require the nurse to adapt manipulative skills to the particular product available. A complete discussion of administration sets in common use is not within the scope of this work; however, the manufacturers' information includes diagrams and complete directions for use of the product.

Intermittent Intravenous Drug Administration Equipment Intermittent intravenous drugs are usually administered with an in-line burette (e.g., Soluset, Buretrol) or with special secondary administration sets (e.g., Add-A-Line Secondary Set, Secondary Piggyback Venoset).

IN-LINE BURETTES Several manufacturers produce in-line burettes, all of which contain a calibrated chamber or burette which is located in the line between the solution bottle or bag and the tubing. Since these in-line devices deliver 60 drops per milliliter, they permit precise control of drug and intravenous solution administration. After preparation of the drug and its dilution in the chamber, the in-line device is attached ("piggybacked") to the primary intravenous infusion administration set at an appropriate injection site. It is important to point out that the multiplicity of in-line devices available makes it mandatory for the nurse to read the product information for the particular device in use.

SPECIAL SECONDARY ADMINISTRATION SETS Special secondary administration sets consist of short administration tubing which incorporates a regular drip chamber. They are piggybacked to the Y-injection site of primary intravenous administration sets, which incorporate a check valve. Since these secondary administration sets provide no means for drug dilution, they are used with minibags or minibottles which contain reconstituted drug, and are not suitable for drugs which require a second dilution.

Hanging the primary infusion bottle or bag lower than the secondary infusion bottle or bag (i.e., minibottle or minibag which contains the drug) closes the check valve, thereby permitting the drug to infuse first. Once the drug container is empty, the check valve is opened, and the primary infusion resumes its flow. Since the minibag or minibottle contains a single dose, it is discarded after one use, and a new minibag or minibottle of drug is prepared for the next drug administration.

To avoid malfunction of the check valve and entry of air into the primary administration set, it is imperative to read and follow directions included with these sets.

ADMINISTERING INTRAVENOUS DRUGS VIA HEPARIN LOCK

The heparin lock, a needle connected to an injection site by a short length of tubing, is placed into a vein and secured in place with tape. Patency of the vein is maintained by flushing and filling the needle with a dilute heparin and normal saline solution. The precise amount of heparin and saline required to maintain patency varies with the needle size and length of the tubing (Geolot and McKinney, 1975, p. 793). Since continuous infusion of fluid is not necessary, restriction of movement is unnecessary, and the danger of fluid overload is eliminated.

Although the heparin lock has been traditionally utilized for the administration of heparin, it is now used to administer all intravenous drugs by direct injection or intermittent infusion. It may also be used for the withdrawal of serial blood samples when repeated venipuncture is difficult or contraindicated. Advocates of heparin lock use cite not only the comfort and convenience of the device but also suggest that it may actually reduce the incidence of drug-associated phlebitis (Hanson, 1976, p. 1102).

BIBLIOGRAPHY

AMA Department of Drugs: *AMA Drug Evaluations*, 3d ed., Publishing Sciences Group, Littleton, Mass., 1977.

American Academy of Pediatrics: "Inaccuracies in Administering Liquid Medications," *Pediatrics*, vol. 56, no. 2, 1975, pp. 327–328.

Asnes, R. S., and B. Grebin: "Pharmacotherapeutics: A Rational Approach," *Pediatric Clinics of North America*, vol. 21 no. 1, 1975, pp. 81–94.

Brandt, P. A., et al.: "IM Injections in Children," *American Journal of Nursing*, vol. 72 no. 8, 1972, pp. 1402–1406.

Brown, M. S., and M. A. Murphy: *Ambulatory Pediatrics For Nurses*, McGraw-Hill, New York, 1975.

Chezem, J. L.: "Locating the Best Thigh Injection Site," *Nursing 73*, December, 1973, pp. 20–21.

Crawford, J. D., et al.: "Simplification of Drug Dosage Calculation by Application of the Surface Area Principle," *Pediatrics*, vol. 5, no. 4, 1950, pp. 783–789.

Dison, N.: *Clinical Nursing Techniques*, 3d ed., Mosby, St. Louis, 1975.

Erikson, E. H.: *Childhood and Society*, 2d ed., Norton, 1963.

Geolot, D. H., and N. P. McKinney: "Administering Parenteral Drugs," *American Journal of Nursing*, vol. 75, no. 5, 1975, pp. 788–793.

Godwin, N. N.: "Intermittent and Direct I.V. Push: Rationale and Procedures," *American Journal of I.V. Therapy*, December 1974–January 1975, pp. 27–30.

Greenblatt, D. J., and M. D. Allen: "Intramuscular Injection-Site Complications," *Journal of the American Medical Association*, vol. 240, no. 6, 1978, pp. 542–544.

——— and J. Koch-Weser: "Intramuscular Injection of Drugs," *The New England Journal of Medicine*, vol. 295, no. 10, 1976, pp. 542–546.

Gruber, D. L.: "Helping the Child Accept I.V. Therapy," *American Journal of I.V. Therapy*, March 1977, pp. 50–51.

Hanson, R. L.: "Heparin-Lock or Keep-Open I.V.?" *American Journal Journal of Nursing*, vol. 76, no. 7, 1976, pp. 1102–1103.

Hays, D.: "Do It Yourself the Z-Track Way," *American Journal of Nursing*, vol. 74, no. 6, 1974, pp. 1070–1071.

How to Give an Intramuscular Injection, Pfizer Laboratories, New York, 1967.

"Injection Accidents: Sometimes No Liability," *The Regan Report on Nursing Law*, vol. 17, no. 10, March 1977.

Intramuscular Injections, Wyeth Laboratories, New York, 1964.

"IV Filters," *The Medical Letter*, vol. 17, no. 8, April 11, 1975, pp. 35–36.

Kendig, E. L.: *Disorders of the Respiratory Tract in Children*, 2d ed., Saunders, Philadelphia, 1972.

Lang, S. H., et al.: "Reducing Discomfort from IM Injections," *American Journal of Nursing*, vol. 76, no. 5, 1976, pp. 800–801.

Leifer, G. H.: *Principles and Techniques in Pediatric Nursing*, 3d ed., Saunders, Philadelphia, 1977.

Lewis, L. W.: *Fundamental Skills in Patient Care*, Lippincott, Philadelphia, 1976.

Maki, D. G., et al.: "Infection Control in Intravenous Therapy," *Nursing Digest*, vol. 3, no. 3, 1975, pp. 5–10.

Marlow, D. R.: *Textbook of Pediatric Nursing*, 5th ed., Saunders, Philadelphia, 1977.

McCloskey, J. R., and M. K. Chang: "Quadriceps Contracture as a Result of Multiple Intramuscular Injections," *American Journal of Diseases of Children*, vol. 131, 1977, pp. 416–417.

Nowak, M. M., et al.: "Rectal Absorption from Aspirin Suppositories in Children and Adults," *Pediatrics*, vol. 54, no. 1, 1974, pp. 23–26.

Pitel, M., and M. Wemett: "The Intramuscular Injection," *American Journal of Nursing*, vol. 64, no. 4, 1964, pp. 104–109.

"Plastic Containers for Intravenous Solutions," *The Medical Letter*, vol. 17, no. 10, May 9, 1975*b*.

Poole, H. H.: "Drugs in Infusion Fluids," *Adverse Drug Reaction Bulletin*, no. 62, February 1977, pp. 216–219.

Prue, B., and R. K. Elliott: "Bethesda Hospital I.V. Reference," *American Journal of I.V. Therapy*, December 1976–January 1977, pp. 22–34.

"Research Leads to More Effective Way of Administering

Eyedrops," *Journal of the American Medical Association*, vol. 236, no. 21, 1976, p. 2371.

Scipien, G. M., et al.: *Comprehensive Pediatric Nursing*, McGraw-Hill, New York, 1975.

Shirkey, H. C.: *Pediatric Dosage Handbook*, American Pharmaceutical Association, Washington, D.C., 1973.

_____: "Drug Therapy," in V. C. Vaughn and J. R. McKay (eds.), *Textbook of Pediatrics*, 10th ed., Saunders, Philadelphia, 1975, pp. 284–288.

Snider, M. A.: "Helpful Hints on I.V.'s," *American Journal of Nursing*, vol. 74, no. 11, 1974, pp. 1978–1981.

United States Pharmacopeia XIX, Mack, Easton, Pa., 1975.

Wood, A. J. J: "Continuous Drug Infusions: Problems and Solutions," *Drug Therapy (Hosp.)*, February 1977, pp. 14–20.

3

Drugs Used to Treat Pediatric Infections

ANTIBIOTICS

Definition

Antibiotics are complex chemicals produced by microorganisms or synthesized in the laboratory. They are used to treat a wide variety of bacterial and nonbacterial infections.

Antibiotic Groups

The numerous antibiotics available for use are divided into groups of chemically related agents (*families*) which share similar characteristics. Major antibiotic groups include the penicillins, cephalosporins (e.g., Keflin), tetracyclines, and aminoglycosides (e.g., gentamicin).

Mechanisms of Action

Antibacterial action of these agents is directed against bacterial structures not found in humans; thus, they are relatively nontoxic to human beings. The method by which an antibiotic inhibits bacteria is known as the agent's *mechanism of action*.

Bactericidal antibiotics (e.g., penicillin, cephalosporins) destroy bacteria and are effective against actively multiplying pathogens. *Bacteriostatic* antibiotics (e.g., tetracyclines, chloramphenicol) weaken bacteria and are effective against both active and resting strains.

Spectrum of Activity

The range of microorganisms susceptible to an antibiotic is expressed figuratively as the drug's *spectrum of activity.* Broad-spectrum antibiotics (e.g., tetracyclines, chloramphenicol) are effective against a wide range of pathogens, while narrow-spectrum ones (e.g., penicillins, aminoglycosides) are effective against a limited range. Some strains of a usually susceptible bacteria may develop resistance to an antibiotic by undergoing changes. Laboratory culture and susceptibility studies are used to determine whether or not bacteria are resistant to an antibiotic.

Clinical Uses

Since infections are major health problems in infants and children, the antibiotics are important drugs in pediatrics. In addition to use in treating infections antibiotics are used also to prevent infections in children (e.g., rheumatic fever, bacterial endocarditis).

Adverse Reactions

Adverse reactions associated with antibiotic administration include hypersensitivity (allergic reaction) and superinfection. Hypersensitivity reactions vary from mild (e.g., oral lesion, skin rashes) to serious (e.g., serum sickness, angioedema, and anaphylactic reactions).

Hypersensitivity Reactions   Serum sickness, characterized by rash, joint pain, generalized edema, and fever, usually persists for 1 to 2 weeks.

Angioedema is manifested by swelling of eyes,

tongue, and lips, urticaria, and asthmatic breathing. Respiratory tract obstruction may occur.

Anaphylactic reaction consists of bronchial constriction, abdominal pain, generalized weakness, hypotension, and circulatory collapse. Immediate nursing action is necessary to avoid disaster.

Superinfection   Large doses of an antibiotic or prolonged administration of antibiotics alters the normal flora of the gastrointestinal tract, upper respiratory tract, and genitourinary tract. This alteration in flora may result in a new infection (i.e., superinfection) caused by a resistant strain (usually fungi and gram-negative rods). Superinfections are more frequent with broad-spectrum antibiotics and in children who are immunosuppressed (i.e., patients with diabetes, wounds, burns, catheters or tubes of any kind, or tracheostomies, or who are receiving cortisone or anticancer drugs; or who are infants).

Nursing Interventions During Antibiotic Therapy

1. Before administering an antibiotic obtain a nursing history with particular attention to whether child has received the antibiotic before and whether or not there was any hypersensitivity reaction. Inform the physician if the nursing history reveals previous hypersensitivity.

2. Have emergency drugs (i.e., cortisone, vasopressors, epinephrine, and bronchodilators) and emergency equipment (i.e., pediatric-size endotracheal tubes, suction machine, oxygen, tracheostomy tubes) available and in working condition.

3. Obtain specimen for culture and susceptibility studies before initiating antibiotic therapy.

4. Identify child at high risk of superinfection and provide meticulous aseptic care for all wounds, tubes, etc.

5. Prepare, administer, and store the antibiotic according to recommendations of the package insert.

6. Assess child frequently for evidence of hypersensitivity and superinfection.

7. Assess effectiveness of the antibiotic and communicate any evidence of antibiotic resistance to the physician.

PENICILLINS (See Table 3-1)

General Considerations

The penicillins are a large group of bactericidal antibiotics which share a common basic structure. They inhibit synthesis of the bacterial cell wall and are closely related to the cephalosporins (e.g., Keflin). The various penicillins vary in their acid stability, antibacterial spectrum, and susceptibility to destruction by enzymes (i.e., penicillinases).

Clinical Uses

Penicillins are effective against many gram-positive and gram-negative cocci, strains which cause many of the infections that occur in children. They are prescribed

(Text continued on page 117.)

Table 3-1   Penicillins

Drug and Dose	Comments	Nursing Actions
PENICILLINASE-SUSCEPTIBLE PENICILLINS		
Penicillin G, sodium, potassium: Neonates: 30,000 U/kg IM or IV every 12 h Older infants and children: 6250 to 12,500 U/kg IM or IV every 6 h Up to 300,000 to 400,000 U/kg continuous IV infusion daily	An aqueous penicillin; short duration of action. 1,000,000 U potassium salt (yields 1.6 meq potassium). 1,000,000 U sodium salt (yields 1.68 meq sodium). More effective against gram-positive cocci.	Dry powder stable at room temperature. Solutions stable 1 week under refrigeration.

Table 3-1   Penicillins (Continued)

Drug and Dose	Comments	Nursing Actions
Procaine penicillin G (Wycillin, Duracillin): Neonates: not recommended Older infants and children: 500,000 to 1,000,000 U/m² IM once daily	Long-acting, slowly absorbed penicillins. Both contain particulate matter and should never be injected intravenously.	Administer only after aspirating carefully. Stable 6 to 12 months under refrigeration.
Penicillin G benzathine (Permapen, Bicillin): Usual pediatric dose: 600,000 to 1,200,000 U IM as single dose 1,200,000 U IM once a month	Higher incidence of hypersensitivity reactions than with other penicillins. Used in prophylaxis of rheumatic fever and bacterial endocarditis.	
Penicillin G benzathine tablets, penicillin G potassium tablets: Children under 12 years: 6250 to 22,500 U/kg PO every 6 h Children 12 years and over: 200,000 to 500,000 U PO every 4 to 6 h	Poorly absorbed from the gastrointestinal tract. Presence of food further decreases absorption. Used for mild infections or for prevention of streptococcal recurrences.	Administer $\frac{1}{2}$ to 1 h before, or 2 to 3 h after, meals
Phenethicillin (Maxipen, Sycillin) (AMA Department of Drugs, 1977, pp. 699–700): Children, mild to moderate infections: 125 to 250 mg PO every 6 h Children, severe infections: 250 mg/kg PO every 6 h Infants: 12.5 to 50 mg/kg PO daily in three to six divided doses		Administer $\frac{1}{2}$ to 1 h before, or 2 to 3 h after, meals.

Table 3-1   Penicillins (*Continued*)

Drug and Dose	Comments	Nursing Actions
Penicillin V (Penvee, Compocillin): Infants and children below 12 years: 6250 to 22,500 U/kg PO every 6 h Children 12 years and over: 250 mg to 1.25 g PO daily	Highly stable in gastric acid. May be better absorbed in the presence of food (Goodman and Gilman, 1975, p. 1142).	Administer after meals.

EXTENDED-SPECTRUM PENICILLINASE-SUSCEPTIBLE PENICILLINS

Drug and Dose	Comments	Nursing Actions
Ampicillin sodium (Omnipen, Principen): Usual pediatric dose: 12.5 to 50 mg/kg PO, IM, or IV every 6 h	Extended-spectrum penicillin effective against gram-negative strains. Presence of food decreases oral absorption. High incidence of rashes and diarrhea.	Administer oral preparations $\frac{1}{2}$ to 1 h before or 2 to 3 h after meals. Oral liquid dosage forms stable 2 weeks under refrigeration. Parenteral solutions must be used within 1 h of preparation.
Amoxicillin (Amoxil, Larotid)	Lower incidence of rashes and diarrhea than ampicillin. Well-absorbed in presence of food.	
Carbenicillin disodium (Pyopen, Geopen) (Rolewicz, 1976b, pp. 733, 734): Neonates: 200 to 400 mg/kg per day IM or IV in four divided doses Older infants and children: 400 to 600 mg/kg per day IM or IV in four divided doses	An expensive penicillin which is used for gram-negative infections (i.e., *Proteus, Pseudomonas, Escherichia coli*). Acts synergistically with gentamicin (Garamycin) against some *Pseudomonas* strains.	Parenteral solutions stable for 24 h at room temperature. Do not mix carbenicillin and gentamicin in same syringe, tubing, etc. Give frequent oral hygiene. Assess for hypernatremia.

Table 3-1   Penicillins *(Continued)*

Drug and Dose	Comments	Nursing Actions
50 to 65 mg/kg per day PO in four doses	May produce an unpleasant taste. One gram of parenteral preparation yields 4.72 meq sodium. Oral carbenicillin also introduces a considerable sodium load.	

PENICILLINASE-RESISTANT PENICILLINS

Drug and Dose	Comments	Nursing Actions
Methicillin sodium (Staphcillin): Usual pediatric dose: 25 mg/kg IM every 6 h	Methicillin is indicated for treatment of infections caused by penicillinase-producing staphylococci. It is prescribed for susceptible infections of skin, soft tissues, and respiratory tract. Reversible bone marrow depression with anemia, neutropenia, or granulocytopenia occurs rarely. Intramuscular methicillin may be more painful than other penicillins.	Monitor serial blood cell studies. Dry powders are stable; however, solutions are unstable in the presence of heat, acidic solutions, and some basic antibiotics. Intravenous solutions are stable for 4 to 8 h depending on drug concentration. Intramuscular solutions are stable for 4 days under refrigeration.
Oxacillin sodium (Bactocil, Prostaphlin): Neonates: 6.25 mg/kg PO every 6 h Children under 40 kg: 12.5 to 25 mg/kg IM, IV, or PO every 6 h Children over 40 kg: 500 to 1000 mg PO every 4 to 6 h	The drug is poorly absorbed from the gastrointestinal tract, and food further reduces absorption.	Administer oral preparations ½ to 1 h before, or 2 to 3 h after, meals. Parenteral oxacillin is more stable in the presence of acid substances than methicillin. Intramuscular solutions

Table 3-1   Penicillins (*Continued*)

Drug and Dose	Comments	Nursing Actions
250 to 1000 mg IM or IV every 4 to 6 h		are stable for 1 week under refrigeration. Intravenous solutions lose less than 10 percent of potency at room temperature over 6 h.
Dicloxacillin sodium monohydrate (Dynapen, Veracillin) Children under 40 kg: 3 to 6 mg/kg PO every 6 h Children over 40 kg: 125 to 250 mg PO every 6 h	The presence of food decreases absorption of dicloxacillin.	Oral solutions are stable for 2 weeks under refrigeration. In spite of vigorous shaking these preparations may form lumps. Administer drug in the fasting state.
Cloxacillin sodium (Tegopen, Cloxapen): Children under 20 kg: 12.5 to 25 mg/kg PO every 6 h Children over 20 kg: 250 to 500 mg PO every 6 h	Gastrointestinal absorption is rapid and erratic, and food decreases absorption.	Administer cloxacillin in the fasting state. Oral solutions are stable for 2 weeks under refrigeration.
Nafcillin sodium (Unipen, Nafcil): Neonates: 10 mg/kg IM or PO every 6 to 12 h Older infants and children: 6 to 12 mg/kg PO every 6 h 25 mg/kg IM every 12 h	Poorly absorbed from the gastrointestinal tract regardless of the presence of food.	Oral solutions are stable for 1 week under refrigeration. Intravenous solutions lose less than 10 percent of potency at room temperature over a 10-min interval. Unused intravenous solutions should be discarded after 24 h. Intramuscular solutions are stable for 1 week under refrigeration.

for susceptible infections of the lung, bone, soft tissues, and other structures. Penicillins are also effective against gonorrhea, syphilis, anthrax, and gas gangrene. Many hospital-acquired staphylococci produce enzymes (penicillinases) which inactivate some penicillins. Penicillinase-resistant penicillins (e.g., methicillin) are prescribed for staphylococcal infections.

Absorption

Penicillins vary in their absorption from the gastrointestinal tract; acid-stable penicillins are well absorbed. Absorption after intramuscular injection is rapid and efficient.

Distribution

Although penicillins readily enter most body fluids and tissues, they do not penetrate the cerebrospinal fluid unless meningeal inflammation or an immature blood-brain barrier are present.

Excretion

Most penicillins are excreted unchanged in the urine. Methicillin (Staphcillin), ampicillin (Omnipen), and nafcillin (Unipen) are partially excreted into the bile.

Neonates and other children with poor renal function accumulate excessive drug plasma concentrations unless penicillin dosage is individualized. Laboratory determination of drug plasma concentration is the most reliable method to adjust penicillin dosage in these children.

Excretion in Breast Milk   Since penicillins are acidic, low concentrations are excreted into breast milk. Penicillin ingested in breast milk may sensitize the infant and cause candidiasis (Savage, 1976, p. 212). There is, however, no agreement on whether breast feeding is contraindicated during penicillin therapy (O'Brien, 1975, p. 23).

Significant Interactions

Administration of probenecid (Benemid) with a penicillin results in reduced urinary excretion of the penicillin, and prolongs its effect. This interaction is used clinically in the treatment of venereal diseases.

Adverse Reactions

Adverse reactions to penicillins include hypersensitivity (allergic) reactions, superinfection, irritative reactions, electrolyte disturbances, and, rarely, renal damage and hematologic disorders.

Hypersensitivity Reactions Hypersensitivity reactions, estimated to occur in 1 to 10 percent of individuals treated with penicillin, are more likely in children with asthma or other allergies, and in those with fungal infections (AMA Department of Drugs, 1977, p. 696). While these reactions occur occasionally after oral administration, they are more likely after parenteral administration. Anaphylaxis, serum sickness, angioedema, oral lesions, skin rashes, fever, and eosinophilia are adverse reactions associated with penicillins. Children with syphilis might have chills, fever, sore throat, joint pain, and exacerbation of syphilitic lesions several hours after the first penicillin dose. This reaction, the *Jarisch-Herxheimer reaction*, abates spontaneously within 12 h. Cross-hypersensitivity to cephalosporins is not rare.

Superinfections Large doses or prolonged therapy with penicillins might cause superinfection with gram-negative rods or fungal strains.

Irritative Reactions Gastrointestinal irritation associated with oral administration of penicillin might produce nausea, vomiting, and diarrhea. Intramuscular administration may cause pain, abscess formation, and other local irritative reactions. Venous irritative reactions include pain, phlebitis, and thrombophlebitis. Large parenteral doses of penicillin G may cause central nervous system irritation, mainly in neonates; however, this may also occur in children with central nervous system lesions or epilepsy. The reaction is characterized by neuromuscular irritability, convulsions, arachnoiditis, and other signs of brain pathology.

Electrolyte Disturbances   Some penicillins contain significant amounts of sodium and potassium; thus, children with renal, cardiovascular, and hepatic disorders may develop electrolyte disturbances with large doses.

Nursing Actions During Penicillin Therapy

1. Before starting penicillin therapy, question parents and older children carefully regarding prior penicillin or cephalosporin allergy. Also inquire about asthma, allergy to any substance, and fungal infections.

2. An affirmative answer to one of these questions places the child at high risk of hypersensitivity. High-risk children must be so identified to all pediatric health workers.

3. Have emergency drugs—epinephrine, vasopressors, corticosteroids, and antihistamines—on hand. Emergency equipment, i.e., endotracheal tubes (pediatric size) and tracheostomy tube, oxygen, and suction machine, must also be readily available in working condition.

4. Observe child carefully after penicillin administration for asthmatic breathing, restlessness, collapse, giant urticaria, and abdominal pain. Evidence of these warrants immediate nursing measures to maintain patent airway and blood pressure.

5. All infants and children receiving large parenteral doses must be evaluated frequently for central nervous system irritation.

6. Infants receiving intrathecal penicillin should be observed and evaluated continually for neurological damage.

7. Children with impaired natural defenses must be identified as being at high risk of superinfection. Scrupulous aseptic care of wounds, catheters, or tubes must be given.

8. Careful inspection of wounds, skin, and body orifices must be made for signs of purulent drainage.

9. Diarrhea, symptoms of urinary tract and respiratory tract infection, or other signs of infection should be communicated to the physician.

10. Neonates and other children with impaired renal or hepatic function must be evaluated continually for penicillin toxicity. Laboratory plasma concentrations are usually determined; however, clinical evidence of toxicity may precede laboratory changes.

11. Careful, frequent inspection of cutaneous and membrane surfaces for candidal infections are important. Any rectal or vaginal scratching should be followed by close visual inspection.

12. Periodic cultures of urine, feces, respiratory tract, or other areas should be made on children receiving long-term therapy.

13. Children receiving potassium or sodium penicillin salts should be watched for electrolyte disturbances. Slow administration of intravenous penicillin will prevent these disturbances.

14. The electrolyte load should be calculated for all children on sodium-restricted diets. Cardiac, hypertensive, or uremic pediatric patients are at risk of electrolyte disturbance.

15. Laboratory reports of serum electrolytes should be noted by all nurses who care for the child.

16. Observation of urine for hematuria and sharp decrease in output may detect early nephrotoxicity.

17. Penicillins for oral and parenteral use must be reconstituted and stored according to manufacturer's directions.

18. Meticulous aseptic technique is necessary to prevent contamination and resulting infection.

19. Parenteral penicillin should never be mixed physically with any other drug.

20. Intramuscular penicillin should be given deep into a large muscle mass. It is important to aspirate before injecting penicillin!

21. Intravenous penicillin should be administered slowly to prevent pain and irritative reactions.

22. Children on oral penicillin should have daily inspection for oral lesions. These children must be evaluated for nausea, vomiting, and diarrhea, also.

23. Children on penicillin must be inspected frequently for skin rashes and evidence of dermatitis.

24. Fever, joint pain, and itching must be reported to the physician.

25. Liquid penicillin must be measured with standardized measuring devices. Vomiting or refusal to take the drug must be reported to the physician.

Parent Teaching for Ambulatory Children Receiving Penicillins

Instruction should be given in clear language that the parent or mothering adult can understand. Since children are unable to take their own medications, it is important that the parent understand the rationale and outcomes of antibiotic therapy. Parents who do not comply usually have reasons, however erroneous, for not doing so. Most parents will do as instructed if they understand the benefits of giving the drug and the risks of not doing so. Written instructions and reminding devices are associated with higher compliance rates. The health worker's estimation of parental reliability does not always correlate with actual compliance; there are no methods by which to predict noncompliance. Some parents believe that oral antibiotics are ineffective and that compliance is of little consequence. Parents should also know that baby-sitters, grandparents, teachers, and other adults with whom the child spends time must be told that the child is receiving or has recently received penicillin.

Children on rheumatic fever or bacterial endocarditis prophylaxis receive parenteral penicillin in clinic or physician's office. Parents or other persons entrusted with the care of the child should be instructed as follows:

1. Penicillin prescriptions should be filled and a standardized measuring device should be requested from the pharmacy for liquid penicillins.

2. Liquid penicillins should be refrigerated according to the pharmacist's directions. Solid dose forms should be stored in a cool, dark place out of children's reach.

3. The drug should be given as directed to the child for whom it is prescribed. The drug must be given until it is all taken even if the child feels better.

4. Asthmatic breathing, facial edema, weakness, and diarrhea with abdominal pain are serious. Child and medication should be brought to nearest emergency room, clinic, or doctor's office. The parent must be prepared to tell physician that the child is taking penicillin.

5. Fever, joint pain, itching, refusal to eat, rashes, and hives should be reported to doctor's office or clinic. Mouth sores, black tongue, or hairy tongue must also be reported. Mouth, rectum, and skin should be checked for signs of thrush.

6. If the child is found to be allergic to penicillin, this information must be recorded with vaccination records. This should be told to all nurses and doctors who take care of the child. If the child is old enough to understand, he or she should be told of the penicillin allergy.

7. If fever, cough, or other signs of infection continue, doctor's office or clinic should be promptly notified.

8. If the child vomits the medicine or refuses to take it, he or she should not be forced to take it, but the clinic or doctor's office should be notified.

9. If there is leftover penicillin, it should be thrown away. It should not be saved for future use.

10. Give the parent best wishes for a speedy recovery for the child.

ERYTHROMYCIN (See Table 3-2)

Indications

Erythromycin, an important drug for pediatric infections, is used as an alternative drug for children who are hypersensitive to penicillin. The drug is indicated for mild to moderately severe susceptible infections caused by gram-positive and gram-negative cocci. It is also used to eradicate the diphtheria carrier state and to prevent rheumatic fever recurrence.

Absorption

Acid-stable preparations are adequately absorbed from the gastrointestinal tract; however, the presence of food may decrease or delay absorption.

Distribution

Erythromycin readily enters most intracellular fluids and tissues. In the absence of meningeal inflammation the drug does not enter the cerebrospinal fluid readily.

Table 3-2   Erythromycin Preparations

Drug and Dose	Nursing Implications
Erythromycin base (E-mycin, Ilotycin): Usual pediatric dose: 7.5 to 25 mg/kg PO every 6 h	Unstable in the gastric pH, and the presence of food delays absorption. Administer the drug $\frac{1}{2}$ to 1 h before, or 2 to 3 h after, meals.
Erythromycin stearate (Bristamycin, Ethril): Usual pediatric dose: 7.5 to 25 mg/kg PO every 6 h	More stable in gastric acid; however, there are individual variations in absorption. Higher concentrations are attained if the drug is administered in the fasting state.
Erythromycin estolate (Ilosone) (AMA Department of Drugs, 1977, p. 729): Children under 10 kg: 10 mg/kg PO every 6 h Children 10 to 25 kg: 125 mg PO every 6 h Children over 25 kg: 250 mg PO every 6 h (maximum 4 g daily)	Stable in gastric fluid, and food does not affect absorption.
Erythromycin ethylsuccinate (EES, Pediamycin): Usual pediatric dose: 7.5 to 25 mg/kg PO every 6 h	Acid-stable, and in children over 2 years of age is well absorbed in the presence of food. Children under 2 years do not absorb the drug adequately in the presence of food. Consequently, the drug may be administered without regard for meals in those over 2 years. Children 2 years of age should receive the drug $\frac{1}{2}$ to 1 h before, or 2 to 3 h after, meals.
Erythromycin lactobionate (Erythrocin): Usual pediatric dose: 5 to 10 mg/kg IV every 12 h Erythromycin gluceptate (Ilotycin): Usual pediatric dose: 5 to 10 mg/kg IV every 12 h	Both the lactobionate and gluceptate are usually administered over an interval of 20 to 60 min to minimize pain and venous irritation. These drugs must be reconstituted and stored according to the recommendations of the package insert.

In neonates and children with meningeal inflammation cerebrospinal fluid concentration may reach therapeutic levels.

Metabolic Fate

The drug is concentrated in the liver, excreted in the bile, and a major portion is excreted unchanged in the feces, while a small portion is excreted in active form in the urine. Neonates and other children with inadequate hepatic and renal function require dosage reduction to avoid accumulation of excessive erythromycin concentrations. Breast milk concentration may be higher than those of the plasma (O'Brien, 1975, p. 25).

Adverse Reactions

Erythromycin causes few adverse reactions; however, hypersensitivity reactions, irritative reactions, and superinfection may occur. Hypersensitivity reactions, which are generally mild, include skin rashes, fever, and eosinophilia.

The estolate ester (Ilosone) may produce liver damage, particularly after prolonged therapy or after repeated use of the drug. This condition is believed to be a hypersensitivity reaction.

Gastrointestinal irritation, associated with the oral route, is manifested by abdominal distress with cramping, pyrosis, nausea, and vomiting.

Intramuscular administration often causes severe, prolonged pain, sterile abscess formation, necrosis, and other local irritative reactions. These reactions make the intramuscular route unsuitable for infants and young children.

Intravenous administration produces pain, phlebitis, and thrombophlebitis.

Dosage Forms

At present there are six erythromycin formations available for clinical use. These preparations differ in acid stability, plasma concentrations produced, route of administration, and adverse reactions. The drug is supplied as chewable tablets, enteric-coated tablets, suppositories, and parenteral solutions.

Nursing Actions During Erythromycin Therapy

1. Promote maximal absorption by administering oral erythromycin preparations according to manufacturers' recommendations.

2. Reconstitute and store parenteral erythromycin preparations according to recommendations of the package insert. Some parenteral preparations must be diluted with solutions which contain no preservatives!

3. Administer intramuscular preparations deep into a large muscle mass.

4. Intravenous erythromycin preparations should be administered over an interval of 20 to 60 min.

CEPHALOSPORINS (See Table 3-3)

General Considerations

The cephalosporins are a group of broad-spectrum, semisynthetic antibiotics which are chemically related to the penicillins. Although cephalosporins are not destroyed by penicillinases, some members of this group are inactivated by the cephalosporinases which some bacteria produce. Some methicillin-resistant *Staphylococcus* strains are cross-resistant to cephalosporins.

Indications

While cephalosporins are not considered antibiotics of first choice, they are widely promoted and prescribed. They are expensive agents and the Veterans' Administration Committee on Antimicrobial Drug Use states that many infections for which cephalosporins are pre-

Table 3-3   Cephalosporins

Drug and Dose	Comments	Nursing Actions
Cephalexin (Keflex): Usual pediatric dose: 6 to 12 mg/kg PO every 6 h	The drug is well absorbed from the gastrointestinal tract; food delays, but does not decrease, absorption.	Administer $\frac{1}{2}$ to 1 h before, or 2 to 3 h after, meals. Solutions should be kept tightly closed and well shaken before using. These preparations are stable for 2 weeks under refrigeration.
Cephaloglycin dihydrate (Kafocin) Children: 25 to 50 mg/kg PO every 6 h (AMA Department of Drugs, 1977, p. 723)	Administered only by the oral route. The presence of food delays but does not decrease absorption.	Administer $\frac{1}{2}$ to 1 h before, or 2 to 3 h after, meals.
Cephalothin sodium (Keflin) Usual pediatric dose: 10 to 45 mg/kg IM or IV every 4 to 6 h	Intramuscular administration may cause pain, fever, induration, tenderness, sterile abscess, or tissue necrosis. The intramuscular route is not considered suitable for infants and young children. One gram of cephalothin contains 2.8 meq of sodium, and susceptible children may have electrolyte disturbances.	Administer intramuscular cephalothin deep into large muscle mass. Do not mix cephalothin and aminoglycoside in the same solution. Monitor serum electrolyte reports. Assess for hypernatremia, and overhydration. Calculate sodium load the drug provides. Solutions are stable for 96 h under refrigeration. If the solution precipitates, it can be redissolved by warming to room temperature with constant agitation. These solutions can be frozen according to recommendations of the package insert.

scribed can be treated by less expensive antibiotics (Veterans' Administration, 1977, pp. 1241, 1243). The oral cephalosporins are among the most expensive oral antibiotics, and the parenteral preparations generate the highest antimicrobial costs in hospitals (Veterans' Administration, 1977, pp. 1241, 1243). There do not appear to be significant differences in the newer and older cephalosporins.

Oral cephalosporins are indicated primarily for long-term treatment of selected staphylococcal infections of bone, urinary tract, and other areas which cannot be treated by less expensive drugs ("The Cephalosporins," 1977, pp. 33, 34). Parenteral cephalosporins are indicated for susceptive gram-negative infections. They are administered concurrently with gentamicin (Garamycin) or another aminoglycoside antibiotic when the infection strain is unknown or the infection is serious. Cephalosporins are also considered alternative antibiotics for susceptive infections in children who are hypersensitive to penicillins (AMA Department of Drugs, 1977, p. 713).

Absorption

The acid-stable cephalosporins are adequately absorbed from the gastrointestinal tract; however, food may delay or decrease absorption. Cephalosporins are well absorbed after intramuscular administration.

Distribution

After absorption these agents are fairly widely distributed throughout body fluids; however, they do not penetrate the cerebrospinal fluid under normal conditions. The permeable blood-brain barrier of the neonate and the child with meningeal inflammation or other cerebral pathology does result in entry of cephalosporins into the cerebrospinal fluid.

Excretion

Cephalosporins are excreted primarily by the kidney, either unchanged or as metabolites; several members of the group are excreted in the bile. Neonates and children with inadequate renal function require dosage adjustment to avoid accumulation of excessive concentrations. These agents are apparently not excreted in breast milk (O'Brien, 1975, p. 25).

Significant Interactions

Concurrent administration of a cephalosporin with furosemide (Lasix) may enhance the nephrotoxicity potential of the cephalosporin (*Evaluations of Drug Interaction*, 1976, p. 391). Administration of probenecid (Benemid) with a cephalosporin decreases urinary excretion of the antibiotic. Combining an aminoglycoside antibiotic (e.g., gentamicin, amikacin) with a cephalosporin results in additive antibacterial activity against some gram-negative rods.

Effects on Urine Glucose Tests

Children receiving cephalosporins may have false-positive reactions for urine glucose if reducing agents (Clinitest tablets, Benedict's solution, etc.) are used. Enzyme reagent strips (Tes-Tape, Dip Stick) are apparently not affected by cephalosporins.

Adverse Reactions

Irritative Reactions Oral cephalosporins may cause anorexia, nausea, vomiting, and severe diarrhea due to gastrointestinal tract irritation. Intramuscular administration is often accompanied by pain, sterile abscess formation, and tissue slough. The intravenous route of administration may produce pain, phlebitis, and thrombophlebitis, particularly with large doses or rapid administration of the drug.

Superinfection   Superinfection caused by *Pseudomonas* and fungal strains, particularly in children with impaired natural defenses, may also occur.

Nephrotoxicity   Cephaloridine (Loridine) has high nephrotoxic potential, and concurrent administration of an aminoglycoside, ethacrynic acid (Edecrin), or furosemide (Lasix) or a decrease in cardiac output increases this nephrotoxic potential ("Adverse Interaction," 1977, p. 6). Cephalothin (Keflin) produces renal damage rarely; however, Appel and Neu suggest that with wider use other cephalosporins may be incriminated in nephrotoxicity (Appel and Neu, 1977, p. 668).

Electrolyte Disturbances   Several cephalosporins are supplied as sodium salts; hence, administration of these drugs may produce electrolyte disorders in susceptible children.

Transient increases in SGOT, SGPT, and alkaline phosphatase has also been reported with cephalosporin therapy.

Nursing Actions During Cephalosporin Therapy

1. While collecting data for the medication history, question the parents carefully about antecedent penicillin or cephalosporin hypersensitivity reaction. Children who have had previous penicillin hypersensitivity reaction require continual nursing evaluation to prevent serious reaction to cephalosporins.

2. Have emergency drugs (epinephrine, bronchodilators, vasopressors, corticosteroids) and equipment on hand at all times.

3. Obtain appropriate laboratory specimens before starting the drug. Interpret baseline and serial lab reports.

4. To prevent loss of potency, store, reconstitute, and administer cephalosporins according to the manufacturers' recommendations. Do not mix parenteral cephalosporins with other drugs.

5. Identify children at risk of interactions, superinfection, and nephrotoxicity. Provide meticulous aseptic care to all wounds, tubes, and catheters, and obtain culture and susceptibility studies if drainage or other signs of superinfection occur. Assess neonates and other children with renal inadequacy for decrease in urine output, hematuria, and proteinuria.

6. Evaluate for diarrhea, nausea, and vomiting. (Nausea and vomiting in an infant can lead to fluid and electrolyte disorders.)

7. Assess frequently for skin rashes, serum sickness, and anaphylaxis. Intervene as indicated.

8. Use Tes-Tape or Dip Stick to ascertain urine glucose.

9. Assess effectiveness of antibacterial action.

TETRACYCLINES (See Table 3-4)

Restrictions of Usage

The tetracyclines are a group of broad-spectrum antibiotics which are toxic to bones and teeth of the fetus and the child under 8 years of age. Their use during this critical period is restricted to serious infections which cannot be treated by less dangerous antibiotics (American Academy of Pediatrics, 1975, p. 142).

Indications

There appear to be few indications for tetracycline use in children under 8 years of age. Most bacterial infections seen in this age group are more susceptible to antibiotics other than the tetracyclines (Yeager, 1977, p. 210).

The Medical Letter consultants recommend tetracyclines as first-choice antibiotics for treatment of cholera,

Table 3-4   Tetracyclines

Drug and Dose	Comments	Nursing Actions
Doxycycline monohydrate (Doxy II, Vibramycin): Children 45 kg and less: 2.2 mg/kg every 12 h for two doses, then 1.1 to 2.2 mg/kg every 12 h Children over 45 kg: 100 mg every 12 h for two doses, then 50 to 100 mg every 12 h	Severe gastrointestinal symptoms are common. Concurrent administration of anticonvulsants and barbiturates decreases half-life of doxycycline.	
Minocycline hydrochloride (Minocin, Vectrin) (AMA Department of Drugs, 1977, p. 745): Children under 12 years: 4 mg/kg PO initially, then 2 mg/kg PO every 12 h Children over 12 years: 200 mg PO initially, then 100 mg PO every 12 h Children: 4 mg/kg IV initially, then 2 mg/kg IV every 12 h	Produces a high incidence of vestibular toxicity with nausea, vomiting, vertigo, and ataxia.	Instruct child not to skateboard and engage in active sports or other activities which increase risk of injury.
Demeclocycline hydrochloride (Declomycin): Infants and children: 6 to 12 mg/kg PO in two to four doses (AMA Department of Drugs, 1977, p. 745)		

brucellosis, relapsing fever, trachoma, psittacosis, inclusion conjunctivitis, lymphogranuloma venereum, melioidosis, primary atypical pneumonia, Rocky Mountain spotted fever, and all other rickettsial infections ("The Choice of Antimicrobial Drugs," 1976).

Available Preparations

The seven tetracyclines presently available have similar antibacterial and pharmacological characteristics; however, there are some variations. These preparations differ in the rate and efficacy of absorption, degree of plasma protein binding, rate and primary route of excretion, and duration of action.

Dosage Schedules

Since all tetracyclines are eliminated slowly, it is usually necessary to initiate therapy with a comparatively large "loading" dose, and then to continue with a smaller maintenance dose. The newer tetracyclines have relatively long half-lives, which permits smaller doses at longer dose intervals. Tetracyclines tend to be present in the blood and tissues long after therapy has been discontinued.

Absorption

Tetracyclines are incompletely absorbed from the gastrointestinal tract; however, food and drugs which contain metal ions (calcium, magnesium, iron, sodium bicarbonate, etc.) decrease absorption. The metal ions in dairy products, vitamins, iron and other mineral preparations, antacids, cathartics, and antidiarrheals form insoluble complexes with tetracyclines, which results in erratic and decreased absorption. Food does not appear to produce decreased absorption of doxycycline (Vibramycin) and minocycline (Vectrin, Minocin).

Distribution

Tetracyclines penetrate most body tissues and fluids readily, and they enter the cerebrospinal fluid in the absence of meningeal inflammation. They have an affinity for growing and metabolically active tissues; thus, they are stored in the liver, spleen, bone, teeth, and in neoplasms. These agents have a particularly high affinity for rapidly developing bones and teeth during the last half of gestation and the first 8 years of life.

Metabolic Fate

Tetracyclines are generally concentrated by the liver, excreted in the bile, and reabsorbed through the intestinal wall into the bloodstream. They then undergo enterohepatic cycling and are ultimately eliminated in the urine. These drugs are also excreted in the feces; however, the amount excreted in the urine and feces varies. Children with renal or hepatic impairment require reduction in tetracycline dosage to prevent accumulation of excessive concentrations.

Excretion in Breast Milk   Significant tetracycline concentrations are excreted in the breast milk. Both Savage and O'Brien state that maternal administration of therapeutic tetracycline doses cause no adverse effects in the nursing infant (Savage, 1976, p. 1212; O'Brien, 1975, p. 25). Hill and Mirkin, on the other hand, state that the adverse effects associated with tetracycline therapy to nursing infants make breast feeding a contraindication to administration of tetracyclines (Hill, 1976, p. 571; Yaffe and Stern, 1976, p. 399).

Adverse Reactions

In the first 8 years of life tetracyclines produce permanent tooth discoloration and reversible bone growth development. Increased intracranial pressure has been seen in infants. Superinfections, liver damage, renal damage, and phototoxicity may occur. Ingestion of outdated tetracycline capsules have produced reversible renal tubular acidosis (AMA Department of Drugs, 1977, p. 743).

Significant Interactions

Concurrent administration of phenytoin (Dilantin), carbamazepine (Tegretol), and barbiturates with a doxycycline (Vibramycin) increases metabolism of the antibiotic. The decreased doxycycline effect produced by this interaction might necessitate an increase in dosage.

Nursing Actions During Tetracycline Therapy

1. Question or view critically tetracycline prescriptions for children under 8 years of age.

2. Differentiate loading dose (if prescribed) from the maintenance dose.

3. Protect child from direct sunlight and ultraviolet light source.

4. Note expiration dates of all tetracycline capsules. Store these dosage forms in tightly closed containers, away from heat, light, and humidity. Reconstitute and administer parenteral tetracyclines according to the recommendations of the package insert. (Do not reconstitute with calcium-containing solutions.)

5. Administer oral tetracyclines 3 h after ingestion of drugs which contain metal ions.

Table 3-5   Antituberculosis Drugs

Drug and Dose	Pharmacology	Nursing Interventions
Ethambutol hydrochloride (Myambutol): no dosage recommendations for children under 13 years.	Synthetic antituberculosis agent which is highly effective. Excreted in the urine; thus, children with renal impairment require dosage reduction. High doses cause ocular toxicity with blurring or fading of vision. Hypersensitivity and gastrointestinal disturbances are rare.	

Isoniazid (INH, Nydrazid):
  Usual pediatric dose: for conversion of tuberculin test with no disease and for prophylaxis: 5 mg/kg PO every 12 h (up to 300 mg daily)
  Usual pediatric dose: for treatment of tuberculosis: 5 to 15 mg/kg PO every 12 h (up to 300 to 500 mg daily)
	Synthetic antituberculosis agent, which is highly effective.
	
	Metabolized by liver enzymes, which are genetically controlled.
	
	Metabolites are excreted in urine. Present in breast milk; infants should be monitored Peripheral neuritis and hepatotoxicity may occur.
		Assess for numbness and tingling of extremites.
		
		Administer total dose once daily.

Rifampin (Rifadin, Rimactane): Children over 5 years: 10–20 mg/kg PO once daily (up to 600 mg daily)	A macrolide antibiotic also used for meningitis carrier state. Food decreases absorption. Metabolized by liver and metabolites excreted into the urine. Colors urine, feces, tears, and saliva a reddish orange.	Administer total dose once daily 1 h before, or 2 h after, meals. Inform child and parents that drug will color excretions.

Table 3-5   Antituberculosis Drugs (*Continued*)

Drug and Dose	Pharmacology	Nursing Interventions
	Liver impairment necessitates dosage reduction.	
	Nausea, vomiting, flatus, and abdominal cramps are not unusual.	
	Jaundice, liver damage, hypersensitivity reactions occur occasionally.	Interpret laboratory reports of liver function.
	Interruption of drug may cause severe flulike syndrome.	
	Concurrent administration with oral anticoagulants and corticosteroids decreases effect of the anticoagulant and corticosteroid.	Monitor prothrombin time reports. Discuss dosage adjustment with physician.
Aminosalicylic acid (Parasal): Children: 0.3 g/kg per 24 h PO in three divided doses (Vaughn and McKay, 1975, p. 1737)	Synthetic antituberculosis agent. Available as sodium calcium and potassium salt. Excreted in the urine, and renal impairment is a contraindication to its use. Nausea, anorexia, abdominal distress, and epigastric pain are common. Severe diarrhea may also occur. Hypersensitivity, acidosis, and hepatic damage have been reported. Electrolyte disturbance may occur with sodium and potassium salt.	Administer drug with meals or aluminum hydroxide to reduce gastrointestinal upset. If tolerated, administer total dose at one time.

Table 3-6   Miscellaneous Antimicrobials

Drug and Dose	Pharmacology	Nursing Interventions
Spectinomycin hydro-chloride (Trobicin): no dosages are available for infants and children.	A bacteriostatic anti-biotic which inhibits bacterial protein synthesis. The drug is indicated for treatment of gonorrheal strains. This drug is not effective for syphilis. Administered by the intramuscular route, and absorption is rapid. The drug is poorly bound to plasma pro-teins and is excreted unchanged in the urine. Intramuscular adminis-tration tends to be quite painful. Nausea, dizziness, chills, insomnia, and oliguria may occur.	Dry powder is stable for 3 to 6 months. Reconstitute drug in accompanying diluent. Suspensions are stable for 24 h at room temperature. Administer spectino-mycin deep into large muscle mass.
Bacitracin (Baciguent): Children: Topical appli-cation to lesion twice a day	A mixture of antibiotics; inhibits bacterial cell wall synthesis. The drug is effective against a variety of bacteria; however, its serious adverse reactions and the availability of less dangerous agents limit its use to topical applica-tion to infected skin and membranes. The drug is available as ointment both alone and in combination with other antimicrobials.	

Table 3-6   Miscellaneous Antimicrobials (*Continued*)

Drug and Dose	Pharmacology	Nursing Interventions
	Since bacitracin has some neuromuscular blocking effects, it may enhance the blocking action of inhalation anesthetics and surgical muscular relaxants.	
	Hypersensitivity reactions are uncommon after topical use.	Observe area for signs of local irritation.
Nystatin (Nilstat, Mycostatin): Premature and low-birth-weight neonates: 100,000 U PO every 6 h Older infants: 200,000 U PO every 6 h Other children: 400,000 to 600,000 U PO every 6 h	A complex antibiotic that is fungistatic and fungicidal against a wide spectrum of yeast and yeastlike strains. The drug is administered orally and topically for fungal infections of skin, mucous membrane, vagina, and gastrointestinal tract. Oral absorption is poor, and nausea, vomiting, and diarrhea are common. Local irritations and hypersensitivity reactions may occur after topical application.	Mycostatin is available as ointment, oral suspension, oral tablets, creams, powders, and vaginal tablets. The drug is also combined in the above dosage forms with other antimicrobial agents.
Pyrvinium pamoate (Povan, Vanquin): Children with pinworms: Single dose of 350 mg PO; repeated in 1 week Children with threadworms: 350 mg PO daily for 5 to 7 days	Drug of choice for pinworm and threadworm infections. The drug is supplied as tablets and oral suspension. Absorption is limited. Nausea, vomiting, and	Instruct older child to swallow tablet without chewing. Refrain from spilling oral suspension on bedding, clothing, etc. Inform child and parents

Table 3-6   Miscellaneous Antimicrobials (*Continued*)

Drug and Dose	Pharmacology	Nursing Interventions
	abdominal distress may follow large doses. Stains clothing, mouth, and feces a bright red color.	that drug will color the feces a bright red.
Griseofulvin (Grisactin, Fulvicin, etc.): Usual pediatric dose: 500 to 1000 mg PO daily	A fungistatic antibiotic selectively effective against ringworm of scalp, palms, soles, nails, etc. The drug does not inhibit bacteria other than tinea. The drug is contra-indicated in children with hepatic impair-ment. Administered by the oral route, absorption is erratic. Deposited in the skin, hair, and nails; and small percentages are excreted in urine and perspiration. Vomiting, diarrhea, photosensitivity, and estrogenlike syndrome occur rarely. Concurrent ingestion of alcoholic beverages produces a minor Antabuse-like reaction ("Interaction of Alcohol," 1977, p. 48).	
Nitrofurantoin (Furadantin, Cyantin): Older infants and children: 1.25 to 1.75 mg/kg PO every 6 h	A synthetic anti-microbial used for urinary tract infections. Available in small crystal (microcrystal-	Administer drug with or after meals, to prolong effect.

Table 3-6   Miscellaneous Antimicrobials (*Continued*)

Drug and Dose	Pharmacology	Nursing Interventions
	line) and large crystal (macrocrystalline) dosage forms.	
	Food increases its therapeutic duration in the body.	
	Excreted in the urine; not usually administered to children with renal impairment.	
	Colors the urine brown.	
	Nausea, vomiting, diarrhea, and rash occur. Hypersensitivity, drowsiness and pulmonary fibrosis, and jaundice occur rarely.	
Sulfisoxazole (Gantrisin): Children over 2 months: 75 mg/kg initially PO, then 37.5 mg/kg PO every 6 h (not to exceed 6 g/daily)	A short-acting sulfonamide, which exerts a wide spectrum of antibacterial activity. Used for uncomplicated urinary tract infections, trachoma, nocardiosis, and inclusion conjunctivitis.	
	Metabolized extensively by liver. Excreted in urine; crystalluria may occur. Children with hepatic or renal impairment require dosage reduction.	Hydrate child to prevent renal damage.
	Excreted in breast milk; infant should not nurse during maternal use of drug.	

Table 3-6   Miscellaneous Antimicrobials (*Continued*)

Drug and Dose	Pharmacology	Nursing Interventions
	In neonate, displaces bilirubin from binding sites.	
	Hypersensitivity reactions, blood dyscrasias, and liver damage occur occasionally.	Assess for skin rashes, fever, and sore throat.
	Nausea, vomiting, diarrhea, and anorexia are common.	
Nalidixic acid (NegGram): Children under 12 years: 55 mg/kg PO daily in four divided doses (AMA Department of Drugs, 1977, p. 793)	Synthetic antimicrobial used for urinary tract infections.	Assess for emergence of resistant strains (i.e., continuation of urinary tract infections).
	Resistance develops rapidly.	
	Metabolized by liver and excreted in urine. Children with liver and renal impairment require dosage reduction.	Obtain urine specimens for susceptibility.
	Excreted into breast milk; infant should be bottle fed during maternal therapy with drug.	
	Nausea, vomiting, rash, and urticaria are common.	
	Large doses may cause insomnia, restlessness, and convulsions in epileptic children.	
	Blood dyscrasia, photosensitivity occur rarely.	
	Increased intracranial pressure has been reported.	Assess young child for bulging fontanels.

Table 3-6   Miscellaneous Antimicrobials (*Continued*)

Drug and Dose	Pharmacology	Nursing Interventions
	Causes false-positive for urinary glucose.	
Trimethoprim-sulfa-methoxazole (Bactrim, Septra) (AMA Department of Drugs 1977, p. 784): Children 2 months to 2 years: $\frac{1}{4}$ tablet PO every 12 h for 12 to 14 days Children 2 to 6 years: $\frac{1}{4}$ to $\frac{1}{2}$ tablet PO every 12 h for 12 to 14 days Children 6 to 12 years: $\frac{1}{2}$ to 1 tablet PO every 12 h for 12 to 14 days Children over 12 years: 2 tablets PO every 12 h for 12 to 14 days	A sulfonamide combination which exerts broad spectrum of antibacterial activity. Limited antifungal and antiprotozoal activity. Used for urinary tract infections, typhoid fever, cholera, and gram-negative infection. Metabolized by liver, excreted in urine; hepatic and renal impairment necessitates dosage reduction. Crystalluria may occur. Liver damage and kidney damage occur occasionally. Produces blood dyscrasias, hypersensitivity reactions. Anorexia, nausea, vomiting, and diarrhea are common.	Force fluids to prevent renal damage. Interpret laboratory reports of renal and liver functions. Assess for rash, fever, and sore throat.
Chloramphenicol (Mychel, Chloromycetin, etc.): Neonates to 2 weeks: 6 mg/kg PO or IV every 6 h Older infants and children: 125 mg/kg PO or IV every 6 h	The serious adverse reactions associated with chloramphenicol restrict its use to specific life-threatening infections which cannot be treated by less dangerous antibiotics.	

Table 3-6   Miscellaneous Antimicrobials (*Continued*)

Drug and Dose	Pharmacology	Nursing Interventions
	Chloramphenicol is effective against a wide spectrum of pathogenic microorganisms; however, the availability of less dangerous, equally effective antibiotics for pediatric infections limit use of chloramphenicol to treatment of typhoid fever and *Hemophilius influenzae* infections. *H. influenzae,* a gram-negative rod, produces life-threatening meningitis, bacteremia, pneumonia, and soft-tissue infections. The drug is considered an important alternate antibiotic for treatment of certain anaerobic infections, brucellosis, and *Neisseria meningitides.* Chloramphenicol base is rapidly absorbed from the gastrointestinal tract; however, the palmitate ester must first be converted to the parent drug. The immature gastrointestinal enzymes of an infant may be unable to perform this conversion; thus, in this age group a major percentage of the drug may be excreted unabsorbed in the feces (Rolewicz, 1976*a*, p. 560). The drug	

Table 3-6   Miscellaneous Antimicrobials (*Continued*)

Drug and Dose	Pharmacology	Nursing Interventions
	enters brain and cerebrospinal fluid in the absence of meningeal inflammation. Other body fluids and most tissues are also well penetrated.	
	Approximately 90 percent of the drug is metabolized in the liver, and metabolites and a small amount of unchanged chloramphenicol are then excreted in the urine.	
	For the first 14 days of life, the neonate has immature, poorly functioning chloramphenicol metabolizing systems; thus, these infants inactivate the drug slowly and inefficiently. The immature, poorly functioning renal system excretes chloramphenicol and its metabolites slowly and inefficiently. Neonates and older infants require special dosage schedules to prevent accumulation of excessive chloramphenicol concentrations and toxicity (gray syndrome). These infants should have periodic serum chloramphenicol determination by microanalytic techniques. Older infants and chil-	

Table 3-6   Miscellaneous Antimicrobials (*Continued*)

Drug and Dose	Pharmacology	Nursing Interventions
	dren with hepatic or renal impairment also metabolize and excrete chloramphenicol slowly and inefficiently. These children also require special dosage reduction and periodic serum determinations to prevent toxicity.	
	Chloramphenicol is also excreted in breast milk, and breast feeding is contraindicated during its administration (Hill, 1976, p. 571).	Advise nursing mother on chloramphenicol to bottle-feed infant and to pump breast and discard the milk.
	Neonates who do not receive special chloramphenicol dosage schedules may accumulate toxic serum concentration, and develop toxicity (gray syndrome). This reaction is characterized by vomiting, diarrhea, hypothermia, ashen skin, cyanosis, and vasomotor collapse. Gray syndrome has occurred in neonates whose mothers received chloramphenicol during labor. There have also been reports of gray syndrome in 6- and 8-month-old infants, as well as in a 25-month-old toddler (Hill, 1976, p. 574; Rolewicz, 1976*a*, p. 563).	Provide constant nursing surveillance of all neonates receiving chloramphenicol. Monitor serum chloramphenicol concentration reports. Withhold drug and communicate with physican as indicated.

Table 3-6   Miscellaneous Antimicrobials (*Continued*)

Drug and Dose	Pharmacology	Nursing Interventions
	Chloramphenicol produces aplastic anemia, superinfections, and hypersensitivity reactions. Stomatitis, bitter taste, diarrhea, perineal irritation, and optic neuritis in children with cystic fibrosis may also occur.	Interpret baseline and serial hematology reports. Assess for lassitude, bleeding tendency, rapid pulse, and sore throat.
	Concurrent administration of chloramphenicol with an oral anticoagulant, oral hypoglycemic, or phenytoinlike anticonvulsant inhibits metabolism of these drugs, thereby increasing their anticoagulant, hypoglycemic, and anticonvulsant effects ("Adverse Interaction of Drugs," 1977, p. 6). This interaction generally necessitates dosage reduction to prevent toxicity.	Identify the child at risk of interaction and discuss feasibility of dose reduction with physician. Monitor closely for evidence of anticonvulsant or anticoagulant toxicity.
	Chloramphenicol inhibits the intermediary metabolism of alcohol; thus, ingestion of alcoholic beverages results in a minor Antabuse-like reaction with abdominal pain, headache, weakness, nausea, and vomiting ("Interaction of Alcohol," 1977, p. 48).	Caution adolescents not to drink alcohol during chloramphenicol therapy.
Metronidazole (Flagyl): Usual pediatric	Synthetic amebicidal agent, used for intesti-	

Table 3-6   Miscellaneous Antimicrobials (*Continued*)

Drug and Dose	Pharmacology	Nursing Interventions
antiamebic dose: 11 to 17 mg/kg PO every 8 h for 10 days	nal and hepatic amebiasis. Metabolized in liver and excreted in the urine. Colors the urine reddish brown. Excreted in breast milk, and breast feeding is contraindicated during therapy. Anorexia, nausea, vomiting, unpleasant metallic taste common. Dizziness, vertigo, and ataxia occur rarely; generally in individuals with central nervous system disorders. Central nervous system disorder is a contraindication to use of the drug. Consumption of alcohol produces Antabuse-like reaction.	

Clindamycin hydro-chloride, phosphate (Cleocin) (AMA Department of Drugs, 1977, pp. 731–732):
  Infants and children over 1 month of age:
    8 to 20 mg/kg PO daily in three divided doses
    15 to 40 mg/kg IM daily in three or four doses
    15 to 40 mg/kg IV daily in three to four doses
	Clindamycin, and its related antibiotic lincomycin are used in treatment of infections caused by *Bacterioides* and *Staphylococcus aureus* strains.
	
	Metabolized by the liver and excreted by bile and feces. Hepatic impairment necessitates dosage adjustment.	

Table 3-6   Miscellaneous Antimicrobials (*Continued*)

Drug and Dose	Pharmacology	Nursing Interventions
	Produces severe colitis which may terminate in ulcerative colitis and death.	
	Parenteral administration may produce hypotension.	Administer IV preparation slowly. Monitor blood pressure.
	Bitter taste, esophageal irritation, and glossitis are not unusual.	Administer oral preparation with one full glass of water to reduce esophageal irritation.
	Administration of clindamycin with Kaopectate results in decreased antibiotic absorption.	

AMINOGLYCOSIDES (See Table 3-7)
General Considerations

The aminoglycosides are a group of antibiotics which are effective against many gram-negative bacteria. These agents share similar antibacterial and pharmacological properties, and their action is increased in the presence of an alkaline medium.

While aminoglycosides are important antibiotics, their potential for toxicity tends to limit their use in infants and children to serious infections which cannot be treated by less dangerous agents.

Indications

Streptomycin and kanamycin are used for treatment of tuberculosis, and other members of the group are administered orally to prevent hepatic coma or to control gram-negative–mediated diarrhea. Paromomycin (Humatin) has direct amebicidal effects. Gentamicin (Garamycin), tobramycin (Nebicin), and amikacin (Amikin) are administered with carbenicillin (Pyopen, Geopen) to treat some serious *Proteus* and *Pseudomonas* infections.

Aminoglycosides are administered parenterally for systemic effects. They are also applied to denuded or burned areas and instilled into closed cavities and wounds. These agents are administered orally for their effects on the gastrointestinal flora. They are administered intrathecally for serious gram-negative bacillary infections of the central nervous system.

When feasible, administration of aminoglycosides is generally limited to 2 weeks or less, to prevent toxicity of these agents.

Absorption

Although aminoglycosides are poorly absorbed from the gastrointestinal tract, some drug absorption does occur after oral administration. After intramuscular adminis-

Table 3-7   Aminoglycosides

Drug and Dose	Comments	Nursing Actions
Amikacin sulfate (Amikin) (AMA Department of Drugs, 1977, p. 765): Neonates: 10 mg/kg IM or IV (loading dose), then 7.5 mg IM or IV every 12 h Older infants and children: 15 mg/kg daily IM or IV in two to three divided doses		A colorless, stable solution which requires no refrigeration. The drug retains potency for 2 years, and a change of color to pale yellow does not indicate decrease in potency.
Gentamicin sulfate (Garamycin): Neonates less than 1 week: 3 mg/kg IM every 12 h Infants and neonates: 2 mg/kg IM every 8 h Children: 1 to 1.7 mg/kg IM every 8 h 1 to 2 mg/kg IV every 8 h		The drug is a clear, stable liquid, which requires no refrigeration.
Tobramycin sulfate (Nebcin) (AMA Department of Drugs, 1977, p. 764): Neonates to 1 week: 4 mg/kg daily IM or IV in two divided doses Older infants and children: 3 to 5 mg/kg daily IM or IV in three divided doses		The drug is supplied as a colorless, stable liquid, which requires no refrigeration.
Streptomycin sulfate: Usual pediatric dose: 10 mg/kg IM every 12 h	Streptomycin is effective against *Brucella*, *Mycobacterium*, *Shigella*, *francisella*, and *Yersinia*.	Dry streptomycin powder is relatively stable and may be stored at room temperature. Solutions are stable for 48 h at room temperature, and 14 days under refrigeration.
	Resistant strains emerge rapidly, and these strains may be-	Assess for effectiveness of antibacterial action. Communicate signs of

Table 3-7   Aminoglycosides *(Continued)*

Drug and Dose	Comments	Nursing Actions
	come streptomycin dependent. Administration of streptomycin is generally reserved for treatment of tuberculosis, tularemia, and plague.	continuation of infection to physican.
Kanamycin sulfate (Kantrex): Neonates: 7.5 mg/kg IM every 12 h Older infants and children: 3 to 7.5 mg/kg IM every 12 h Usual pediatric dose: 12.5 mg/kg PO every 6 h	Seldom used for tuberculosis at the present time. Oral kanamycin used to reduce gastrointestinal flora before surgery and to prevent ammonia production in cirrhotic patients.	Kanamycin is supplied as a water-soluble solution. Darkening of the solution does not effect potency.
Neomycin sulfate (Neobiotic, Myciguent): Neonates: 1.75 to 8.75 mg/kg PO every 6 h Older infants and children: 17.5 mg/kg PO every 6 h	The most toxic of the aminoglycosides, administered orally to treat diarrhea caused by *Escherichia coli* and to reduce ammonia-producing intestinal strains.	
Paromomycin sulfate (Humatin): Children: 15 to 25 mg/kg daily PO in three divided doses with meals for 5 to 10 days (AMA Department of Drugs, 1977, p. 853)	This broad-spectrum aminoglycoside has direct amebicidal effects within the intestinal lumen. Paromomycin is administered alone or with agents for intestinal amebiasis and other forms of amebiasis. The drug must be administered with caution to children with ulcerative lesions of the bowel. It is contraindicated in the presence of intestinal obstruction.	

tration there is rapid absorption, and there is significant absorption after irrigation of wounds and cavities and application to denuded skin.

Distribution

After absorption aminoglycosides are widely distributed in most extracellular fluids; however, they do not enter the intracellular and transcellular fluids. Under normal circumstances aminoglycosides do not enter the cerebrospinal fluid readily; however, in neonates and children with meningitis they cross the permeable blood-brain barrier quite freely. Therapeutic cerebrospinal concentrations are attained only with intrathecal administration of these agents.

Excretion

Aminoglycosides are rapidly excreted unchanged in the urine, and without dosage reduction neonates and children with renal impairment accumulate excessive serum drug concentrations. Dosage in these children is individualized by using laboratory determination of serum aminoglycoside concentrations as the guideline.

A small portion of aminoglycoside dose is excreted into the bile, saliva, and perspiration. Significant concentrations are excreted in breast milk; however, maternal renal impairment will greatly increase breast milk concentrations. (Savage, 1976, p. 212). While aminoglycosides are poorly absorbed from the nursing infant's gastrointestinal tract, the effects of large aminoglycoside doses on the infant are not known (AMA Department of Drugs, 1977, p. xxx). Savage states that up to 1 g streptomycin can be safely administered to the nursing mother with normal renal function (Savage, 1976, p. 212). O'Brien states that infants of nursing mothers receiving kanamycin (Kantrex) must be monitored for possible toxicity, and that streptomycin should be avoided in nursing mothers (O'Brien, 1975, pp. 25, 26).

Significant Interactions

Concurrent administration of aminoglycosides with ether, other inhalation anesthetics, or with tubocurarine or other neuromuscular depressants may enhance the neuroblockade action of the aminoglycoside (*Evaluations of Drug Interactions*, 1976, pp. 70, 254).

Adverse Reactions

Early auditory toxicity is characterized by high-pitched tinnitus and hearing loss of high-frequency sounds. Discontinuing the drugs will prevent permanent hearing loss; however, the tinnitus may persist for a week after therapy is withdrawn.

Careful observation of the child for unsteady gait, difficulty standing or sitting without visual cues, or nausea, vomiting, and headaches will identify early vestibular damage. Caloric testing will confirm this adverse reaction.

Aminoglycosides are potentially toxic to the kidney, particularly in the presence of renal impairment and large doses when administered concurrently with other nephrotoxic agents.

Neuromuscular blockade, which results from interaction of an aminoglycoside with another neuromuscular depressant, usually begins with sudden dyspnea, which rapidly progress to prolonged apnea, and may terminate in prolonged, irreversible respiratory failure.

Hypersensitivity reactions and intramuscular administration of aminoglycosides cause severe pain, fever, tender masses, induration, and other local irritative reactions.

Nursing Actions During Aminoglycoside Therapy

1. Identify significant interactions. Administer other nephrotoxic, ototoxic, or neuromuscular depressant drugs with great caution.

2. Reconstitute, store, and administer aminoglycosides according to recommendations of the package insert. Do not physically mix these agents with other drugs. Administer intramuscular preparations deep into large muscle mass. Use of Z technique may minimize local irritative reactions. Administer intravenous preparation over an interval of 1 to 2 h depending on age of the child. Assess frequently for muscular weakness, dyspnea, or apnea. Monitor blood pressure and respirations during infusion of the drug.

3. Measure urine output and assess urine for presence of protein. Hydrate child to minimize renal damage.

4. Obtain baseline and serial evaluation of audiometric and caloric function. Assess gait, coordination, nausea, vomiting, and other vestibilar signs in the older child. Question child about headaches and "ringing in the ears." Assess infants for difficulty crawling, inability to pull themselves up, other signs of poor coordination, and hearing loss. *Withhold drug should any of the above occur.* Protect child from falls and other injuries.

BIBLIOGRAPHY

"Adverse Interaction of Drugs," *The Medical Letter*, vol. 19, no. 2, 1977, pp. 5–12.

AMA Department of Drugs: *AMA Drug Evaluations*, 3d ed., Publishing Sciences Group, Littleton, Mass., 1977.

American Academy of Pediatrics: "Requiem For Tetracyclines," *Pediatrics*, vol. 55 1975, pp. 142–143.

Appel, G. B., and H. C. Neu: "The Nephrotoxicity of Antimicrobial Agents II," *New England Journal of Medicine*, vol. 296, no. 12, 1977, pp. 663–669.

"The Cephalosporins," *The Medical Letter*, vol. 18, no. 8, 1976, pp. 33–35.

"The Choice of Antimicrobial Drugs," *The Medical Letter*, vol. 18, no. 3, 1976, pp. 9–16.

Evaluations of Drug Interactions, 2d ed., American Pharmaceutical Association, Washington, D.C., 1976.

Hill, R. M.: "Adverse Drug Reactions in Children," *Pediatric Annals*, vol. 5, no. 9, 1976, pp. 566–577.

"Interaction of Alcohol with Drugs," *The Medical Letter*, vol. 19, no. 11, 1977, pp. 46–48.

O'Brien, T. E.: "Excretion of Drugs in Human Milk," *Nursing Digest*, July–August 1975, pp. 23–31.

Rolewicz, T. F.: "A Rational Approach to Antibiotic Therapy in Infants and Children," *Pediatric Annals*, vol. 5, no. 9, 1976*a*, pp. 558–565.

————: "Antibiotic Dosage for Infants and Children," *Pediatric Annals*, vol. 5, no. 11, 1976*b*, pp. 733–734.

Savage, R. L.: "Drugs and Breast Milk," *Adverse Drug Reaction Bulletin*, no. 61, 1976, pp. 212–215.

Vaughn, V. C., and J. R. McKay: *Textbook of Pediatrics*, 10th ed., Saunders, Philadelphia, 1975.

Veterans' Administration Ad Hoc Interdisciplinary Advisory Committee on Antimicrobial Usage: "Audits of Antimicrobial Usage: 3. Oral Cephalosporins. 4. Parenteral Cephalosporins," *Journal of the American Medical Association*, vol. 237, no. 12, 1977, pp. 1241–1245.

Yaffe, S. J., and L. Stern: "Clinical Implications of Perinatal Pharmacology," in B. Mirkin (ed.), *Perinatal Pharmacology and Therapeutics*, Academic, San Francisco, 1976.

Yeager, A. S.: "Why Now? Use of Tetracyclines in Young Children," *Journal of the American Medical Association*, vol. 237, no. 19, 1977, p. 2101.

Drugs Used to Treat Cardiovascular Disorders

DIGITALIS GLYCOSIDES (See Table 4-1)

General Considerations

The term *digitalis* is used to designate a group of drugs derived from digitalis and other plant sources. (AMA Department of Drugs, 1977, p. 1). These drugs have similar therapeutic and adverse effects on the heart; however, they differ in rate and degree of absorption, speed of onset, duration of action, and rate and route of metabolism and excretion.

This group of drugs includes both nonpurified (e.g., digitalis leaf, digitalis tincture) and purified crystalline preparations (e.g., digoxin, digitoxin). Although digitalis leaf and tincture were frequently prescribed in the past, there are few reasons for their use at present (Goodman and Gilman, 1975, p. 672).

While their precise mechanism of action is unknown, it is believed that these agents influence cardiac potentials by increasing the flow of calcium ions into the myocardium (Dipalma, 1976, p. 218). There are differences in oral absorption of the various digitalis preparations (see Table 4-1). Variations in absorption of oral dosage forms from various manufacturers have also been documented.

(Text continued on page 161.)

Table 4-1   Digitalis Glycosides

Drug and Dose	Comments and Relevant Nursing Actions
Digoxin (Lanoxin) (all dosages must be individualized): Oral digitalization, neonates to 1 month: 40 to 60 μg/kg PO in two or more portions at 6- to 8-h intervals Parenteral digitalization, neonates under 2 weeks: 5.5 to 16.5 μg/kg IM or IV initially, then 16.5 μg/kg at 6-h intervals as necessary Oral maintenance, neonates: one-fifth to one-third of total digitalizing dose PO daily Parenteral maintenance, neonates under 2 weeks: 5.5 to 16.5 μg/kg IM or IV daily Oral digitalization, infants 1 month to 2 years: 60 to 80 μg/kg PO total dose divided into two or more portions given at 6- to 8-h intervals Parenteral digitalization, infants 2 weeks to 2 years: 11 to 22 μg/kg IM or IV initially, then 11 to 22 μg/kg at 6-h intervals as necessary Oral maintenance, infants 1 month to 2 years: one-fifth to one-third of total digitalizing dose PO daily Parenteral maintenance, infants 2 weeks to 2 years: 11 to 22 μg/kg IM or IV daily Oral digitalization, children 2 to 10 years: 40 to 60 μg/kg PO total dose divided into two or more portions given at 6- to 8-h intervals Parenteral digitalization, children 2 to 10 years: 5.5 to 16.5 μg/kg initially IM or IV, followed by 5.5 to 16.5 μg/kg at 6-h intervals as necessary	Derived from *Digitalis lanata* leaves and used frequently in pediatrics for its rapid onset of action and rapid rate of elimination. Available as tablets and elixir for oral administration, and as sterile solution for parenteral use. Approximately 60 to 80 percent of an oral dose is absorbed, and therapeutic effects occur within 1 to 2 h. Changes in gastrointestinal motility may decrease rate of absorption, but not total amount finally absorbed. Major portion excreted unchanged in urine. Children with renal impairment require dose reduction. Half-life approximately 32 to 48 h, and duration of action relatively short (i.e., 2 to 6 h). After intravenous administration, effects appear within 5 to 30 min. Digoxin is often favored for intravenous digitalization because of its rapid onset and the fact that changing to oral maintenance is relatively easy.

Table 4-1 Digitalis Glycosides (Continued)

Drug and Dose	Comments and Relevant Nursing Actions
Oral maintenance, children 2 to 10 years: one-fifth to one-third of total digitalization dose PO daily	
Parenteral maintenance, children 2 to 10 years: 11 to 22 μg/kg IM or IV daily	
Oral digitalization, children over 10 years: 1.0 to 1.5 mg (determined by weight) total dose PO divided in two or more portions given over 6- to 8-h intervals	
Parenteral digitalization, children over 10 years: 500 μg to 1 mg IM initially, then 250 to 500 μg at 6-h intervals as necessary 500 μg to 1 mg IV initially, then 250 to 500 μg at 2- to 4-h intervals as necessary	
Oral maintenance, children over 10 years: 125 to 500 μg PO daily	
Parenteral maintenance, children over 10 years: 250 μg IM or IV one to three times daily	
Digitoxin (Purodigin, Crystodigin) (all doses must be individualized):	Derived from *Digitalis purpurea* and *D. lanata* leaves. A slow-acting glycoside with a long duration of action.
Digitalization, neonates to 2 weeks of age: 22 μg/kg total dose PO, IM, or IV in three or more portions given at least 6 h apart	Available as tablets and elixir for oral use and as sterile solution for parenteral injection.
Digitalization, infants 2 weeks to 1 year: 45 μg/kg PO, IM, or IV total dose in three or more portions given at least 6 h apart	Completely absorbed after oral administration; thus, oral and parenteral doses are identical. Effects achieved in 1 to 4 h after oral ingestion with maximal effects in 8 to 12 h. Half-life approximately 7 days.
Digitalization, children 1 to 2 years: 40 μg/kg PO, IM, or IV total dose in three or more portions given at least 6 h apart	Extensively metabolized by the liver, undergoes enterohepatic recircula-

Table 4-1   Digitalis Glycosides (*Continued*)

Drug and Dose	Comments and Relevant Nursing Actions
Digitalization, children over 2 years: 30 μg/kg PO, IM, or IV total dose in three or more portions given at least 6 h apart Maintenance: one-tenth of digitalization dose PO, IM, or IV per day	tion, and ultimately is excreted in urine and feces. Children with hepatic impairment require dosage reduction to avoid excessive plasma concentrations. Two weeks or more are required for complete regression of therapeutic effects. After intravenous administration of a digitalization dose, drug requires 4 h or more to produce maximal effects. The long duration of action increases the risk of cumulative toxicity. Such toxicity persists even after the drug is discontinued.
Ouabain (Strophanthin G) (all doses must be individualized): Usual pediatric dose: 10 μg/kg IV total dose; one-half taken initially, then fractions thereof every 30 min until desired response attained or total dose given	A rapid-acting glycoside derived from seeds of the *Strophanthus gratus* vine. Not absorbed from the gastrointestinal tract; thus, used for emergency digitalization by the intravenous route. After digitalization the child must be changed to an oral preparation. Onset of action requires 3 to 10 min, and maximal effects occur within 30 to 60 min. Most of ouabain is excreted unchanged in the urine. The rapid digitalization produced by the drug increases the risk of toxicity. Monitor apical and radial pulses, and assess for cardiac toxicity.

Absorption

Absorption of digitalis glycosides after intramuscular injection is slow, erratic, and occasionally no faster than oral absorption (Greenblatt and Koch-Weser, 1976, p. 544). Since the intramuscular route is associated with pain, induration, and other evidence of local inflammation, intramuscular administration of these drugs is not usually recommended (Singh, 1976, p. 584).

Onset of Action

While intravenous injection of rapid-acting digitalis glycosides (e.g., digoxin, ouabain) produces fast action, intravenous injection of slow-acting preparations (e.g., digitoxin) requires several hours for maximal cardiac effects.

Clinical Uses

Digitalis glycosides are used in treatment of congestive heart failure, for treatment of atrial flutter and atrial fibrillation, and to prevent congestive heart failure during cardiac surgery and cardiac catheterization.

Effects

These agents increase myocardial contractility, an effect which is termed *inotropic* and which results in increased cardiac output, reduction of blood volume, increased urine output, and relief of pulmonary congestion.

The increase in vagal tone produced by these drugs increases both atrioventricular nodal conduction time and refractory period. Vagal effects also shorten atrial and ventricular refractory time.

Dosage

An appropriate dose of a digitalis glycoside is that which restores the highest degree of cardiac efficiency and relieves failure. Digitalis glycosides have a narrow margin of safety, i.e., the difference between therapeutic and toxic doses is small; there are wide variations in response to identical doses; and dosage requirements for the same child will vary as cardiac status changes. In severe congestive heart failure, an optimal dose might even border on toxicity and can produce some adverse reactions.

Dosage for these drugs must be carefully titrated by close assessment of clinical response, serum drug concentration, and interpretation of ECG changes.

Age and Dosage There are poorly understood age-related differences in pediatric dosage requirements of digitalis glycosides. Premature and full-term infants with congenital heart disorders are very sensitive to these drugs. The total daily dose of digoxin required for an infant is twice the adult dose calculated on the basis of kilograms of body weight (Mirkin, 1976, p. 557). Children require approximately 50 percent more drug calculated on the basis of body weight than adults to obtain similar effects. (Goodman and Gilman, 1975, p. 676).

It has been suggested that decreased myocardial receptor sensitivity to digitalis preparations might explain these age-dependent variations in dosage (Singh, 1976, p. 579).

Digitalization Since digitalis preparations are excreted slowly, obtaining optimal therapeutic effects (*digitalization*) requires a comparatively long period if these drugs are administered according to usual dosage schedules. Administration of digoxin at usual rates requires approximately 1 week for digitalization, while digitoxin requires approximately 1 month (Goodman and Gilman, 1975, p. 673). Such slow digitalization is suitable for chronic congestive heart failure and other nonemergency situations.

In pulmonary edema and other critical situations rapid digitalization may be necessary. Rapid digitalization is achieved by administering a comparatively large "loading" dose in divided portions over a period of hours. The child is then placed on a smaller daily *maintenance* dose, to replace the amount inactivated or eliminated.

CAUTIONS Intravenous digitalization with rapid-acting preparations (digoxin, ouabain, etc.) produces prompt response; however, toxicity is much more likely to occur. Oral digitalization doses may also be administered to achieve rapid therapeutic response.

Hypokalemia, hypercalcemia, hypomagnesemia, hypoxemia, and metabolic alkalosis increase the risk of adverse drug reactions (Singh, 1976, p. 584).

Adverse Reactions

Early digitalis toxicity is often evidenced by extracardiac manifestations; however, in infants and children these manifestations can be misleading. Anorexia, nausea, vomiting, and abdominal discomfort are early signs. Fatigue, weakness, nightmares, and visual disturbance may also occur.

Cardiac manifestations of digitalis toxicity consist of *any* rhythm disturbance; however, heart block atrioventricular junctional rhythms, and ventricular tachycardia are common. In the presence of hypokalemia, treatment of cardiac reactions includes cautious administration of potassium. The arrhythmia is then abolished by administration of antiarrhythmic drugs (e.g., lidocaine, quinidine) or electric cardioversion.

Nursing Actions

Nursing care during digitalis therapy consists of close evaluation during both digitalization and maintenance therapy.

During digitalization, when cardiac toxicity is likely to occur, excessive slowing or acceleration of apical and radial pulse, dizziness, or palpitations must be immediately communicated to the physician. Clinical response to the drug must be evaluated by noting changes in edema, pulmonary congestion, and urine output, as well as rate and strength of pulse. Continuation of these conditions must be communicated to the physician.

Apical and radial pulses should be taken for a full minute before administration of the drug. In the presence of significant slowing or acceleration of pulse, the drug should be withheld and the physician notified. (Specific pulse rates will vary with age, size, cardiac status, and normal pulse rate.)

Interpretation of laboratory blood gas and electrolyte values (potassium, calcium, pH, etc.) is mandatory to prevent conditions which increase risk of toxicity.

Communicate gastrointestinal upset, fatigue, nightmares, and visual disturbances to the physician.

Significant Interactions

Administration of digoxin or digitoxin with aluminum-containing antiacids and cholestyramine (Questran) decreases absorption of the digitalis glycoside. Administration of digoxin or digitoxin at least $1\frac{1}{2}$ h before cholestyramine avoids this interaction. Administration of antacids 3 h before or after cardiac glycosides prevents decreased absorption.

Concurrent administration of potassium-losing diuretics [e.g., furosemide (Lasix), chlorothiazide (Diuril)] increases the risk of digitalis toxicity unless potassium is administered.

Consult package insert for reconstitution of parenteral digitalis glycosides.

Table 4-2   Antiarrhythmic Drugs

Drug and Dose	Comments and Relevant Nursing Actions

Lidocaine hydrochloride (Xylocaine) (AMA Department of Drugs, 1977, p. 18):
  Children:
    0.5 to 1 mg/kg IV every 5 min for maximum of three doses
    Solution of 5 mg/ml infused at rate of 0.03 mg/kg per minute
	A rapid-acting antiarrhythmic agent which is used for emergency treatment of ventricular arrhythmias. Lidocaine is also used as a local anesthetic.
	
	Cardiac effects include depression of diastolic depolarization and automaticity of the ventricles. The drug has minimal effects on atrial activity and atrioventricular conduction.
	
	Lidocaine is not absorbed from the gastrointestinal tract; thus, it is administered by intravenous infusion with the child on a cardiac monitor at a specific dose per kilogram of body weight per minute. Onset of action is rapid, and duration of action is short; thus, the drug is infused, but it is terminated in presence of cardiac depression. The drug is rapidly metabolized by the liver, and metabolites are excreted in the urine. Half-life is approximately 2 h. Children with liver or renal impairment require dosage reduction to avoid excessive accumulation.
	
	Lidocaine is contraindicated in complete heart block.
	
	Drowsiness, muscular twitching, and convulsions may occur. Respiratory depression, hypotension, and sensations of heat or numbness have also been reported.
	
	Bradycardia and depression of myocardial contractility have also occurred.
	
	Nursing action includes reconstitution of lidocaine according to recommendations of the package insert. (Do not confuse with topical dosage forms!) Administration of precise dosage and interpretation of cardiac monitor are also essentials. At the first evidence of myocardial depression (e.g., prolongation of PR interval and QRS complex) the infusion should be temporarily stopped. Restart drug if arrhythmia recurs. Have

Table 4-2   Antiarrhythmic Drugs (*Continued*)

Drug and Dose	Comments and Relevant Nursing Actions
	parenteral diazepam (Valium) and short-acting barbiturates on hand to treat convulsions.
	Assess level of consciousness and muscular reflexes and communicate changes to the physician.
	Monitor blood pressure and urine output and communicate significant decrease of either to the physician.
Procainamide hydrochloride (Pronestyl): Usual pediatric dose: 12.5 mg/kg PO every 6 h	A synthetic compound related to the local anesthetic procaine (Novocaine) and used to treat ventricular arrhythmias.
	The drug depresses atrial and ventricular response to electrical stimulation. Conduction time is slowed, and myocardial refractory period is increased.
	While procainamide is available for oral and parenteral administration, the oral route produces fewer adverse reactions and is therefore preferred. Should parenteral administration be required, when feasible the intramuscular route is preferred over the intravenous route (Goodman and Gilman, 1975, p. 676).
	Procainamide is rapidly and well absorbed after oral administration and is metabolized by the liver; metabolites are excreted by the urine. Half-life is 3 to 4 h. Children with renal impairment or congestive heart failure require dosage reduction to avoid excessive accumulation. Procainamide is contraindicated in the presence of complete heart block.
	Nausea, vomiting, anorexia, and diarrhea occur. After prolonged administration, a reversible lupus erythematosus–like syndrome occurs frequently. Fever, skin rashes, and agranulocytosis occur occasionally. Severe hypotension, heart block, and rapid ventricular rate occur rarely.

Table 4-2   Antiarrhythmic Drugs (*Continued*)

Drug and Dose	Comments and Relevant Nursing Actions
	Nursing care during procainamide therapy includes frequent checking of blood pressure and communicating all significant drops to the physician. During intravenous administration the drug should be terminated if widening of the QRS complex occurs.
Quinidine (Cardioquin, Quinaglute): Usual pediatric dose: 6 mg/kg PO five times a day	An alkaloid which is chemically related to quinine and is obtained from the bark of the cinchona tree. Quinidine's complex cardiac effects include depression of myocardial automaticity, slowing of conduction velocity, and increasing myocardial refractory period.
	The drug is used to treat atrial flutter and atrial fibrillation and to prevent ventricular tachycardia. Clinical use is limited by its toxicity (AMA Department of Drugs, 1977, p. 16). Since the oral route is associated with a lower incidence of cardiovascular toxicity, this route is preferred over parenteral routes.
	Quinidine is well absorbed after oral administration and after extensive metabolism by the liver, metabolites are excreted in the urine. Half-life is approximately 5 h, and acidification of the urine increases urinary excretion of the drug.
	Children with renal or hepatic impairment require dose reduction to avoid excessive accumulation.
	The drug is contraindicated in complete heart block or in the presence of bleeding tendency with previous quinidine exposure.
	Nausea, vomiting, and diarrhea are common with the drug. Visual disturbances, tinnitus, headache, and vertigo also may occur. Thrombocytopenic purpura, fever, and hepatitis occur rarely. Tachycardia, heart failure, severe hypotension, heart block, and cardiac arrest have also occurred.

Table 4-2   Antiarrhythmic Drugs (*Continued*)

Drug and Dose	Comments and Relevant Nursing Actions
	Administration of quinidine with aluminum-containing antacids may decrease absorption of the antiarrhythmic agent.
	Drugs which alkalinize the urine (e.g., sodium bicarbonate, thiazide diuretics) decrease urinary excretion of quinidine, thereby increasing its effects.
	Parenteral administration of quinidine with or shortly after muscle relaxants [e.g., succinylcholine (Anectine), tubocurarine (Tubarine)] may cause respiratory depression and apnea.
	Administration of warfarin (Coumadin) with quinidine may cause hemorrhage.
	Nursing care during quinidine therapy includes careful checking of blood pressure and communication of significant decrease to the physician. Apical and radial pulses should be checked before administration, and the drug withheld if a significant increase or decrease occurs. Notification of the physician is mandatory.
	Careful assessment of child for bruises and bleeding from body orifices is essential. In the presence of such manifestations the drug should be withheld and the physician notified.

Table 4-3   Drugs Used in Shock

Drug and Dose	Comments and Relevant Nursing Actions
Dopamine hydrochloride (Intropin): There are no pediatric dosage recommendations at present; however, the drug is undergoing clinical trials in infants and children.	A naturally occurring precursor of norepinephrine, which is present in the central nervous system. The drug is administered by careful intravenous infusion as a temporary measure in shock. Dopamine has a rapid onset of action, and its duration is brief. Dopamine action on alpha- and beta-adrenergic receptors produces a positive inotropic effect and a release of norepinephrine. There is an increase in blood flow to the kidney and to the mesentery. The drug is not effective after oral administration; thus, it is administered by intravenous infusion. A specific dose per kilogram of body weight per minute is administered by careful titration. Response is assessed by cardiac monitor, blood pressure, and urine output. Dopamine is rapidly metabolized by the liver, and metabolites are excreted in the urine. Nausea, vomiting, headache, palpitation, and dyspnea may occur. Tachycardia, ectopic beats, and vasoconstriction, with gangrene of fingers and toes, may occur after large doses. Infiltration of large amounts into subcutaneous tissues causes necrosis and tissue slough. Injection of phentolamine (Regitine) into the area of infiltration may prevent necrosis and tissue slough. Concurrent administration of dopamine with cyclopropane and related anesthetics may increase the risk of tachycardia and ectopic beats. Furazolidone (Furoxone) used with dopamine may cause hypertensive crisis. Nursing actions during dopamine therapy include careful administration of drug according to ECG pattern, blood pressure, and urine output. Widening of the QRS complex, bradycardia, tachycardia, and ectopic beats are contraindications to continuation of dopamine infusion.

Table 4-3   Drugs Used in Shock (*Continued*)

Drug and Dose	Comments and Relevant Nursing Actions
	Measure urine output every hour and notify physician if output decreases. Take blood pressure at least every 15 min, and if diastolic pressure rises disproportionately, decrease infusion rate and notify physician.
	Immobilize extremity in which the infusion is located and assess the site frequently for infiltration. Should infiltration occur, remove infusion immediately, notify physician, and prepare phentolamine for injection into area of infiltration.
	Assess fingers and toes for temperature and color changes which indicate vasoconstriction.
	Dopamine is unstable in the presence of alkaline media (e.g., sodium bicarbonate), iron salts, and oxidizing agents. Dilute and store drug according to directions of the package insert.

Levarterenol bitartrate (Levophed):
  Usual pediatric dose:
  2 mg/m² per minute IV
	An endogenous catecholamine which is liberated at postganglionic adrenergic nerves.

	Administered by careful intravenous infusion for temporary treatment of shock. Onset of action is rapid; however, duration of action is short (i.e., 1 to 2 min).
	The drug increases the force of myocardial contractions; however, a reflex bradycardia may occur. Systolic and diastolic blood pressures are increased; however, cardiac output is not increased. Peripheral vascular resistance is increased; thus, blood flow to brain, liver, and kidney are decreased.
	Levarterenol is ineffective when administered by mouth. The drug is rapidly metabolized by the liver and other tissues, and metabolites are excreted in the urine.
	Since the drug is a potent vasoconstrictor, necrosis and tissue sloughing may occur at the site of infiltration. Injection of phentolamine (Regitine) and warm packs to area may reduce these reactions.
	Anxiety, respiratory difficulty, headache, and hypertension may also occur.

Table 4-3   Drugs Used in Shock (Continued)

Drug and Dose	Comments and Relevant Nursing Actions
	Ischemia to vital organs (i.e., brain, kidney, liver), intense sweating, vomiting, and photophobia occur occasionally.
	Concurrent use of furazolidone (Furoxone) may result in hypertensive crises.
	Nursing actions during levarterenol therapy include continual monitoring of blood pressure and stopping infusion when blood pressure rises rapidly.
	Assess infusion site for evidence of infiltration and vasoconstriction and keep extremity immobilized.
	Consult package insert for reconstitution directions.

Table 4-4   Antihypertensive Drugs

Drug and Dose	Comments and Relevant Nursing Actions
Methyldopa (Aldomet): Usual pediatric dose: 3.3 mg/kg PO every 8 h initially, increased to 65 mg/kg daily if necessary	An effective antihypertensive which lowers blood pressure by a poorly understood mechanism. The drug is combined with a diuretic to treat mild to moderate hypertension. It is believed that the drug inhibits decarboxylase, thereby depressing sympathetic activity and producing reduction in systolic and diastolic pressures. Cardiac rate, cardiac output, and peripheral resistance are decreased. While standing and lying blood pressures are both reduced, the decrease in standing pressure is the greater. Methyldopa is adequately absorbed after oral ingestion, and is excreted in urine, primarily in the active form. Small amounts are metabolized in the liver, and metabolites are excreted in the urine. Half-life is approximately 12 h. Children with renal impairment accumulate excessive concentrations during chronic administration. The onset of action is slow; maximal effects occur 4 to 6 h after oral ingestion, and persist for up to 24 h. After intravenous administration, effects do not appear for 1 to 2 h. Drowsiness, slowing of thought processes, and nightmares may occur in the first weeks of therapy. Abnormal liver functions tests may also occur. Nasal congestion, dry mouth, vomiting, and nausea are not uncommon. Reversible hemolytic anemia, orthostatic hypotension, positive Coombs' tests, and liver damage may occur with chronic administration.

Table 4-4   Antihypertensive Drugs (*Continued*)

Drug and Dose	Comments and Relevant Nursing Actions
	Nursing care during methyldopa therapy includes avoiding accidents by teaching parents to guard child from falls and other injuries.
	Close observation of the child for fever, malaise, and other evidence of liver damage is essential.
Hydralazine hydrochloride (Apresoline): Usual pediatric dose: 425 to 875 μg/kg IM or IV every 6 h 187.5 μg/kg PO every 6 h initially and for maintenance increased over 3 to 4 weeks up to 10 times the initial dose, if necessary	Hydralazine reduces blood pressure by direct relaxation of vascular smooth muscle. The drug has not been extremely successful in childhood hypertension. Peripheral vascular resistance is decreased; however, heart rate, cardiac output, and stroke volume are also increased. Renal blood flow is not affected.
	The drug is well absorbed after oral administration, and after hepatic metabolism, metabolites are excreted in the urine. Children with severe renal impairment may accumulate excessive drug concentrations.
	Hydralazine is contraindicated in children with congestive heart failure or coronary artery disease.
	Headache, nausea, anorexia, sweating, and palpitation are common. Adverse effects can be reduced by slowly increasing dosage to optimal levels.
	Blood dyscrasias, rash, and peripheral neuritis are rare.
	Reversible systemic lupus erythematosus (SLE)–like syndrome occurs with prolonged administration. Limiting the dosage during long-term therapy usually prevents this reaction (Sinaiko and Mirkin, 1976, p. 596).

Table 4-4   Antihypertensive Drugs (*Continued*)

Drug and Dose	Comments and Relevant Nursing Actions
	During hydralazine therapy, assess child carefully for fever, joint pain, and edema. Communicate these signs of SLE to the physician.
Propranolol hydrochloride (Inderal): Pediatric dose: 0.5 to 1.0 mg/kg daily PO in four divided doses initially, followed by dosage increments at 3 to 4 days (Sinaiko and Mirkin, 1976, p. 593)	A beta-adrenergic receptor blocking agent, which decreases vasomotor tone and suppresses renin release from the kidney.
	The drug is also used as an anti-arrhythmic agent and as a coronary artery dilator. It reduces cardiac rate, cardiac output, and myocardial contractility.
	Propranolol has been used successfully with diuretics for treatment of adult hypertension and may also become an important drug for childhood hypertension. Dosage is slowly increased until optimal effects are attained. The drug is contraindicated in children with congestive heart failure, asthma, and diabetes mellitus.
	Propranolol decreases both standing and supine blood pressures. The drug is well absorbed after oral administration and after extensive metabolism is excreted in the urine. Half-life is approximately 3 h.
	Nausea, anorexia, vomiting, mild diarrhea, and constipation may occur.
	Insomnia, nightmares, and depression occur rarely.
	Bradycardia and heart failure in individuals with inadequate cardiac reserve may occur. Children with asthma may have asthmatic attacks. In children with diabetes or on restricted food intake propranolol may produce hypoglycemia.

Table 4-4   Antihypertensive Drugs (*Continued*)

Drug and Dose	Comments and Relevant Nursing Actions
	During propranolol therapy, assess for bronchial constriction, hypoglycemia, and evidence of congestive heart failure.
Guanethidine sulfate (Ismelin): Usual pediatric dose: 200 μg/kg PO initially, then gradually increased every 7 to 10 days in increments of the initial dose up to five to eight times the initial dose	A potent antihypertensive agent which inhibits responses to sympathetic adrenergic nerve activation and responses to indirect-acting sympathomimetic amines [e.g., amphetamine (Dexedrine)]. Cardiac output is decreased, and there is also a drop in peripheral vascular resistance. In pediatrics, guanethidine is used for severe hypertension which does not respond to other forms of antihypertensive therapy. Since the drug is effective only when the child is upright, it is not suitable for hypertension in neonates and infants.
	Oral absorption varies, and the drug is metabolized and excreted in the urine. The extremely long half-life results in a delayed onset of action; once antihypertensive effects are obtained, a single daily dose usually suffices.
	Orthostatic hypotension, exercise hypotension, diarrhea, and bradycardia may occur.
	Ingestion of alcohol increases antihypertensive effects of the drug; however, phenothiazines (Thorazine, etc.) and dextroamphetamine (Dexedrine) decrease this antihypertensive effect.
	Nursing actions during guanethidine therapy include teaching parents and older children that sudden changes in posture, ingestion of alcohol, exposure to heat, and prolonged standing increase the risk of hypotensive episodes. Additional teaching includes the neces-

Table 4-4   Antihypertensive Drugs (*Continued*)

Drug and Dose	Comments and Relevant Nursing Actions
	sity of sleeping with the head elevated, of avoiding prolonged exercise periods, and of sitting or lying down when dizziness occurs.
	Blood pressure should be taken in the lying position, the upright position, and after exercise.

Table 4-5   Diuretics

Drug and Dose	Comments and Relevant Nursing Actions
Furosemide (Lasix) (dose must be carefully individualized): Children: 2 mg/kg PO once or twice daily initially and if necessary increased gradually by 1 mg/kg per dose (AMA Department of Drugs, 1977, p. 88)	A nonthiazide, sulfonamide diuretic; inhibits sodium and chloride reabsorption in the ascending limb of the loop of Henle. Its potent short-acting diuretic action is not affected by acid-base disturbances.
	The drug is used to treat edema associated with congestive heart failure in children who do not respond to less potent diuretics. It is also prescribed for edema of nephrotic syndrome and liver damage, as well as for treating hypertensive children with reduced renal clearance.
	Furosemide is well absorbed from the gastrointestinal tract and after hepatic metabolism is excreted in the urine. Diuretic action appears within 1 h of oral administration and persists for approximately 6 h.
	After intravenous administration, effects occur immediately and persist for approximately 2 h. Intravenous use is generally reserved for treatment of pulmonary edema and hypertensive crises.
	Overdosage produces dehydration, hypotension, hypokalemia, and hypochloremic alkalosis.
	Hyperglycemia and hyperuricemia may also occur.
	Rapid administration may cause reversible deafness in children with renal impairment. Concurrent administration of another ototoxic drug [e.g., gentamicin (Garamycin), streptomycin] increases the risk of ear damage. Skin rashes and bleeding tendency occur rarely.
	Children receiving a digitalis glycoside (e.g., digoxin) with furosemide are at risk of cardiac toxicity if hypokalemia occurs.
	Furosemide administered to children receiving long-term anticonvulsant therapy may produce decrease in urinary sodium loss (AMA Department of Drugs, 1977, p. 87).
	Nursing actions during furosemide therapy include interpretation of serum electrolyte reports,

Table 4-5   Diuretics (*Continued*)

Drug and Dose	Comments and Relevant Nursing Actions
	assessment of fluid and electrolyte status, monitoring of blood pressure, and administration of potassium preparations as prescribed.
	Careful assessment of hearing, particularly after intravenous administration, is also essential.
Chlorothiazide (Diuril): Usual pediatric dose: 10 mg/kg PO twice daily Hydrochlorothiazide (Esidrix, Hydrodiuril): Usual pediatric dose: 1 mg/kg PO twice daily	Chlorothiazide (Diuril) and hydrochlorothiazide (Esidrix, Hydrodiuril) are sulfonamide compounds which have diuretic effects. They belong to a large group of chemically related drugs which are designated the *thiazide diuretics*. At present there are eight thiazide diuretics and three closely related sulfonamide, nonthiazide diuretics. These diuretics differ in the dosage required for optimal therapeutic response and in duration of action.
	The thiazide diuretics and their related compounds increase urinary sodium and water excretion by preventing sodium reabsorption in the loop of Henle and the distal tubule. Urinary loss of potassium, chloride, and small amounts of bicarbonate also occurs. These actions reduce the extracellular fluid volume and prevent its reexpansion.
	These agents are utilized in treatment of edema associated with congestive heart failure, hypertension, nephrotic syndrome, and occasionally chronic renal failure. They are also prescribed for edema of premenstrual tension and corticosteroid administration. They are well absorbed from the gastrointestinal tract and are excreted in the urine within 3 to 6 h.
	Direct effects begin within 1 h after oral ingestion.
	Thiazides and their related diuretics tend to produce increase in blood urea nitrogen (BUN) and hypokalemia with hypochloremic alkalosis. (This decrease in potassium increases the risk of digitalis toxicity.) Increase in serum uric acid, aggravation of diabetes with hyperglycemia, which are common in adults, are unusual in children (Sinaiko and Mirkin, 1976, p. 593).

Table 4-5   Diuretics (Continued)

Drug and Dose	Comments and Relevant Nursing Actions
	Blood dyscrasias, hypersensitivity reactions, and pancreatitis occur rarely.
	These diuretics increase the neuromuscular blocking effects of tubocurarine (Tubarine); however, they decrease the arterial effects of norepinephrine.
	Nursing action during thiazide diuretic therapy includes interpretation of serum electrolyte reports. Assess child for anorexia, leg cramps, muscular fatigue, thirst, etc., and communicate such evidence of electrolyte disturbances to the physician.
	Assess diabetic children for evidence of hyperglycemia. Measure urine output, and communicate any decrease in output to physician.
	Evaluate for hypersensitivity reactions.
	Administer potassium preparations as prescribed.
Chlorthalidone (Hygroton): Usual pediatric dose: 2 mg/kg PO three times a week	A sulfonamide diuretic which differs chemically from the thiazides (e.g., Hydrodiuril) and shares many of their pharmacological properties.
	The drug promotes urinary excretion of sodium and water by inhibiting their reabsorption in the distal tubules and the ascending limb of Henle's loop.
	Chlorthalidone is used to produce diuresis in congestive heart failure, the nephrotic syndrome, and in treatment of hypertension.
	After oral administration, the drug is slowly absorbed from the gastrointestinal tract and is excreted unchanged in the urine. Its prolonged duration of action permits decreased dosing, an advantage for children of all ages.
	(See earlier discussion of thiazide diuretics for details.)

Table 4-6   Heparin and its Antagonist

Drug and Dose	Comments and Relevant Nursing Actions

Heparin sodium injection:
  Usual pediatric dose:
  50 U/kg initially by IV
  infusion followed by
  100 U/kg six times daily
	A sulfated mucopolysaccharide found in the mast cells of mammals. Heparin of commercial use is obtained from lungs, intestinal mucosa, and other tissues of food animals (i.e., beef, pork).
	
	Heparin inhibits the formation of thrombin and also blocks the enzymatic action of activated thrombin in the conversion of fibrinogen to fibrin. Whole-blood clotting time, thrombin time, and one-stage prothrombin time are prolonged, and thrombo-plastin generation is also affected.
	
	The drug is used primarily to prevent clotting during open heart surgery, renal hemodialysis, and orthopedic surgery.
	
	Dosage is prescribed in units rather than milligrams, since potency varies according to the heparin source (AMA Department of Drugs, 1977, p. 119).
	
	Heparin is contraindicated for use in children with bleeding disorders, open wounds, peptic ulcer, sub-acute bacterial endocarditis, severe hypertension, and severe liver or renal disease. It should not be used during or after surgery of the spinal cord, brain, and the eye.
	
	While heparin can be administered by the intra-venous, deep subcutaneous (intrafat), and intra-muscular routes, the intravenous route is generally utilized. Absorption from deep subcutaneous injec-tion sites is slow, and hematoma formation and tissue slough may occur (Goodman and Gilman, 1975, p. 1354). The intramuscular route produces a high incidence of bleeding, erratic absorption, and painful hematoma formation at the injection site. Heparin is not effective when administered orally; it is adequately absorbed from intramuscular and deep subcutaneous injection sites. The drug is metabolized by the liver; metabolites and a portion of unchanged drug are excreted in the urine. Onset of action after intravenous administration is immedi-ate, in contrast to 20- to 30-min delay after sub-cutaneous administration. Half-life is relatively short

Table 4-6   Heparin and its Antagonist (*Continued*)

Drug and Dose	Comments and Relevant Nursing Actions
	(100 U per kilogram of body weight administered intravenously has a half-life of 56 min). The drug is usually administered by continuous intravenous drip, or by intermittent intravenous infusion or intermittent intravenous injection. Intermittent administration may be facilitated by an indwelling needle (heparin lock).
	The heparin lock has been advocated as a method to maintain a patent vein in patients who require intravenous medications but do not require continual intravenous fluids. It is also used to avoid repeated venipuncture for patients requiring frequent blood sampling (Hanson, 1976, p. 1103). Heparin dosage is determined by whole-blood clotting time (Lee-White) or the activated partial thromboplastin time (PTT). There is no agreement on which test is more reliable, and it has been stated that the PTT and newer tests have not been shown to be superior to Lee-White determination, which is conducted under well-controlled conditions (AMA Department of Drugs, 1977, p. 113).
	The most serious adverse reaction associated with heparin therapy is hemorrhage. Careful laboratory control minimizes this risk; however, hematuria, gastrointestinal bleeding, or bleeding into joint spaces has occurred. This risk is increased by concurrent administration of aspirin.
	Major hemorrhage is treated by administrations of protamine sulfate. Asthma, giant urticaria, and fever have occurred occasionally; however, anaphylactoid reactions are rare. Osteoporosis and alopecia occur rarely after prolonged administration of heparin.
	Nursing action during heparin therapy includes careful assessment of the child for evidence of bleeding. Inspection of oral cavity, body orifices, excreta, joints, and skin surfaces for blood or subcutaneous bleeding is mandatory. The child must be protected from falls and injuries.

Table 4-6   Heparin and its Antagonist (*Continued*)

Drug and Dose	Comments and Relevant Nursing Actions
	Blood for laboratory tests must be obtained at intervals appropriate to the route and frequency of heparin administration.
	The child must be evaluated for evidence of hypersensitivity (i.e., fever, asthma, urticaria).
Protamine sulfate injection: Usual pediatric dose: 1 mg for each 80 or 100 U heparin activity derived from lung tissue or intestinal mucosa, respectively, in 1 to 3 min, up to a maximum of 50 mg in any 10-min period; repeated as necessary	Protamine, a strongly basic protein found in the sperm of salmon and other fish, antagonizes the anticoagulant activity of heparin. When administered alone, protamine exerts anticoagulant activity; however, in the presence of strongly acidic heparin, the two drugs (i.e., protamine and heparin) form a stable complex which has no anticoagulant activity. This drug should always be available when heparin is utilized.
	The drug is administered by careful intravenous injection to treat major hemorrhage associated with heparin therapy, and to neutralize large heparin doses used during surgical procedures. Therapeutic effects appear immediately after intravenous administration and persist for approximately 2 h. Hypotension, flushing, dyspnea, and bradycardia may occur.

BIBLIOGRAPHY

AMA Department Of Drugs: *AMA Drug Evaluations,* 3d ed., Publishing Sciences Group, Littleton, Mass., 1977, pp. 1–10.

Dipalma, J. R.: *Basic Pharmacology in Medicine,* McGraw-Hill, New York, 1976.

Gifford, R. W.: "A Guide to the Practical Use of Diuretics," *Journal of the American Medical Association,* vol. 235, no. 17, 1976, pp. 1890–1893.

Goodman, L. S., and A. Gilman: *The Pharmacological Basis of Therapeutics,* 5th ed., Macmillan, New York, 1975, pp. 653–679.

Greenblatt, D. J., and J. Koch-Weser: "Intramuscular Injection of Drugs," *New England Journal of Medicine,* vol. 295, no. 10, 1976, pp. 542–546.

Hanson, R. L.: "Heparin—Lock or Keep-Open I.V.?" *American Journal of Nursing,* vol. 76, no. 7, 1976, pp. 1102–1103.

Mirkin, B. L.: "Drug Disposition and Therapy in the Developing Human Being," *Pediatric Annals,* vol. 5, no. 9, 1976, pp. 542–557.

Sinaiko, A. R., and B. L. Mirkin: "Pediatric Hypertension: Current Therapeutic Considerations," *Pediatric Annals,* vol. 5, no. 9, 1976, pp. 587–596.

Singh, S.: "Clinical Pharmacokinetics of Digitalis Glycosides: A Developmental Viewpoint," *Pediatric Annals,* vol. 5, no. 9, 1976, pp. 578–585.

5

Drugs Used for Respiratory Disorders and Hypersensitivity Reactions

GENERAL CONSIDERATIONS

Respiratory disorders and hypersensitivity (allergic) reactions produce increased secretions, nasal congestion, bronchospasm, cough, and other responses which require drug therapy.

Drugs used to treat these conditions include expectorants and mucolytics, decongestants, antitussives, bronchodilators, and antihistamines. Most of these drugs are administered orally or parenterally; however, some are administered as oral inhalants (aerosols) or as nasal solutions. Oral inhalation of bronchodilators by way of hand-held devices is suitable for children over 6 years of age, but these devices should only be used with the assistance of a knowledgeable adult. Nasal solutions must be instilled in a manner which will minimize systemic absorption (see "Critical Steps in Instillation of Pediatric Nasal Solutions" in Chap. 2).

Table 5-1   Theophylline Bronchodilators

Drug and Dose	Comments and Relevant Nursing Actions
Aminophylline (theophylline ethylenediamine): Children over 41 kg of body weight: 300 mg rectally one or two times a day, or 4 mg/kg rectally three or four times a day Usual pediatric dose: 4 mg/kg IV three times a day	A soluble salt of theophylline, which is a safe drug for pediatric patients. Theophylline, a xanthine, is closely related to caffeine and theobromine, drugs which share its properties. Aminophylline relaxes smooth muscle, particularly the muscles of the bronchi. The drug also stimulates the central nervous system, produces mild diuresis, and stimulates the myocardium. The drug is available as sterile injection, rectal suppositories, rectal solution, and enteric-coated tablets. Aminophylline is administered for the prevention and treatment of asthma attacks, and for treatment of status asthmaticus. It can be safely administered concurrently with adrenergic bronchodilators (e.g., epinephrine) for additive effects. The drug is also utilized for treatment of pulmonary edema and biliary colic. Wide variations in response to aminophylline are presumably related to unpredictable absorption and metabolism of the drug. Careful individualization of dosage during long- or short-term administration is necessary to prevent adverse reactions. Monitoring of plasma or saliva concentrations is an important part of individualizing dose and preventing toxicity. Since plasma and saliva concentrations are constant, monitoring of saliva is possible (Gibaldi and Levy, 1976, p. 1991). Oral absorption of aminophylline is highly unreliable; thus, this route is not a preferred one (AMA Department of Drugs, 1977, p. 638). Rectal absorption is also variable; however, this route may be necessary. Administration of the drug as a retention enema may decrease the risk of overdose (AMA Department of Drugs, 1977, p. 637). Since intramuscular administration of aminophylline produces severe, persistent pain, this route of administration is not used.

Table 5-1 Theophylline Bronchodilators (Continued)

Drug and Dose	Comments and Relevant Nursing Actions
	The drug is metabolized in the liver and is excreted in the urine. Metabolism of aminophylline is known to vary widely from child to child.
	Adverse effects may occur with any route of administration, and death has followed administration of aminophylline suppositories to children.
	Concurrent administration of theophylline-containing cough medications increases the risk of adverse reactions.
	Intravenous administration at rapid rates produces hypotension, headache, palpitations, precordial pain, and cardiac arrest.
	Oral administration causes nausea, vomiting, and epigastric distress; however, these reactions might occur after parenteral administration.
	Repeated rectal administration of aminophylline may result in irritation of the rectum.
	Insomnia, nervousness, vomiting, gastrointestinal bleeding, shock, and convulsions may also occur.
	All children receiving aminophylline must be constantly assessed for cardiovascular and central nervous system toxicity. Frequent monitoring of blood pressure, apical rate, and respiration and evaluation for precordial pain are essential.
	Evaluation of the child for headache, restlessness, nervousness, and alterations in state of consciousness must be made continually.
	Notation of frequent urination, vomiting, fever, and dehydration must be made.
	The child must be evaluated for sudden increase of theophylline absorption, particularly after rectal administration.
	The nurse should also note the presence of theophylline in cough medications which the child is receiving.

Table 5-1   Theophylline Bronchodilators (*Continued*)

Drug and Dose	Comments and Relevant Nursing Actions
Oxtriphylline (Choledyl): Children: 15 mg/kg PO daily in four divided doses (AMA Department of Drugs, 1977, p. 639)	A choline salt of theophylline which is both stable and soluble. The drug stimulates the central nervous system, produces mild diuresis, relaxes bronchial smooth muscle, and produces relaxation of other smooth muscle. Oxtriphylline is available as enteric-coated tablets and elixir for oral administration. Since the drug is stable in the gastric fluid, it is more completely absorbed than aminophylline and other poorly soluble theophyllines. The drug is used for treatment of acute bronchial asthma and other conditions which cause spasm of the bronchi. Since tolerance is not common, oxtriphylline can be used for long-term therapy of bronchospasm. After oral administration the drug is readily absorbed from the gastrointestinal tract. Oxtriphylline is less irritating than aminophylline, and gastric irritation is minimal. After partial metabolism by the liver, the drug is excreted in the urine. Nervousness and restlessness might occur, particularly in young children. Anorexia, mild epigastric distress, and nausea occur occasionally. Since oral absorption is predictable, there is less risk of sudden increase in plasma drug concentration. The child must still be evaluated for evidence of central nervous system stimulation (e.g., insomnia, restlessness).
Dyphylline (Neothylline, Airet) (AMA Department of Drugs, 1977, p. 638): Infants: 4 to 6 mg/kg PO daily divided doses	Dyphylline is a stable, soluble derivative of theophylline. As a theophylline drug it shares the actions and properties of the parent compound.

Table 5-1   Theophylline Bronchodilators (*Continued*)

Drug and Dose	Comments and Relevant Nursing Actions
Children: 14 mg/kg PO daily in divided doses	The drug is used to relieve bronchospasm associated with chronic bronchitis; however, its most important use is for acute bronchial asthma.
	Oral dosage forms include elixir and tablets. Since the drug is neutral, it is also available as sterile solution for intramuscular administration. Dyphylline is the only theophylline derivative suitable for administration by the intramuscular route.
	Absorption of the drug from the gastrointestinal tract is consistent and more complete than that of aminophylline, and the incidence of gastric upsets is much lower.
	Insomnia, nervousness, and restlessness might occur in young children.

Table 5-2   Adrenergic Bronchodilators

Drug and Dose	Comments and Relevant Nursing Actions
Epinephrine, hydrochloride (Adrenalin, etc.): Usual pediatric dose: 10 μg/kg SC, repeated as necessary up to six times a day	A naturally occurring catecholamine which produces sympathetic nervous system—like responses (i.e., relaxation of bronchial muscle, acceleration of heart rate with strengthening of contraction, dilation of pupil, constriction of somatic blood vessels, and stimulation of the central nervous system).
	The drug is available in a variety of dosage forms and concentrations. Sterile preparations for injection, nonsterile nasal solutions, sterile ophthalmic solutions, and solutions for oral inhalation are available for use.
	Small doses of epinephrine are administered for treatment of acute asthma attacks and status asthmaticus.
	The drug is also used for treatment of hypersensitivity (allergic) reactions, angioedema, and anaphylactic shock.
	Epinephrine is utilized to maintain adequate heart rate in heart block and for emergency cardiac resuscitation.
	Ophthalmic preparations are used to reduce congestion of blood vessels and to produce mydriasis for examination.
	The drug is destroyed by the gastrointestinal tract and thus is not suitable for oral administration. In infants and young children significant absorption of epinephrine ophthalmic solution and inhalation across conjunctiva and nasal mucosa may occur. Subcutaneous absorption, while adequate, is slower and more sustained than absorption from the muscle.
	After rapid metabolism by the liver and other tissues, excretion occurs by way of the urine.
	Epinephrine must be administered cautiously to children with hypertension, diabetes, and cardiac disorders.

Table 5-2   Adrenergic Bronchodilators (Continued)

Drug and Dose	Comments and Relevant Nursing Actions
	Repeated administration of parenteral and inhalation dosage forms may result in tolerance and refractoriness to the drug's bronchodilating action.
	The risk of adverse reactions is increased by the administration of another adrenergic drug [e.g., ephedrine, isoproterenol (Isuprel)] concurrently with epinephrine.
	Administration of nasal solutions is associated with rebound congestion, drying of mucosa, and irritation of membranes.
	Inhalation of epinephrine tends to dry mucus, thereby forming mucous plugs, which are viscid and extremely difficult to dislodge.
	Excessive, prolonged inhalation of the drug may precipitate severe asthma attacks in some children.
	Anxiety, tremor, palpitation, respiratory difficulty, and restlessness occur with usual doses of epinephrine. Placing the child in the recumbent position in a quiet environment promotes rapid resolution of these reactions.
	Hypertension and cardiac arrhythmias may occur after administration of large doses.
	Epinephrine preparations must be protected from strong light, alkalies, and oxidizing agents. Solutions which contain a precipitate or which have turned brown should not be used!
	Accidental injection of the drug into the vein must be avoided by careful aspiration before parenteral administration.
	After administration of the drug the child must be evaluated for effectiveness of epinephrine action, hypertension, cardiac reactions, and central nervous system reactions.
	Asthmatic children should be hydrated and encouraged to cough in order to dislodge mucus from bronchioles.

Table 5-2   Adrenergic Bronchodilators *(Continued)*

Drug and Dose	Comments and Relevant Nursing Actions
Isoproterenol (Isuprel, Norisodrine): Usual pediatric dose: 5 to 10 mg SL three times a day	A synthetic drug which is chemically similar to epinephrine and which produces sympathetic nervous system–like responses. Isoproterenol relaxes the smooth muscle of the bronchi, skeletal muscle, and gastrointestinal tract. The drug also increases the heart rate and the force of myocardial contraction. Available dosage forms include sterile parenteral solution, sublingual tablets, oral tablets, and solution for oral inhalation. Isoproterenol is used for the prevention and treatment of asthma. The drug is also used in heart block to maintain the cardiac output before pacemaker insertion. Absorption of oral and sublingual tablets is incomplete and unreliable; however, the drug is readily absorbed after parenteral and aerosol administration. After metabolism by the liver and other tissues, isoproterenol is excreted by the kidney. Excessive use of isoproterenol inhalations can produce dryness and irritation of mucosa, and severe, prolonged asthma attacks. Tolerance and refractoriness to the bronchodilating actions of the drug may also occur with overuse. Headache, flushing, palpitation, and tachycardia occur frequently. Tremor, nausea, and serious cardiac arrhythmias occur occasionally. After administration of isoproterenol the child should be evaluated for response to the drug, cardiac reactions, and central nervous system reactions.
Ephedrine sulfate: Usual pediatric dose: 750 μg/kg PO, SC, or IV four times a day	A synthetic preparation whose sympathetic effects resemble those of epinephrine. The drug relaxes bronchial smooth muscle, dilates the pupil, increases the cardiac rate, and stimulates the central nervous system. While the actions of ephedrine are less potent than those of epinephrine, their duration is significantly longer.

Table 5-2   Adrenergic Bronchodilators (*Continued*)

Drug and Dose	Comments and Relevant Nursing Actions
	The drug is available as syrup, tablets, and capsules for oral administration. It is also supplied as sterile solution for parenteral administration, ophthalmic solution, and as nasal solution.
	Ephedrine is administered to prevent mild episodes of asthma, particularly to patients with chronic conditions which require long-term medication.
	The drug is applied to the conjunctiva to produce mydriasis for eye examination, and to relieve ocular congestion.
	While topical application of ephedrine to nasal mucosa produces decongestion of swollen membranes, the drug is seldom used for this purpose at present.
	In adults the drug is used to prevent hypotension during spinal anesthesia, and to maintain cardiac output during heart block.
	Insomnia, nervousness, and urinary retention are common during ephedrine administration.
	Hypertension and palpitation occur with large doses.
Metaproterenol (Alupent, Metaprel) (AMA Department of Drugs, 1977, p. 635): Children 6 to 9 years (under 60 lb): 10 mg syrup PO three or four times daily Children over 9 years (over 60 lb): 20 mg syrup PO three or four times daily	A synthetic drug which produces selective adrenergic responses of prolonged duration. The drug relaxes bronchial smooth muscle more effectively than does isoproterenol. Bronchodilation produced by metaproterenol is of long duration, and tolerance to this action has not been reported. Since the drug produces minimal cardiovascular effects, few adverse reactions involving this system occur.
	Metaproterenol is available as syrup and tablets for oral administration, as well as micronized powder for oral inhalation.
	Absorption of oral metaproterenol is apparently reliable.
	Tremor, nervousness, hypertension, and tachycardia may occur after administration of the drug.

Table 5-2   Adrenergic Bronchodilators (*Continued*)

Drug and Dose	Comments and Relevant Nursing Actions
Pseudoephedrine (Sudafed, Novafed) Children: 4 mg/kg per 24 h in four divided doses (Vaughn and McKay, 1975, p. 1755)	A bronchodilator decongestant which is closely related to ephedrine, a drug which shares its therapeutic and adverse effects. The drug is supplied as tablets and syrup for oral administration. Pseudoephedrine is administered for relief of bronchospasm and congestion of upper respiratory tract mucosa. While the drug produces few serious adverse reactions, nausea, insomnia, nervousness, and headache occur occasionally. Hypertension may occur with large doses.

Table 5-3   Nasal Decongestants

Drug and Dose	Comments and Relevant Nursing Actions

Phenylephrine hydrochloride (Neo-Synephrine, Isophrin)
  Pediatric decongestant dose:
  0.05 to 0.15 ml of a 0.125 to 0.25% solution in each nostril six to eight times a day as necessary
  Pediatric vasopressor dose:
  100 μg/kg IM or SC
	A synthetic drug which produces adrenergic actions on the heart, blood vessels, and peripheral vessels. The drug elevates both systolic and diastolic pressures, the heart rate is increased, most vascular beds are constricted, and mydriasis occurs.
	
	Phenylephrine is available as sterile solution for injection, nasal solution, sterile ophthalmic solution, and as capsules and elixir for oral administration.
	
	The drug is widely used as a topical nasal decongestant, and is available in over-the-counter preparations.
	
	Sterile parenteral dosage forms are used to treat shock, orthostatic hypotension, and tachycardia.
	
	Ophthalmic solutions are applied to the conjunctiva to produce mydriasis for eye examination.
	
	Topical application of phenylephrine to nasal mucosa may cause drying and irritation of membranes as well as rebound congestion.
	
	Severe hypertension, tachycardia, palpitation, and cardiac arrythmias may occur with large doses administered by any route.

Tuaminoheptane sulfate (Tuamine Sulfate)
(The preparation is instilled in each nostril not more than 4 or 5 times daily for a maximum of 3 or 4 consecutive days) (AMA Department of Drugs, 1977, p. 652):
  Infants under 1 year: 1 or 2 drops
  Children 1 to 6 years: 2 or 3 drops
  Children over 6 years: 4 or 5 drops
	An effective nasal decongestant which has been used for infants and children.
	
	Available as oral inhalant and nasal solution; however, the latter is usually used for pediatric patients.
	
	The drug produces the adverse reactions associated with other adrenergic drugs, i.e., hypertension, rebound mucosal congestion, drying and irrita-

Table 5-3   Nasal Decongestants (*Continued*)

Drug and Dose	Comments and Relevant Nursing Actions
	tion of membranes, and central nervous system stimulation.
Xylometazoline hydrochloride (Otrivin) (The drug is placed in each nostril 2 or 3 times daily) (AMA Department of Drugs, 1977, p. 653): Infants under 6 months: 1 drop of 0.05% solution Children 6 months to 12 years: 2 or 3 drops of 0.05% solution	A nasal decongestant which is effective and produces mild, infrequent adverse reactions. Rebound congestion, drowsiness, headache, hypotension, and bradycardia occur with overuse.

Table 5-4   Drugs Which Promote Removal of Respiratory Tract Secretions

Drug and Dose	Comments and Relevant Nursing Actions
Pancreatic dornase (Dornavac): Inhalation: 50,000 to 100,000 U dissolved in 2 ml of normal saline, and administered in aerosol form one to four times daily for 1 to 7 days (AMA Department of Drugs, 1977, p. 659)	A mucolytic agent which is derived from beef pancreas, and rapidly liquefies purulent sputum. The drug is supplied as a powder to be dissolved in normal saline, and the resulting solution is administered by oral inhalation. While it is ineffective for mucoid sputum, pancreatic dornase is used to liquefy purulent secretions associated with bronchopulmonary infections. Local and systemic sensitivity reactions may occur with repeated use of the drug.
Acetylcysteine (Mucomyst): Inhalation: 2 to 20 ml of a 10% solution nebulized into a face mask or mouthpiece every 2 to 6 h	A mucolytic which is derived from a naturally occurring amino acid and which lowers the viscosity of some mucus. The drug's action actually alters the structure of mucus, and its effectiveness is increased in the presence of an alkaline medium. Acetylcysteine is supplied as a sterile solution in 10 and 20% concentrations. The drug is administered as an aerosol or is instilled directly into the trachea, bronchi, or other portion of the respiratory tract. The drug is used to decrease secretions associated with bronchopulmonary infections, and to obtain secretions for laboratory study. After administration of the drug the sudden increase in secretions may result in aspiration or airway obstruction. It is essential to have on hand a suction machine and other means of maintaining a patent airway (e.g., endotracheal tube). Acetylcysteine may cause asthmatic attacks in sensitive children. The unpleasant odor of the drug may produce nausea, vomiting, and gastric distress in some children.

Table 5-4   Drugs Which Promote Removal of Respiratory Tract Secretions
(Continued)

Drug and Dose	Comments and Relevant Nursing Actions
	Stomatitis, runny nose, and hemoptysis occur also.
Sodium chloride	Nebulized normal saline solution liquefies viscid secretions in the respiratory tract. Since sodium chloride solution evaporates after the mist is generated, the preparation is usually hypertonic when it comes into contact with the lower respiratory tract.
	The drug is not irritating to the respiratory membranes; tolerance apparently does not develop; and sensitivity reactions have not been reported.
	Normal saline is also used as a nasal decongestant for infants and children. Topical application of the drug produces adequate decongestion, and it avoids the central nervous system and cardiovascular reaction of the adrenergic nasal decongestants.
Ammonium chloride: Children: 75 mg/kg per 24 h PO in four divided doses (Vaughn and McKay, 1975, p. 1715)	A combination of a labile cation and a fixed anion which has expectorant actions, as well as mild diuretic actions.
	The drug is available as sterile parenteral solution, enteric-coated tablets, and syrup, and is contained in many cough medications.
	Ammonium chloride is administered orally for its expectorant and diuretic effects. It is occasionally used to acidify the urine in treatment of metabolic alkalosis.
	The drug must be administered cautiously in infants and in children with hepatic or renal impairment.
	Nausea, anorexia, and vomiting occur with large doses of oral ammonium chloride.
	Metabolic acidosis may occur, particularly in infants.

Table 5-4 **Drugs Which Promote Removal of Respiratory Tract Secretions**
(*Continued*)

Drug and Dose	Comments and Relevant Nursing Actions
Potassium iodide solution: Pediatric expectorant dose: 0.06 to 0.25 ml PO four times a day	An inorganic iodide preparation which is used as an expectorant, an antifungal agent, and as a source of iodine. The official solution of the drug contains 1 g potassium iodide per milliliter. Potassium iodide irrates the gastric mucosa, an action which reflexly stimulates respiratory tract secretion. The drug is used for short-term treatment of thyroid crisis, and its action is due to its ability to prevent synthesis and release of thyroid. It is also effective against fungal (i.e., cutaneous lymphatic sporotrichosis) infections. Potassium iodide produces a brassy, unpleasant taste, and gastric upset, sore mouth, excessive salivation, and runny nose occur frequently. Rash, fever, edema of larynx, and anaphylaxis occur occasionally. The drug should not be administered, and the physician should be notified, if these reactions appear. The drug may produce either thyroid enlargement or decrease in thyroid function.

Table 5-5   Cromolyn Sodium

Drug and Dose	Comments and Relevant Nursing Actions
Cromolyn sodium (Aarane, Intal): Children over 5 years: 80 mg/24 h by insufflation (inhalation), divided into four doses (Vaughn and McKay, 1975, p. 1721)	A unique antiasthmatic agent which prevents release of histamine and other spasmogens from respiratory tract mast cells. Since the drug does not dilate the bronchi, it is not effective for asthma attacks. Cromolyn is supplied as gelatin capsules which contain 20 mg active drug. The drug is not to be swallowed, but rather is placed in a special inhaler where the capsule is punctured. As the child inhales through the mouthpiece, a rotary device creates a vortex which forces the powder into the current of air. The drug is administered to prevent asthma attacks, and many children with severe asthma respond to the drug. While some children show improvement several days after cromolyn therapy has been initiated, an occasional child might require approximately 1 month of therapy before demonstrating positive response. Tolerance to cromolyn does not develop, and use of the drug decreases the requirement for other drugs (i.e., bronchodilators, expectorants, and corticosteroids). After inhalation cromolyn is incompletely absorbed from the lung, and is excreted unchanged in the bile and urine. Wheezing, nasal congestion, bronchospasm, and cough are the most frequently reported adverse reactions associated with readministration of cromolyn ("Adverse Reactions to Cromolyn Sodium," 1978, p. 24). Urticaria, rash, angioedema, headache, swelling of the parotid gland, and lacrimation have also occurred.

Table 5-6   Antitussives

Drug and Dose	Comments and Relevant Nursing Actions

Guaifenesin (Robitussin, Expectran, etc.) (AMA Department of Drugs, 1977, p. 668):
    Children 2 to 6 years: 25 mg PO every 3 to 8 h
    Children 6 to 12 years: 50 mg PO every 3 to 8 h
	A nonnarcotic cough preparation which is often effective for dry, unproductive cough.
	
	The drug is available as the syrup, tablets, and capsules for oral administrations. Guaifenesin is also an ingredient of many over-the-counter mixtures which contain expectorants. Some manufacturers market the drug as glyceryl guaiacolate.
	
	While adverse reactions are rare, drowsiness and nausea may occur after large doses.

Hydrocodone bitartrate (Codone, Dicodid): Children: 0.6 mg/kg daily PO in three or four divided doses (AMA Department of Drugs, 1977, p. 665)	A highly effective antitussive drug, which acts on the medullary cough center. While the drug is a more effective antitussive than codeine, the risk of dependence is much greater with hydrocodone. Hydrocodone is available as tablets for oral administration. The drug is also contained in numerous antitussive mixtures, which are supplied as syrups, capsules, and tablets. The drug does not usually produce adverse reactions; however, nausea, dizziness, and constipation may occur.
Dextromethorphan hydrobromide (Romilar, Tussade, etc.): Children: 1 mg/kg daily PO in three or four divided doses (AMA Department of Drugs, 1977, p. 667)	A nonnarcotic antitussive drug which acts on the medullary cough center. Dextromethorphan is as effective an antitussive as codeine, and is not addicting. The drug is available as tablets, capsules, and syrup for oral administration. It is also contained in many over-the-counter cough remedies. Serious adverse reactions are unusual with dextromethorphan; however, slight drowsiness, mild nausea, and dizziness may occur.

ANTIHISTAMINES (See Table 5-7)

The antihistamines are a large group of drugs which antagonize the action of histamine at smooth-muscle receptor sites. Antihistamines in present use can be divided into several chemical classes; however, they share many similarities and differ only in potency and adverse reactions. Children may differ in their response to the various antihistamines, as well as in their susceptibility to their adverse effects.

Antihistamines are available in a variety of solid and liquid dosage forms for oral administration, and several are also supplied as sterile solution for injection. Diphenyhydramine (Benadryl) is supplied as cream and lotion for topical application.

Some antihistamines are also available in over-the-counter cold remedies, sleep aids, and other preparations.

Absorption

Oral antihistamines are well absorbed from the gastrointestinal tract and, after hepatic metabolism, are excreted in the urine.

Indications

Antihistamines are utilized for preoperative sedation, for prevention and treatment of nausea and vomiting, for allergic reactions, and for relieving the local discomfort of insect bites.

Adverse Reactions

The most common adverse reaction associated with administration of antihistamines is central nervous system depression. Varying degrees of drowsiness, ataxia, dizziness, and difficulty in concentrating are frequent. Antihistamines increase the central nervous system depression of alcohol and other drugs.

Table 5-7 Antihistamines

Drug and Dose	Comments

Brompheniramine maleate (Dimetane, Veltane):
   Children: 0.5 mg/kg PO daily in three or four divided doses
   Children under 12 years: 0.5 mg/kg IM, IV or SC daily in three or four divided doses
	The most common adverse reaction is drowsiness.

Chlorpheniramine maleate (Chlor-Trimeton, Teldrin, etc.):
   Infants: 1 mg PO three or four times daily
   Children under 12: 2 mg PO three or four times a day
	Causes a low incidence of drowsiness.

Cyproheptadine hydrochloride (Periactin): Children: 0.25 mg/kg daily PO in three or four doses (AMA Department of Drugs, 1977, p. 681)	Useful in treating pruritis and cold allergy. Increases weight gain and linear growth.
Diphenhydramine hydrochloride (Benadryl, Histex): Usual pediatric dose: 1.25 mg/kg PO or IM four times daily, not to exceed 300 mg daily	Useful as an adjunctive drug in allergic anaphylaxis. Applied topically for pruritis. Produces significant sedation and anticholinergic activity.

Hydroxyzine hydrochloride (Atarax, Vistaril) (Vaughn and McKay, 1975, p. 1779):
   Pediatric preoperative dose: 1 mg/kg IM
   Pediatric antiemetic dose, under 6 years: 50 mg PO daily in four divided doses
	Useful for prevention and treatment of nausea and vomiting, and for allergic reactions.
	
	 Produces a low incidence of drowsiness.
	
	 Highly irritating; administration by Z technique may prevent local inflammatory reactions after intramuscular use.

Promethazine hydrochloride (Phenergan, Methazine): Pediatric antiemetic dose: 250 to 500 μg/kg PO or IM four to six times daily	Produces the heaviest sedation of the antihistamines. Useful for preoperative sedation and prevention and treatment of nausea and vomiting.

Table 5-7   Antihistamines (*Continued*)

Drug and Dose	Comments
Pediatric antihistaminic dose: 6.25 to 12.5 mg PO or IM three times daily, or 25 mg once at bedtime	
Trimeprazine tartrate (Temaril): Children 6 months to 2 years: 1.25 mg PO one to four times daily, not to exceed 5 mg daily Children 3 to 6 years: 2.5 mg PO one to four times daily, not to exceed 10 mg daily Children 7 to 12 years: 2.5 to 5 mg PO one to three times daily, not to exceed 15 mg daily	Produces a low incidence of drowsiness. Useful as an antipruritic.

In children anticholinergic reactions are likely to occur, particularly with large doses and in young children. These reactions include insomnia, tremor, irritability, urinary retention, and palpitation.

Fever, toxic nephrosis, and blood dyscrasia (e.g., hemolytic anemia) occur rarely.

Hypersensitivity (allergic) reactions may follow topical application of antihistamine lotions and creams.

Nursing Care

Nursing care during antihistamine therapy includes protecting the child from injury and careful evaluation for adverse reactions.

BIBLIOGRAPHY

"Adverse Reactions to Cromolyn Sodium," *FDA Drug Bulletin,* vol. 8, no. 3, May–July 1978, p. 24.

AMA Department of Drugs: *AMA Drug Evaluations*, 3d ed., Publishing Sciences Group, Littleton, Mass., 1977.

American Academy of Pediatrics: "Adverse Reactions to Iodide Therapy of Asthma and Other Pulmonary Diseases," *Pediatrics*, vol. 57, no. 2, 1976, pp. 272–273.

"Azatadine (Optimine)—A New Antihistamine," *The Medical Letter*, vol. 19, no. 19 (issue 448), September 23, 1977.

Gibaldi, M., and G. Levy: "Pharmacokinetics in Clinical Practice, II," *Journal of the American Medical Association*, vol. 235, no. 18, 1976, pp. 1987–1992.

Goodman, L. S., and A. Gilman: *The Pharmacological Basis of Therapeutics*, 5th ed., Macmillan, New York, 1975.

Hendles, L., et al.: "Guide to Oral Theophylline Therapy for the Treatment of Chronic Asthma," *American Journal of Diseases of Children*, vol. 132, 1978, pp. 876–880.

Marks, M. B.: "Therapeutic Efficacy of Cromolyn in Childhood Asthma," *American Journal of Diseases of Children*, vol. 128, 1974, pp. 301–304.

"Oral Theophylline Drugs for Asthma," *The Medical Letter*, vol. 17, no. 3 (issue 419), January 31, 1975.

Speer, F.: "The Allergic Child," *American Family Physician*, vol. 11, no. 2, 1975.

Thompson, H. C., et al.: "New Advances in Drug Therapy of Asthma in Childhood," *Arizona Medicine*, vol. 33, no. 5, 1976, pp. 369–372.

Vaughn, V. C., and J. R. McKay: *Textbook of Pediatrics*, 10th ed., Saunders, Philadelphia, 1975.

Wilson, A. F.: "Drug Treatment of Acute Asthma," *Journal of the American Medical Association*, vol. 237, no. 11, 1977, pp. 1141–1143.

Vitamins, Fluids, and Electrolytes

GENERAL CONSIDERATIONS

Vitamins are organic substances which are obtained from foods and are essential for normal metabolic processes. They are divided into the fat-soluble and water-soluble vitamins, and the former require bile for their absorption. Since vitamins K and B_{12} play important roles in hemopoiesis, they are included in Chap. 9, "Drugs Which Affect the Blood."

Dietary Allowances

A comprehensive review of recommended dietary allowances of vitamins and of vitamin deficiency states is beyond the scope of this work. The interested reader is directed to the many excellent nutrition texts on this subject.

Vitamin Supplementation

Vitamin supplementation is recommended for healthy infants and children throughout the growth years; however, some children receive excessive vitamin doses. Some parents mistake "extra" vitamins as preventative and curative measures for a wide variety of conditions.

Fluids and Electrolytes

Fluid and electrolyte needs of infants and children are quite distinct from those of adults, and they are also extremely complex. Since it is not feasible to present a complete discussion of fluid and electrolyte disorders, the reader is directed to works which present these disorders in their entirety.

Table 6-1   Fat-Soluble Vitamins

Vitamin and Dose	Comments and Relevant Nursing Actions
Vitamin A: Prophylactic pediatric dose: 600 μg to 1.35 mg PO once daily Therapeutic pediatric dose: 3 to 15 mg PO once daily	Vitamin A is obtained from dairy products, eggs, fish liver oils, meat (particularly liver), and fortified margarine. The provitamins contained in green and yellow fruits and vegetables are converted to vitamin A in the body. This vitamin is essential for the growth and development of bones and teeth, for normal function of the retina, and for the integrity of mucosal and epithelial surfaces. While the diet received by the average American infant and child supplies sufficient vitamin A, premature infants, children with malabsorption disorders (e.g., celiac disease, cystic fibrosis), and children receiving low-fat diets require supplementation. Most normal children also receive a small supplemental dose to prevent vitamin A deficiency during the growth years. Children with symptoms of vitamin A deficiency require doses appropriate to the severity of the deficiency. Vitamin A is available alone, in combination with vitamin D, and as a component of multivitamin preparations. It is supplied as tablets, capsules, and drops for oral administration. The parenteral dosage form, which is indicated for children unable to swallow oral preparations, is administered intramuscularly. Excessive concentrations of the vitamin, *hypervitaminosis A,* develops rapidly in infants; however, in older children its appearance requires a longer period of exposure as well as a much larger dose. In the infant hypervitaminosis A is manifested by bulging fontanels, drowsiness, vomiting, papilledema, and other symptoms of increased intracranial pressure. Irritability, loss of hair, dryness of skin and mucous membranes, abdominal pain, tender swelling of bones, desquamation of palms and soles, and suppression of growth occur with excessive vitamin administration to older children. It is important that parents understand that vitamin A preparations are to be administered only as directed by the pediatric prescriber. Nurses should also assess infants and children frequently for evidence of hypervitaminosis A.

Table 6-1   Fat-Soluble Vitamins (*Continued*)

Vitamin and Dose	Comments and Relevant Nursing Actions

Vitamin D (Vaughn and McKay, 1975, p. 204):
  Pediatric prophylactic dose: 400 IU PO daily
  Pediatric therapeutic dose: 1500 to 5000 IU PO daily
	Vitamin D is obtained from dairy products, fish liver oils, eggs, and animal fats, and the vitamin can also be derived from exposure to sunlight or ultraviolet light. Many cereals and other foods received by infants and children are fortified with vitamin D.
	
	The vitamin regulates the absorption and deposition of calcium and phosphorus, possibly by altering intestinal permeability to these substances. It controls normal calcification of teeth and bone by maintaining plasma calcium concentrations within specific limits, and by directly influencing bone mineralization.
	
	Infants and children usually receive vitamin D supplementation during the growth years to avoid symptoms of deficiency.
	
	Requirements for premature infants, black children, and children receiving long-term therapy with anticonvulsants are larger.
	
	Therapeutic doses of vitamin D are indicated for treatment of hypocalcemia in infants (infantile tetany), rickets, and osteomalacia.
	
	Vitamin D is available alone, combined with vitamin A, or as an ingredient of multivitamin preparations. Tablet, capsules, and drops are supplied for administration by the oral route.
	
	Excessive vitamin D concentrations, *hypervitaminosis D,* may result not only from administration of larger than necessary doses of the vitamin but also from feeding children large amounts of vitamin D—fortified foods. The margin between a beneficial and a toxic dose of vitamin D is narrow, and there are individual differences in susceptibility to excessive doses.
	
	Chronic hypervitaminosis D in the infant is characterized by mental and physical retardation, elfin features, and renal failure. Suppression of linear growth, hypercalcemia, weakness, fatigue, dehydration, and irritability also occur in this condition.
	
	It is important that parents be taught that vitamin D—fortified milk and foods are not necessary with vitamin

Table 6-1   Fat-Soluble Vitamins (*Continued*)

Vitamin and Dose	Comments and Relevant Nursing Actions
	supplementation. Some parents will require instructions on identification of fortified foods. All children should be assessed for manifestations of hypervitaminosis D.
Vitamin E (AMA Department of Drugs, 1977, p. 187): Therapeutic dose for children: 40 to 150 IU PO or IM daily Infants fed formula high in polyunsaturated fats: 5 to 7 IU per liter of formula	Vitamin E is found in grains, eggs, vegetable oils, margarine, legumes, liver, and whole milk. Although the functions of the vitamin are far from clear, it appears to facilitate utilization of vitamin A, to promote metabolism of steroids, and to inhibit oxidative destruction of polyunsaturated fats. There is no evidence that vitamin E prevents aging, cures cancer, provides protection from heart disease, or minimizes the risk of developing numerous diseases. Premature and other infants fed diets high in polyunsaturated fats require vitamin E supplementation. Vitamin E requirements may be increased in children receiving iron or large doses of thyroid and in those placed in high-oxygen environments. Vitamin E is available as capsules for oral administration and as a sterile preparation for intramuscular administration. Overdosage with vitamin E seldom produces serious consequences; however, weakness, fatigue, and gastrointestinal distress may occur.

Table 6-2   Water-Soluble Vitamins

Vitamin and Dose	Comment and Relevant Nursing Actions
Vitamin C (ascorbic acid) (AMA Department of Drugs, 1977, p. 189): Neonates fed formula: 35 mg PO daily during the first few weeks of life Therapeutic pediatric dose: 300 to 1000 mg PO or IM daily for at least 2 weeks	Vitamin C is abundant in fresh fruits, fresh vegetables, and liver. The vitamin is essential for collagen formation, tissue repair, and for synthesis of proteins and fats. It promotes metabolism of iron and folic acid and plays a role in the maintenance of blood-vessel integrity. Formula-fed infants and children with malabsorption usually receive vitamin C supplementation. Vitamin C requirements are increased in the presence of burns and trauma, and after surgical procedures. Since atropine, barbiturates, and salicylates increase the urinary excretion of vitamin C, children receiving long-term therapy with these drugs may require vitamin C supplementation. Therapeutic doses are administered to children with vitamin C deficiency (scurvy), a condition seldom seen in the United States. Vitamin C is available alone and combined in multivitamin preparations as capsules, tablets, and drops for oral administration. The vitamin is also supplied as a sterile preparation for intramuscular injection. Excessive doses of vitamin C increase the rate at which the vitamin is metabolized and excreted. Sudden withdrawal of such excessive doses may precipitate vitamin C–deficiency states, but gradual reduction of dosage does not produce this condition. There is no agreement on the adverse effects of vitamin C overdosage; however, the condition is associated with diarrhea, renal calculi, and interference with warfarin (Coumadin) anticoagulant activity. Children receiving large doses of vitamin C may have false-negative reactions for urine glucose when Clinistix is used, and false-positive reactions when Clinitest or Benedict's solution is used (Hansten, 1976, p. 337).
Vitamin B complex:	The vitamin B complex consists of a large group of chemically unrelated factors which serve different

Table 6-2   Water-Soluble Vitamins (Continued)

Vitamin and Dose	Comment and Relevant Nursing Actions
	physiological functions. While deficiency states of thiamine, riboflavin, niacin, and pyridoxine are well understood, it is common to find several vitamin B deficiencies in the same child. For this reason the child with a vitamin B deficiency is often treated with a preparation which contains the entire complex.
	While the functions of some factors of the vitamin B complex (e.g., biotin, choline, pantothenic acid) are understood, no deficiency states have been identified in human populations.
	Two members of the vitamin B complex, folic acid and vitamin B_{12}, play important roles in the formation of blood cells and thus are discussed in Chap. 9.
Thiamine (vitamin B_1): Prophylactic dose: 5 to 10 mg IM or PO once daily Therapeutic dose: 10 to 20 mg IM three times a day 10 to 35 mg PO three times a day	Thiamine is obtained from wheat germ, whole-grain and enriched cereals, liver, legumes, and nuts. The vitamin is necessary for carbohydrate metabolism and for preventing accumulation of pyruvic acid in body tissues. Requirements for thiamine are increased during fever, stress, prolonged diarrhea, and in the presence of a high carbohydrate intake. Therapeutic doses are administered for treatment of thiamine deficiency (beriberi), a condition which is often mild in the United States. Administration of large doses by the oral route is followed by rapid urinary excretion of the vitamin with no adverse effects. Intravenous administration of large doses, on the other hand, may produce fatal anaphylactic reactions.
Riboflavin: Prophylactic dose: 2 mg PO or IM once daily Therapeutic dose: 5 to 10 mg PO or IM once daily	Riboflavin is obtained from liver and other organ meats, milk, nuts, green leafy vegetables, and whole or enriched grains. This vitamin plays a vital role in the metabolism of numerous respiratory proteins, in several biological oxidations, and in the maintenance of erythrocyte integrity. The factor is administered for deficiency states, which usually occur with niacin deficiency (pellagra). No adverse reactions are associated with oral or intramuscular administration of riboflavin.
Niacin (niacinamide): Prophylactic dose: 10 to 20 mg IM or PO	Niacin is obtained from milk, eggs, green vegetables, peanuts, and cereals (whole-grain and enriched). It plays an important role in tissue respiration, and in

Table 6-2   Water-Soluble Vitamins (Continued)

Vitamin and Dose	Comment and Relevant Nursing Actions
once daily Therapeutic dose: 25 to 50 mg IM 2 to 10 times a day 50 mg PO 3 to 10 times a day	energy transfer during glycolysis and lipid metabolism. Therapeutic doses of this vitamin are indicated for niacin deficiency (pellagra), a condition which usually occurs concurrently with other vitamin B complex deficiencies. Therapeutic doses of niacin produce flushing, sensation of local heat, pruritis, headache, and gastrointestinal distress. Large doses are associated with reversible liver damage and elevation of serum uric acid levels. Intravenous administration of the vitamin may cause anaphylactic reactions in sensitive children.
Pyridoxine (vitamin B_6): Prophylactic dose: 2 mg IM, IV, or PO once daily Therapeutic dose: 10 to 150 mg IM, IV, or PO one to three times a day	Pyridoxine plays a primary role in the metabolism of proteins and amino acids, and a smaller role in the metabolism of fats and carbohydrates. Whole grains, meats, fish, poultry, peanuts, soybeans, and corn supply the vitamin. Nursing infants of mothers on therapy with isoniazid (INH); children receiving isoniazid (INH), hydralazine (Apresoline), or penicillamine (Cuprimine) may require pyridoxine to prevent peripheral neuritis. The drug is also administered for the treatment of deficiency states and infantile epileptiform convulsions. Administration of large doses of pyridoxine by the oral and parenteral routes does not produce adverse reactions.

Table 6-3   Intravenous Fluids

Solution	Comments and Relevant Nursing Actions
Intravenous solutions containing single electrolytes: Sodium chloride 0.33% with dextrose 5%. (Each liter supplies 56 meq of both sodium and chloride, as well as 50 g glucose.) Sodium chloride 0.45% with dextrose 5%. (Each liter supplies 77 meq of both sodium and chloride, as well as 50 g glucose.) Intravenous solutions containing multiple electrolytes: Pediatric electrolyte "number 48" with dextrose 5%. (Each liter supplies 25 meq sodium, 20 meq potassium, 3 meq magnesium, 22 meq chloride, 3 meq HPO$_4$, 23 meq lactate, as well as 50 g glucose.) Ringer's lactate (Hartmann's) solution. (Each liter supplies 103 meq sodium, 4 meq potassium, 3 meq calcium, 109 meq chloride, and 28 meq lactate.)	Intravenous fluids and electrolytes are administered to replace usual losses in children unable to take food and fluids orally (*maintenance* fluids and electrolytes). They are also indicated for replacement of unusual losses which occur during vomiting, diarrhea, and other abnormal states (*supplementary* or *replacement* fluids and electrolytes). Intravenous fluids are also used to maintain a patent vein [keep vein open, (KVO)] for administration of drugs by the intravenous route (e.g., antibiotics, bronchodilators, adrenocorticosteroids). Pharmaceutical firms produce a wide variety of single-electrolyte solutions which contain sodium chloride in varying doses (sodium chloride, 0.33% and 0.45%), and multiple-electrolyte solutions which contain several electrolytes (e.g., pediatric electrolyte number 48, Ringer's solution). Since children with fluid and electrolyte disorders also often need calories, these solutions may also contain dextrose. In some institutions electrolytes are added to intravenous solutions by nursing or pharmacy staff. Addition of any drug to an intravenous solution increases the risk of microbial contamination, particularly if carried out in a contaminated environment. While adding electrolytes and other drugs to intravenous fluids under controlled environmental conditions (laminar flow hood) minimizes the risk of contamination, the 17 percent contamination rates found when drugs are added under these hoods indicates that they by no means eliminate this risk (Wood, 1977, p. 16). Electrolytes can be added to intravenous fluids by the manufacturer, after which the solution is sterilized and sealed. Since these products

Table 6-3   Intravenous Fluids (*Continued*)

Solution	Comments and Relevant Nursing Actions
	eliminate the risk of microbial contamination, they are recommended over hospital-prepared solutions (Wood, 1977, p. 20; Poole, 1977, p. 217).
	Intravenous fluids are available in glass bottles and in plastic bags (polyvinyl chloride). Plastic bottles do not require an air vent for adequate flow; however, they may be as susceptible to contamination as are glass bottles ("Plastic Containers," 1975, p. 44). While these plastic bags are unbreakable and conveniently stored, chemicals from the bag may be leached from the plastic, enter the solution, and be infused into the bloodstream (Wood, 1977, p. 17). Significant amounts of some drugs may be attracted to and held (adsorbed) by the bag's plastic surface ("Plastic Containers," 1975, pp. 43–44). Incomplete mixing of the electrolyte with the intravenous fluid is more likely to occur with plastic bags; however, it may also occur with a glass bottle if the drug is added slowly ("Plastic Containers," 1975, p. 44). Such incomplete mixing occurs when the electrolyte is added with the solution container (i.e., bag or bottle) hanging in the down (infusion) position. With the container in this position, adding a drug which varies in specific gravity from the intravenous solution results in formation of a layer of drug immediately above the administration set. This undiluted electrolyte will enter the bloodstream in the first minutes of the infusion and can have serious effects.
	To avoid microbial contamination of plastic bags, the bag should be squeezed before preparation for administration, and bags with holes must be discarded.
	Electrolytes and other drugs should be added to intravenous fluids with the container in the upright position (opposite of infusion position) to avoid incomplete mixing.

Table 6-3   Intravenous Fluids (*Continued*)

Solution	Comments and Relevant Nursing Actions
	Addition of drugs should be performed under strict aseptic conditions, i.e., using aseptic technique and under a laminar flow hood, to decrease the risk of microbial contamination.
	The physician's order should specify not only the solution and electrolyte but also the rate at which it should be infused. Since many physicians prescribe a specific number of milliliters per hour, the nurse must convert this to drops per minute. The child's age and body mass, fluid and electrolyte status, and cardiac and renal status are the major determinants of the flow rate. During administration of the infusion, the order will be changed as the child responds to intravenous therapy.
	Infants have a larger portion of total body water, more rapid turnover of water, and a higher fluid requirement per unit of body mass than do older children. They are more susceptible to fluid and electrolyte disorders (e.g., dehydration, acidosis) than are older children. Although infants have higher fluid requirements in terms of body mass, their total plasma compartment is much smaller than that of older children; thus, their total fluid requirements are much smaller. The kidneys of the infant might also be unable to remove excess fluids and electrolytes as quickly and efficiently as those of the older child.
	As the child matures, the percentage of total body water decreases and the turnover of body water decelerates; thus, fluid requirements per kilogram of body weight decrease. The total fluid needs are larger than those of the infant, and the kidneys remove excess fluids and electrolytes more quickly and effectively.
	Infants not only receive smaller amounts of intravenous fluids but the rate at which they

Table 6-3   Intravenous Fluids (*Continued*)

Solution	Comments and Relevant Nursing Actions
	receive fluids is much slower than the rate for older children.

Infants and children with severe fluid and electrolyte disorders (e.g., severe dehydration, metabolic acidosis, etc.) may require larger amounts of fluids in a comparatively short period of time to replace severe deficits. Such large fluid volumes are administered only after careful evaluation of renal function and cardiovascular status. Children with cardiac disorders will receive sodium with utmost caution to avoid excessive expansion of the extracellular compartment.

During administration of intravenous fluids and electrolytes, the child's response is evaluated by laboratory determination of the pH, electrolytes, tests of hemoconcentration (i.e., plasma proteins, hematocrit), Pco_2, and bicarbonate levels. Frequent taking of blood pressure and central venous pressure readings, determination of body weight, accurate recording of intake and output with urine specific gravity, and monitoring of ECG changes (for children with potassium disorders) also help to evaluate the response to fluid and electrolyte therapy. Careful assessment of skin turgor, inspection of mucous membranes, and examination of fontanels are essential to determine hydration status. A flow sheet on which all laboratory reports, nursing assessments, and other information is recorded is a helpful tool.

Administration of fluids and electrolytes to infants and children is best achieved by use of small-volume (e.g., 250-ml, 500-ml) bottles or bags. It is also advisable to use volume-controlled administration sets, which deliver 60 drops per milliliter (microdrop) and which permit more precise regulation of infusion flowrates than do regular administration sets. Use of small-volume containers and volume-

Table 6-3 Intravenous Fluids (*Continued*)

Solution	Comments and Relevant Nursing Actions
	controlled administration sets (e.g., Soluset, Volutrol) not only decrease the risk of over-hydration but also decrease risk of too rapid administration rates. During administration of the infusion, the child must be assessed at least every 15 min and the flowrate adjusted (if necessary); the site must be evaluated for evidence of infiltration; and the child's fluid and electrolyte status must be determined. Since administration sets in common usage do not deliver accurate fluid rates a variety of volume pumps are available for use. These volume pumps (e.g., the IVAC 600/601) deliver precise amounts of intravenous fluids and also alarm should infiltration occur.
	Adverse reactions associated with administration of intravenous fluids and electrolytes include volume overload with pulmonary edema in susceptible children. This reaction results from administration of large amounts of fluid and/or sodium within a short period of time to a child whose kidneys are unable to remove the excess fluid and/or sodium. Careful regulation of flowrate and assessment of renal function and of cardiac status will prevent this reaction. Labeling the bottle or bag with a strip which indicates the specific time at which specific amounts should infuse may also eliminate this reaction.
	Microbial contamination of the solution can be avoided by use of asepsis in preparing the solution, use of filters which prevent some bacterial access to the bloodstream, and by changing administration sets at least every 24 h.
	Problems of incompatibility of additives can be eliminated by use of commercially prepared solutions, or by confirming compatibility of additives with pharmacy before preparation.

Table 6-3   Intravenous Fluids (*Continued*)

Solution	Comments and Relevant Nursing Actions
	Infiltration can be avoided by gently immobilizing the extremity (if an extremity is the site), and by proper use of a board for the extremity or protection for a scalp vein site.
	Phlebitis may result from reaction to the needle or plastic venous cannula, or from irritation caused by the solution. Proper dilution of electrolytes and changing the site every 48 h will minimize this risk.
	Contamination of the solution with rubber and glass particles can occur either during commercial manufacture or during hospital addition of drugs. Use of filters may prevent entry of these particulate contaminants into the bloodstream; however, the effects of infusing these particles is uncertain.

Table 6-4   Electrolytes

Electrolyte	Comments and Relevant Nursing Actions
Oral electrolyte preparations (Pedialyte, Lytren)	These oral electrolytes are suitable for infants and children with mild to moderate fluid and electrolyte losses.
	Pedialyte solution is supplied in cans and in nursing bottles. The solution contains sodium, potassium, calcium, magnesium, chloride, citrate, and dextrose. Each 100 ml Pedialyte contains 20.8 calories.
	Lytren is supplied as a powder which is to be dissolved in water. Each dose of the preparation contains sodium, potassium, calcium, magnesium, citrate, sulfate, chloride, phosphate, lactate, and dextrose. A dose of 8 oz Lytren supplies 240 calories.
	These preparations are not recommended for severe fluid and electrolyte losses, nor for use in children with renal impairment. They should not be added to fruit juices, milk, or other oral electrolytes.
Potassium chloride injection: Usual pediatric dose: up to 3 meq/kg daily (Vaughn and McKay, 1975, pp. 258, 269) Potassium chloride oral solution (KayCiel, K-Lor, etc.)	Potassium, the major intracellular cation, regulates muscular contraction, conduction of nerve impulses, cell membrane function, and enzyme action.
	Potassium chloride is indicated for hypokalemia associated with diarrhea, gastric suction, upper gastrointestinal tract obstruction, diuretic usage, and digitalis toxicity.
	The drug is diluted in the intravenous infusion, and infused slowly over a prolonged period of time. It is never administered by "IV push," or in concentrated amounts. Addition of potassium chloride to intravenous fluids with the plastic bag in the down position (infusion position) may result in inadequate mixing of the electrolyte, with the child receiving an excessive amount of potassium chloride in the first few minutes of the infusion (Wood, 1977, p. 17).

Table 6-4   Electrolytes (*Continued*)

Electrolyte	Comments and Relevant Nursing Actions
	Potassium is excreted by the kidney; thus, renal impairment results in retention of excessive potassium concentrations. Before starting any intravenous solution which contains potassium, confirmation of adequate renal function (BUN, voiding of sufficient amount of urine) is absolutely essential. Renal function must also be assessed frequently during administration of potassium.
	Dosage of potassium chloride is carefully individualized by using the urine and blood electrolyte levels and the ECG. Changes in serum potassium concentration are reflected in ECG conduction defects. Most children receive a potassium chloride solution which contains from 20 to 40 meq electrolyte per liter of fluid.
	Adverse reactions associated with potassium chloride administration include muscular weakness and paralysis, abdominal distension, diarrhea, and ECG changes which range from peaked T waves to ventricular fibrillation and cardiac arrest.
	Uncoated tablets for oral administration have caused gastric irritation; enteric-coated tablets of former usage were poorly absorbed, and produced small-bowel ulceration. Oral solutions do not usually produce gastric irritation if they are adequately diluted with water or fruit juice. Administration of oral potassium chloride dosage forms after meals also reduces gastric irritation.
	Administration of intravenous potassium chloride may produce irritation and pain, particularly if the solution is administered into a small vein.
	Nursing evaluation of renal function before and during potassium chloride administration is critical. Careful reading of the ampule will avoid errors in dosage, and addition of the electrolyte with the plastic bag in the upright (noninfusion) position rather than in the down (infusion) position avoids the risk of inadequate mixing. Label the bag or bottle with the electrolyte, dose, date, and

Table 6-4   Electrolytes (*Continued*)

Electrolyte	Comments and Relevant Nursing Actions
	time started, as well as specific times that specific amounts should have infused. Remain with child for the first minutes of the infusion and evaluate for hyperkalemia. Administer slowly, keeping a careful record of urine output and a careful eye on ECG changes. Decrease flow at first evidence of renal impairment or changes in cardiac conduction as reflected in the ECG.

Calcium preparations:
 	
  Calcium gluconate:
    Usual pediatric dose:
    125 mg/kg PO or IV up to
    four times daily
 	
  Calcium chloride:
    Usual pediatric dose:
    75 mg/kg IV four times
    daily as a 2% solution
    (rarely used)
 	
  Calcium lactate:
    Usual pediatric dose: 125
    mg/kg PO up to four
    times daily
	Calcium, the most abundant cation in the body, is found in large amounts in bones and teeth and in small amounts in the plasma. The plasma concentration of calcium is regulated by vitamin D, parathyroid hormone, and calcitonin. Calcium concentrations of the plasma compartment are closely related to those of phosphorus.
	
	The calcium ion is necessary for neuromuscular transmission, blood coagulation, cardiac function, and cell membrane function.
	
	Administration of calcium salts is indicated for treatment of hypocalcemic tetany associated with malabsorption syndromes, rickets, chronic renal failure, prolonged administration of anticonvulsants, and parathyroid hormone deficiency. A calcium preparation is also administered during cardiac arrest to increase the force of myocardial contraction. Hypocalcemia may result from complexation of plasma calcium with citrated blood during exchange transfusions or massive transfusions.
	
	Calcium preparations for intravenous administration must be diluted and administered slowly, and since they are very irritating to subcutaneous tissues, they should never be permitted to infiltrate. Since the calcium concentration of the various preparations varies, they must be prepared with attention to accuracy of dosage. Since these intravenous dosage forms are used for correction of severe calcium deficits, the child must be carefully evaluated for overdosage during administration.

Table 6-4   Electrolytes (*Continued*)

Electrolyte	Comments and Relevant Nursing Actions
	Oral dosage forms are indicated for treatment of mild to moderate calcium deficits, and for maintenance therapy. These preparations tend to cause gastric distress; thus, they should be administered after meals.
	Excessive doses of calcium produces weakness, polyuria, gastric upset, constipation, stupor, azotemia, and coma. Administration of calcium to digitalized children enhances the effects of the digitalis preparation and increases the risk of cardiac arrhythmias. Addition of tetracyclines to calcium-containing solutions and simultaneous administration of oral tetracyclines with oral calcium preparations decreases the effectiveness of the tetracycline. This interaction can be avoided by administering intravenous tetracycline at a different time interval, and by administering oral tetracyclines 3 h before administration of oral calcium preparations.
Sodium bicarbonate: Usual dose: 2 to 5 meq/kg IV in a 1.4 to 5% solution over 4 to 8 h 325 mg to 16 g PO daily	Bicarbonate, an extracellular anion, maintains normal pH of the bloodstream by buffering hydrogen ions.
	This anion may be administered as lactate or acetate, precursors which are metabolized to bicarbonate by the liver. Children with hypoxia or circulatory insufficiency might metabolize precursors inadequately, and thus might require sodium bicarbonate.
	Sodium bicarbonate is indicated for treatment of metabolic acidosis due to cardiac arrest, sickle-cell crisis, diabetic ketosis, and severe diarrhea. The drug is widely used by the laity as an antacid and as an antipruritic.
	Intravenous sodium bicarbonate is diluted and administered slowly, during which time plasma bicarbonate concentrations and pH determinations are used as guides to flowrate. In severe metabolic acidosis the drug may be administered rapidly until acidosis is corrected.

Table 6-4   Electrolytes (*Continued*)

Electrolyte	Comments and Relevant Nursing Actions
	Oral dosage forms may be used for children with mild to moderate acidosis, provided the child can retain the drug.
	Sodium bicarbonate is not indicated for children losing chloride ion by vomiting or gastric suction or for those with alkalosis associated with diuretic usage.
	The drug should be administered cautiously to children with hypertension, renal impairment, congestive heart failure, and other cardiovascular disorders.
	Rapid correction of metabolic acidosis with sodium bicarbonate may produce metabolic alkalosis with movement of potassium out of the cell into the bloodstream.

BIBLIOGRAPHY

AMA Department of Drugs: *AMA Drug Evaluations,* 3d ed., Publishing Sciences Group, Littleton, Mass., 1977.

Evaluation of Drug Interactions, 2d ed., American Pharmaceutical Association, Washington, D.C., 1976.

Fluids and Electrolytes: Some Practical Guides to Clinical Use, Abbott Laboratories, North Chicago, 1970.

Gruber, D. L.: "Helping the Child Accept I.V. Therapy," *The American Journal of Intravenous Therapy,* March 1977, pp. 50–51.

Hanid, T. K.: "Intravenous Injection and Infusion in Infants," *Pediatrics,* vol. 56, no. 6, 1975, p. 1080.

Hansten, P. D.: *Drug Interactions,* 3d ed., Lea & Febiger, Philadelphia, 1976.

Krupp, M. A., and M. J. Chatton: *Current Medical Diagnosis and Treatment,* Los Altos, Calif., 1976.

Leifer, G.: *Principles and Techniques in Pediatric Nursing,* 3d ed., Saunders, Philadelphia, 1977.

"Plastic Containers for Intravenous Solutions," *The Medical Letter,* vol. 17, no. 110, May 9, 1975.

Poole, H. H.: "Drugs in Infusions," *Adverse Drug Reaction Bulletin,* no. 26, February 1977.

Snider, M. A.: "Helpful Hints on I.V.'s," *American Journal of Nursing,* vol. 74, no. 11, 1974, pp. 1978–1981.

Stroot, V. R., et al.: *Fluids and Electrolytes: A Practical Approach,* 2d ed., Davis, Philadelphia, 1977.

Vaughn, V. C., and J. R. McKay: *Textbook of Pediatrics,* 10th ed., Saunders, Philadelphia, 1975.

Wood, A. J. J.: "Continuous Drug Infusions: Problems and Solutions," *Drug Therapy (Hospital),* February 1977, pp. 14–20.

7

Immunizing Agents

GENERAL CONSIDERATIONS

Bacterial and viral vaccines are biological preparations which stimulate production of active immunity to infectious diseases. Only 7 of the 19 available vaccines are recommended for routine use in infants and children. The American Academy of Pediatrics recommends the routine administration of diphtheria, tetanus, pertussis (whooping cough), poliomyelitis, measles, mumps, and rubella vaccines according to a specific schedule. Administration of two multiple vaccines, diphtheria-tetanus-pertussis (DTP) and measles-mumps-rubella, is favored over administration of single vaccines unless there is a specific rationale for avoiding a vaccine contained in these multiple preparations.

Routine Immunization

Schedules for these routine immunizing agents consist of those for infants and those for children not immunized during the first year of life. Routine immunization is usually deferred during infections, and live virus vaccines (measles, mumps, etc.) are withheld in the presence of immunosuppression or immunodeficiency; thus, schedules are often individualized.

Special Immunization

Special immunizing agents (influenza virus vaccine) and agents which provide passive immunity (immune serum human globulin) are indicated for high-risk children under specific circumstances.

Storage

To assure retention of maximal potency, all biologicals must be stored, reconstituted, and administered according to the directions of the package insert. It is also prudent to note not only lot number but also the expiration date of the product. Since concentration and dosage of biologicals vary from one manufacturer to another, it is mandatory to read the package insert for dosage concentration information.

Adverse Reactions

Some immunizing agents evoke hypersensitivity reactions in susceptible children; thus, epinephrine and emergency equipment must always be available.

Parent Teaching

Parents should be taught not only the importance of immunization but also the value of maintaining current immunization records and the rationale for keeping these records in an accessible location.

Table 7-1   Routine Immunizing Agents

Agent and Schedule	Comments

Diphtheria and tetanus toxoids with pertussis vaccine (DTP) (American Academy of Pediatrics, 1974):
    Primary immunization, infants: Injections at 2, 4, and 6 months, and also at 1½ years
    Booster (recall) dose: 5 or 6 years
	DTP is a sterile suspension of tetanus and diphtheria toxoids with killed pertussis bacilli. These three antigens are combined in proportions which provide an immunizing dose for each.
	
	This combination is recommended for primary immunization and booster doses for children up to 6 years of age; however, it is not recommended for use in children over 6 years of age. DTP contains 10 or more flocculating units of diphtheria toxoid, an amount which produces increased local and systemic reactions in children over 6 years of age.
	
	The preparation should be well shaken before administration to assure even distribution of contents. Careful aspiration before injecting the agent is essential to avoid accidental intravenous injection. Since the dose and concentration of DTP from different manufacturers are not always identical, the package insert must be consulted for appropriate doses. Unused DTP should be stored under refrigeration, and freezing of the preparation should be avoided.
	
	Transient fever with induration, tenderness, and erythema of the injection site are the most common adverse reactions to DTP. These reactions indicate the necessity for reduction of subsequent doses of DTP.
	
	Screaming spells, infantile massive spasms, convulsions, and other central nervous system reactions occur rarely; they are considered contraindications to further use of pertussis vaccine.

Diphtheria and tetanus toxoids (DT)	DT is a sterile suspension of diphtheria and tetanus toxoids which is used for primary immunization and booster doses in children under 6 years of age. The large amount of diphtheria toxoid (10 or more flocculating units) in DT produces a high incidence of undesirable reactions

Table 7-1   Routine Immunizing Agents (*Continued*)

Agent and Schedule	Comments
	in children over 6 years of age; thus, the preparation is not suitable for use in this age group.
	This combination is indicated for use in children who do not tolerate pertussis vaccine or who should have this vaccine separately.
Tetanus and diphtheria toxoids (Td)	Td is a sterile suspension of tetanus toxoid with a smaller amount of diphtheria toxoid than DTP and DT. This preparation does contain enough diphtheria toxoid (2 flocculating units) to produce adequate primary immunization and booster doses in children over 6 years of age.
	Fever, malaise, and mild local inflammatory reactions (e.g., induration and tenderness of injection site) occur occasionally after administration of the preparation.
Tetanus toxoid	Tetanus toxoid is a sterile, bacteria-free preparation of tetanus bacillus growth products. Since most children receive primary tetanus vaccination with a multiple antigen (e.g., DTP, DT), the single tetanus toxoid is usually indicated for recall (booster) doses. For clean, minor wounds no booster dose is required provided the child has received complete primary immunization (at least two doses) within 10 years. In the event of a severe, contaminated wound a booster dose is indicated if more than 5 years has elapsed since the last dose.
	Erythema, induration, and tenderness of the injection site occur occasionally. Fever and malaise may occur rarely after administration of tetanus toxoid.
Pertussis vaccine	Pertussis vaccine is an aqueous preparation of killed bacteria which contains most of the constituents of the microorganism. The vaccine is a relatively crude preparation, and it has not been purified because the distinct bacterial antigenic components have yet to be identified (Krugman and Katz, 1977, p. 2229).

Table 7-1   Routine Immunizing Agents (*Continued*)

Agent and Schedule	Comments
	The single pertussis vaccine is indicated for children who have manifested a reaction to an earlier injection of DTP, and for children with neurological disorders (e.g., epilepsy, brain tumors).
	Since both the incidence and severity of whooping cough decrease with age, administration of pertussis vaccine to children over 6 years of age is not advisable.
	Convulsions, fever, malaise, myalgia, and sterile abscess formation occur rarely after administration of pertussis vaccine.
Measles, mumps, and rubella virus vaccine (live) (American Academy of Pediatrics, 1974) Primary immunization, infants: A single injection at 15 months	This preparation is a lyophilized combination of live, attenuated measles, mumps, and rubella viruses which provides immunization with a single dose. The vaccine, which produces antibody levels comparable to those attained after administration of the three separate vaccines, can be used in children from 15 months to puberty.
	Measles, mumps, and rubella vaccine is contraindicated for use in children with impaired cellular immunity, those with active, untreated tuberculosis, and those who have received immune serum globulin (gamma globulin), whole blood, or plasma within 3 months. Since transplacentally acquired antibodies may interfere with antibody production in the first year of life, the vaccine is not administered until the child reaches 15 months of age. This vaccine should be administered to children with cerebral disorders (i.e., history of febrile convulsions, cerebral trauma) with extreme caution.
	Measles, mumps, and rubella vaccine is supplied as a freeze-dried solid, with a special preservative-free diluent which does not inactivate the vaccine. The preparation must be stored under refrigeration and protected from

Table 7-1   Routine Immunizing Agents (*Continued*)

Agent and Schedule	Comments
	light to avoid loss of potency. Failures of measles vaccines have been attributed to poor refrigeration or excessive exposure to light and heat after reconstitution (Krugman and Katz, 1977, p. 2228). After reconstitution with its special diluent, measles, mumps, and rubella vaccine is stable for 8 h, provided the vaccine is refrigerated and protected from light. Although the reconstituted vaccine usually ranges from pink to reddish in color, a yellowish color is acceptable provided the preparation is crystal clear.
	Moderate fever, mild local inflammatory reactions (e.g., tenderness, induration, and erythema), and regional lymphadenopathy may occur after administration of the vaccine.
	Nongeneralized rash and urticaria may also occur. Arthritis, arthralgia, and polyneuritis have occurred within 2 months of administration of the preparation.
	High fever with convulsions and encephalitis have been reported rarely after administration of measles, mumps, and rubella vaccine.
	The vaccine should be administered subcutaneously in the outer lateral aspect of the arm, after careful aspiration to avoid accidental intravenous administration.
Trivalent oral poliovirus vaccine (TOPV) (American Academy of Pediatrics, 1974): Primary immunization, infants: 2, 4, and 6 months, and at $1\frac{1}{2}$ years Follow-up dose: 4 to 6 years, or upon entering school	TOPV is a liquid preparation which contains live, attenuated viruses of types I, II, and III. The vaccine produces immunity in 90 percent of recipients, and is the polio vaccine of choice for routine immunization of infants and children. It is convenient to administer, well accepted by children, and does not require periodic recall (booster) doses.
	Children with impaired immunity (i.e., those receiving immunosuppressive therapy and those who are immunodeficient) should not

Table 7-1   Routine Immunizing Agents (*Continued*)

Agent and Schedule	Comments
	receive TOPV; however, they may receive a trivalent inactivated polio vaccine (IPV) (Krugman and Katz, 1977, p. 2228). Since persistent vomiting and diarrhea prevent proliferation of the virus in the intestine, TOPV should not be administered in the presence of vomiting and diarrhea. While some enteroviruses may interfere with antibody production, TOPV can be administered simultaneously with diphtheria, tetanus, and pertussis vaccine (DTP).
	TOPV must be stored in the freezer compartment of a refrigerator to avoid loss of potency. Frozen preparations should be thawed before use, and an unopened container of the vaccine can be frozen and refrozen 10 times providing the total thaw time does not exceed 24 h and the temperature during thawing does not exceed 46°F (8°C). Vaccines which do not meet these criteria may be used for 30 days, provided they are refrigerated at 46°F. The usual color of the thawed vaccine varies from reddish pink to yellow; however, a change in color from red or pink to yellow after the container has been entered indicates contamination.
	This vaccine is suitable for oral administration only! It may be mixed with milk, distilled water, or chlorine-free water. The vaccine also may be placed directly on the child's tongue or placed on a sugar cube, bread, or cake.
	Recipients of TOPV and their close contacts have developed vaccine-associated poliomyelitis. The incidence of vaccine-associated polio has apparently increased over the past 15 years, and a large proportion of polio cases are vaccine related (Basilico and Bernat, 1978, p. 2275). It is important to point out that the incidence of vaccine-associated polio is very low; between 1968 and 1976 193 million doses of TOPV were administered, and 10 cases of

Table 7-1   Routine Immunizing Agents (*Continued*)

Agent and Schedule	Comments
	polio occurred in vaccine recipients and 34 cases of polio occurred in healthy contacts (Wolman, 1978, p. 313). Children with impaired immunity should avoid close contact with TOPV recipients for at least 2 or 3 weeks after vaccination.

Table 7-2   Special Immunizing Agents

Agent and Schedule	Comments
Influenza virus vaccine (*United States Pharmacopeia XIX,* p. 252): Children 3 months to 6 years: 2 injections of 0.1 ml SC or IM 2 weeks apart, followed by a third injection 2 months later Children 6 to 10 years: 2 injections of 0.25 ml SC or IM 2 months apart	Influenza virus vaccine is a sterile aqueous suspension of inactivated influenza virus or virus subunits which stimulates antibody production in individuals with some circulating antibodies. This vaccine contains influenza strains specified by the Food and Drug Administration Bureau of Biologics, and the strains are changed periodically when mutants emerge or the seasonally prevalent strain changes.

The preparation does not provide dependable or long-term protection from influenza. It produces a comparatively high incidence of febrile reactions, and thus, it is not recommended for routine vaccination of healthy children. Influenza vaccination is recommended for high-risk children (e.g., children with rheumatic fever, cystic fibrosis, nephrosis, acquired and congenital cardiac disorders) when an epidemic is imminent or is present (Vaughn and McKay, 1975, p. 684). The reappearance of the swine influenza strain and the continued improvement of influenza vaccine preparations may alter vaccination recommendations for normal children in the future.

Newer, more purified influenza vaccines contain more viral protein and lower concentrations of contaminant (e.g., egg protein); thus, they produce fewer and milder adverse reactions. Children who are sensitive to chick embyro protein rarely manifest urticaria, vascular purpura, or other hypersensitivity reactions.

Fever, malaise, myalgia, and local reaction involving the injection site (pain, induration, erythema) are common after administration of influenza vaccine.

Encephalitis has occurred rarely after administration of this vaccine.

Influenza virus vaccine is a liquid or suspension, the color of which varies from reddish to yellow.

Table 7-2   Special Immunizing Agents (*Continued*)

Agent and Schedule	Comments
	To assure full retention of potency the vaccine must be stored under refrigeration and protected from light.
Pneumococcal polysaccharide vaccine (Pneumovax)	This recently approved vaccine consists of purified polysaccharide antigens of the 14 pneumococcal strains responsible for 80 percent of the serious pneumococcal infections in the United States. Each 0.5 ml of the vaccine contains 50 μg of each polysaccharide type dissolved in a normal saline solution which contains a preservative of 0.25% phenol.
	After subcutaneous or intramuscular administration of the vaccine each antigen produces an independent antibody response, with protection from infection developing within approximately 14 days (Klein and Mortimer, 1978, p. 322). Children under 2 years of age, however, manifest unsatisfactory serologic response to single-dose administration of pneumococcal vaccine.
	Pneumococcal vaccine is presently recommended for use in children over 2 years of age who are at risk of severe or life-threatening pneumococcal infections (i.e., those with sickle-cell anemia, splenectomy, and lipoid nephrosis). The emergence of antibiotic-resistant pneumococcal strains in Minnesota and South Africa may increase the importance of this vaccine in the future.
	Serious adverse reactions are rare after administration of pneumococcal vaccine to children; however, mild fever and local reaction involving the injection site (e.g., pain, induration, and erythema) have occurred.

Table 7-3   Passive Immunizing Agents

Agent and Schedule	Comments
Immune human serum globulin (ISG, gamma globulin)	ISG, a sterile solution of globulins which contain concentrated antibodies present in adult human blood, is derived from a plasma or serum pool from normal donors.
	This preparation is indicated chiefly to prevent or modify (attenuate) measles and rubella, and to prevent infectious hepatitis (type A) in nonvaccinated and/or susceptible children and hospitalized contacts. The drug is also used to prevent communicable diseases and invasive bacterial infection in immunodeficient and immunosuppressed children.
	ISG provides temporary passive protection, and since its half-life is 2 weeks, the preparation is usually effective for 2 to 3 weeks. The effectiveness of ISG varies with the antibody content of the serum-plasma pool; thus, its effectiveness is not always reliable or predictable.
	The drug is administered intramuscularly, after cautious aspiration to prevent accidental intravenous administration.
	Dosage and schedules for administration of ISG vary greatly with the objective of the therapy (whether for prevention or modification), and the infectious state for which it is indicated.
	Serious adverse reactions are rare; however, pain, induration, and erythema of the injection site are common.

Tetanus immune human globulin (TIG) (*United States Pharmacopeia XIX*, p. 493):
    Prophylactic pediatric dose: 4 U/kg IM
    Therapeutic pediatric dose: 3,000 to 10,000 U IM
	TIG is a sterile solution of globulins derived from plasma of adult donors, previously immunized with tetanus toxoid.

	This preparation provides passive immunity to tetanus, and is the agent of choice for preventing tetanus in children with contaminated wounds. Under these circumstances, TIG is indicated if the child has been incompletely immunized, has never been immunized, or if the immunization history is not clear. Large doses of TIG are also indicated for the treatment of clinical tetanus.

Table 7-3   Passive Immunizing Agents (*Continued*)

Agent and Schedule	Comments
	Since TIG is derived from human sources, it avoids the serious hypersensitivity reactions associated with equine tetanus antitoxin, another passive immunizing agent for tetanus. TIG also has a longer half-life than equine tetanus antitoxin; consequently, smaller doses of TIG provide protection for longer durations of time.
	TIG is administered by the intramuscular route, and care must be taken to avoid inadvertent intravenous injection.

BIBLIOGRAPHY

American Academy of Pediatrics: *Report of the Committee on Infectious Diseases,* 17th ed., 1974.

Basilico, F. C., and J. L. Bernat: "Vaccine-Associated Poliomyelitis in a Contact," *Journal of the American Medical Association,* vol. 239, no. 21, 1978, p. 2275.

Furste, W., and A. Aguirre: "The Prevention of Tetanus," *American Journal of Nursing,* vol. 78, no. 5, 1978, pp. 835–837.

Klein, J. O., and E. A. Mortimer: "Use of Pneumococcal Vaccine in Children," *Pediatrics,* vol. 61, no. 2, 1978, pp. 321–322.

Krugman, S.: "Measles Immunization: New Recommendations," *Journal of the American Medical Association,* vol. 237, no. 4, 1977, p. 366.

_____ and S. L. Katz: "Childhood Immunization Procedures," *Journal of the American Medical Association,* vol. 237, no. 20, 1977, pp. 2228–2230.

Smit, P., et al.: "Protective Efficacy of Pneumococcal Polysaccharide Vaccine," *Journal of the American Medical Association,* vol. 238, no. 24, 1977, pp. 2613–2616.

Vaughn, V. C., and J. R. McKay: *Textbook of Pediatrics,* 10th ed., Saunders, Philadelphia, 1975.

Wolman, I. J. (ed.): "Clinical Pediatrics Handbook II, the Latest on Poliomyelitis Prevention," *Clinical Pediatrics,* vol. 17, 1978, pp. 311–316.

Yeager, A. S., et al.: "Measles Immunization: Successes and Failures," *Journal of the American Medical Association* vol. 237, no. 4, 1977, pp. 347–351.

Drugs Which Affect the Central Nervous System

GENERAL CONSIDERATIONS

Fever, inflammatory conditions, and seizures are indications for use of central nervous system drugs in infants and children. These drugs produce a broad range of effects which vary from relief of pain and fever to loss of consciousness. The potency, efficacy, and dose of the drug, as well as the child's maturational level, are essential factors in effects produced.

Definitions

Central nervous system drugs prescribed for children include analgesics, sedatives, hypnotics, anesthetics, analeptics, anticonvulsants, and psychotropics. *Analgesics* are drugs which relieve pain by altering perception of painful stimuli but do not produce loss of consciousness. These drugs are divided into the *nonnarcotic analgesics* [e.g., aspirin, acetaminophen (Tylenol)] and the *narcotic analgesics* (e.g., codeine, morphine). *Sedatives* reduce nervous excitement, while *hypnotics* produce sleep. Some drugs (e.g., barbiturates, paraldehyde) produce sedation at small doses and hypnosis at larger doses. *Anesthetics* (e.g., nitrous oxide, halothane) produce reversible neural depression with loss of consciousness. *Analeptics* [e.g., dextroamphetamine (Dexedrine)] produce stimulation of the central nervous system. *Anticonvulsants* [phenytoin (Dilantin)] are drugs which prevent or arrest convulsions. Some sedative-hypnotics (e.g., barbiturates, paraldehyde) and antianxiety drugs [e.g., diazepam (Valium)] are also effective as anticonvulsants. *Psychotropics* include the antipsychotics [chlorpromazine (e.g., Thorazine)] formerly termed major tranquilizers; antianxiety agents [e.g., diazepam (Valium)] formerly known as minor tranquilizers; and the antidepressants [imipramine (Tofranil)].

Drug Distribution to the Central Nervous System

Drugs which affect the central nervous system are highly lipid soluble; thus, they readily penetrate the blood-brain barrier. They also tend to accumulate in adipose tissue, and such accumulation may persist for several hours after termination of the drug's effect. These agents are metabolized in the liver, and metabolites are excreted in the urine. They may also have significant effects on the metabolism of other drugs. Hepatic and renal impairment are indications for dosage reduction.

Age and Drug Response

While many central nervous system drugs have been extensively used, their effects on the maturing central nervous system of the infant and child are not always consistent. While many pediatric patients manifest increased susceptibility to stimulants and depressants, paradoxical responses to these agents are not unusual. In some children increased susceptibility to central nervous system drugs results in excessive sedation and increased adverse reactions. Central nervous system stimulants [e.g., dextroamphetamine (Dexedrine)] produce excitement in adults; however, small doses of these agents quiet hyperkinetic children. Drugs which produce central nervous system depression in adults [e.g., phenobarbital (Luminal)] may produce excitement in some normal children.

The increased susceptibility and paradoxical responses manifested by pediatric patients may be due to differential development of the central nervous system. Maturation of the central nervous system, a complex process, occurs throughout childhood. Neural immaturity of the neonate is evidenced by the permeable blood-brain barrier, poor body temperature control, vasomotor instability, and the presence of birth reflexes. Maturation of the central nervous system is reflected by abolition of the birth reflexes, and by subsequent development of motor skills and hand-eye coordination. By the second year of life 90 percent of total brain growth has occurred and myelinization of the system is complete. Continued development of the system is manifested by development and refinement of gross and fine motor skills, development of speech, and development of cognitive skills.

Controlled Substances

Distribution and dispensing of central nervous system drugs which have potential for abuse is regulated by the Comprehensive Drug Abuse, Prevention, and Control Act of 1970 (Controlled Substances Act). Since small doses of these drugs are prescribed for children, drug abuse is not a major concern in pediatric use of these agents.

Relevant Nursing Actions

Since all central nervous system drugs may cause sedation and lethargy in children, it is important that the child be protected from falls and other injuries. Diazepam (Valium) increases salivary and bronchial secretions; thus, children receiving this drug must be encouraged to cough and deep-breathe frequently. Since anticonvulsants are administered for prolonged periods, dosage is regulated and compliance occasionally assessed by monitoring plasma drug concentrations.

Table 8-1   Nonnarcotic Analgesics

Drug and Dose	Comments and Relevant Nursing Actions
Aspirin (acetylsalicylic acid): Analgesic and antipyretic pediatric dose: 11 to 16 mg/kg PO six times (maximum dose 3.6 g daily) Antirheumatic pediatric dose: 16 mg/kg PO six times daily or 25 mg/kg PO four times daily initially (up to 125 mg/kg daily) After complete relief, in absence of toxicity, dose reducible to 10 mg/kg six times daily or 15 mg/kg four times daily (up to 100 mg/kg daily)	Aspirin, sodium salicylate and other related drugs have similar analgesic, antipyretic, anti-inflammatory, and antirheumatic properties. Of the group, aspirin is the drug of choice, while sodium salicylate is an alternative for children who are sensitive to aspirin (AMA Department of Drugs, 1977, p. 380). Aspirin is available as chewable tablets, enteric-coated tablets, rectal suppositories, combined with other analgesics, and buffered with antacids. The drug is used extensively in the home for mild to moderate pain of headache, muscle aches, and other discomforts. Aspirin is utilized for juvenile rheumatoid arthritis, acute rheumatic fever, to reduce fever, and, in adults, is used investigationally to prevent thrombus formation. Topical salicylates, methyl salicylate and salicylic acid, are applied locally for painful joints and as a keratolytic agent, respectively. Systemic salicylates relieve pain by inhibiting synthesis of prostaglandins within inflamed tissues. This action prevents sensitization of the pain receptors to chemical or mechanical stimulation. These drugs also act at hypothalamic sites for analgesic and antipyretic effects. Aspirin and other salicylates are rapidly absorbed from the gastrointestinal tract. Taking the drug with a meal delays absorption and prolongs the therapeutic effect; however, it does not decrease the amount of drug eventually absorbed. Absorption of enteric-coated tablets is often incomplete. Rectal absorption of aspirin suppositories is slow, unpredictable, and highly unreliable. Topical application of methyl salicylate results in absorption through the skin and has produced systemic toxicity. Salicylates enter synovial and spinal fluids, in addition to most other body tissues and fluids. Metabolism takes place in the liver and many other tissues, and excretion occurs primarily by way of the urine.

Table 8-1   Nonnarcotic Analgesics (*Continued*)

Drug and Dose	Comments and Relevant Nursing Actions
	Salicylates displace methotrexate and sulfonamides from plasma protein binding sites, thereby increasing their therapeutic effects (*Evaluations of Drug Interactions,* 1976, p. 342). Aspirin and other salicylates enhance the effects of anticoagulants.
	Gastrointestinal disturbances, i.e., nausea, vomiting, and gastric distress, occur frequently. Gastric ulceration with occult bleeding occurs in approximately 70 percent of individuals who receive aspirin. Administration of enteric-coated tablets or choline salicylate (Arthropan) may reduce these reactions.
	While usual doses of aspirin inhibit platelet aggregation and prolong bleeding time, large doses prolong the prothrombin time. Administration of salicylates to children with bleeding disorders or vitamin K deficiency or to those receiving anticoagulants is contraindicated.
	Large doses may produce tinnitus, reversible hearing loss, lethargy, dizziness, confusion, and liver toxicity.
	Salicylate poisoning, the most common poisoning emergency in children, is characterized by acid-base disturbance, hyperpyrexia, hypoglycemia, and metabolic acidosis in infants and young children; respiratory alkalosis is common in older children. Treatment consists of correction of electrolyte disturbances, monitoring serum salicylate levels, and measures to remove the drug from the body.
	Hypersensitivity to aspirin with rash, asthmatic episodes, or anaphylactic reactions occurs rarely. These reactions are more likely in children with asthma, hay fever, or allergy to other substances. Children who are allergic to aspirin can usually tolerate sodium salicylate without incident.
	Administration of salicylates with food, milk, or a full glass of water will reduce gastric irritation. The sodium ion is contraindicated in cardiovascular disorders; thus, children with rheumatic heart disease should not receive sodium salicylate.
	Careful assessment of the child for diminution of rheumatic manifestations will reduce the time that the

Table 8-1   Nonnarcotic Analgesics (*Continued*)

Drug and Dose	Comments and Relevant Nursing Actions
	child receives large salicylate doses. Evaluation of the child for lethargy, ringing in the ears, and electrolyte disorders will identify toxicity early in its course.
Acetaminophen (Tylenol, Tempra, etc.): Children under 1 year: 60 mg PO four times a day Children, 1 to 3 years: 60 to 120 mg PO four times a day Children, 3 to 6 years: 120 mg PO four times a day Children, 6 to 12 years: 240 mg PO four times a day	Acetaminophen and phenacetin, two chemically related agents, have weak anti-inflammatory properties and no antirheumatic effects. Since acetaminophen is safer, it is preferred over phenacetin; however, the latter agent is present in several analgesic combinations.

These drugs are utilized to reduce fever and to relieve headache and muscle and joint pain of moderate intensity. Acetaminophen is available as tablets, oral liquid, rectal suppositories, and in combination with codeine.

Acetaminophen reduces fever by inhibiting the action of endogenous pyrogen on temperature-regulating centers of the hypothalamus. The mechanism of analgesic effects is not certain. Both phenacetin and acetaminophen are well absorbed from the gastrointestinal tract. Approximately 75 percent of phenacetin is rapidly metabolized to acetaminophen, and the remainder is converted to other metabolites.

Acetaminophen enters most body fluids and is metabolized extensively by the liver, after which metabolites are excreted in the urine.

These drugs do not cause gastrointestinal distress or bleeding, nor do small doses enhance the effects of anticoagulants.

Skin rash and other hypersensitivity reactions occur occasionally with both drugs. Large doses of acetaminophen have caused hepatic necrosis and death.

Phenacetin in large doses has produced hemolytic anemia and nephrotoxicity. |

Table 8-2 Narcotic Analgesics

Drug and Dose	Comments and Relevant Nursing Actions
Codeine phosphate: Analgesic pediatric dose: 500 μg/kg PO or SC four to six times a day as necessary Antitussive pediatric dose: 175 to 250 μg/kg PO or SC four to six times a day as necessary	A purified alkaloid of opium, utilized to control mild to moderate pain and for its antitussive actions. The drug is frequently combined with nonnarcotic analgesics (e.g., aspirin) and included in cough preparations. Classified as a controlled drug, codeine has limited potential for abuse. While codeine is usually administered orally, it can also be given subcutaneously. Well absorbed from the gastrointestinal tract, the drug is metabolized by the liver and excreted chiefly in the urine. Approximately 10 percent of the drug is converted to morphine by metabolic reactions. Constipation, nausea, vomiting, drowsiness, and dizziness may occur in ambulatory children.
Meperidine hydrochloride (Demerol): Usual pediatric dose: 1 mg/kg PO or IM six times a day as necessary up to a maximum of 100 mg per dose	A synthetic narcotic which is subject to the regulations of the Controlled Substances Act. Meperidine is utilized to produce preoperative sedation and to relieve pain in infants and children. The drug is available combined with mild analgesics (e.g., acetaminophen). Although meperidine resembles morphine in its effects, it is less potent, and its duration of action is shorter. The drug not only relieves pain but also produces sedation, euphoria, and mental clouding. Meperidine is well absorbed after oral and intramuscular administration, and after its metabolization by the liver, metabolites are excreted in the urine. Children with hepatic impairment require dosage reduction to prevent toxicity. Dizziness, nausea, and vomiting, particularly in ambulatory children, may occur with usual doses. In ambulatory children fainting due to sharp drop in blood pressure is not uncommon. Placing the child in the recumbent position increases blood pressure, thereby resolving the reaction. Hypersensitivity reactions occur rarely.

Table 8-2 Narcotic Analgesics (Continued)

Drug and Dose	Comments and Relevant Nursing Actions
	While tolerance and addiction occur, a longer exposure to meperidine is required than for addiction to morphine.
	The drug increases the central nervous system depression of psychotropics, sedatives, and other drugs. Concurrent administration of meperidine with furazolidone (Furoxone) or other monoamine oxidase inhibitors may result in delirium, fever, and coma.
	After administration of meperidine, keeping the child on bed rest prevents gastrointestinal upsets and falls.
	Children with bronchial secretions should be encouraged to cough and deep-breathe at regular intervals to prevent pulmonary complications. Those unable to cough spontaneously must be suctioned gently and frequently.
Morphine sulfate: Usual pediatric dose: 100 to 200 μg/kg SC up to a maximum of 15 mg per dose	A purified alkaloid of opium which has high potential for addiction, and thus is included under the Controlled Substances Act.
	Morphine is used in pediatrics as a preoperative medication and to relieve severe pain not controlled by less potent analgesics.
	The precise mechanism by which the drug relieves pain is unknown; however, it is believed that morphine and other opium derivatives interact with neurotransmitters (e.g., epinephrine, norepinephrine) either directly or indirectly.
	In therapeutic doses morphine alters psychological response to pain, suppresses anxiety and apprehension, and produces euphoria, drowsiness, and mental clouding. The drug also suppresses the cough reflex, depresses respiration, and produces antiperistaltic actions on the gastrointestinal tract.
	Morphine is well absorbed from subcutaneous and intramuscular injection sites, and after hepatic metabolism is rapidly excreted in the urine. Children with liver impairment require dosage reduction to prevent accumulation of excessive concentrations.

Table 8-2   Narcotic Analgesics (*Continued*)

Drug and Dose	Comments and Relevant Nursing Actions
	The drug is contraindicated in children with respiratory depression or excessive bronchial secretions.
	Concurrent administration of another central nervous system depressant (e.g., antianxiety agent, sedative-hypnotic) increases the depressing effects of morphine.
	Respiratory depression, increased intracranial pressure, gastrointestinal tract disturbances (i.e., nausea, vomiting, and constipation), and hypotension occur with morphine administration.
	Urinary retention, biliary spasm, and constriction of pupils may also occur.
	Hypersensitivity (allergic) reactions are rare.
	Children with respiratory disorders or excessive bronchial secretions, or those at risk of respiratory depression, must be assessed frequently for respiratory depression. These children also require nursing measures to mobilize secretions, e.g., suctioning, frequent turning, as well as measures to promote ventilation.
	Decrease in bowel sounds, urinary retention, and evidence of biliary spasm should be communicated to the physician.
	Morphine should be administered to children with severe pain; however, those for whom a less potent analgesic will suffice should not receive morphine.

Table 8-3   Sedative-Hypnotics

Drug and Dose	Comments and Nursing Actions
BARBITURATES	

Secobarbital, sodium (Seconal):
   Pediatric sedative dose:
     2 mg/kg PO three times a day
     1.1 to 1.65 mg IM
   Pediatric hypnotic dose: 2.2 mg/kg IM or IV
	Secobarbital, pentobarbital, and amobarbital are short- to intermediate-acting barbiturates which differ in duration of action. They produce sedation and hypnosis; however, since they possess no analgesic properties, administration to a child in pain increases response to painful stimuli.

Pentobarbital, sodium (Nembutal): Sedative pediatric dose: 2 mg/kg PO or IM three times a day	Tolerance, dependence, and addiction develop with long-term administration of barbiturates; thus, the drugs are controlled substances.
Amobarbital, sodium (Amytal): Pediatric sedative dose: 2 mg/kg PO three times a day	Secobarbital and pentobarbital in combination with a narcotic or belladonna alkaloid (i.e., atropine, scopolamine) are frequently used as preanesthetic sedatives. These barbiturate preanesthetics decrease apprehension and provide ease of induction, as well as reducing postoperative vomiting and delayed awakening.
	Amobarbital is used occasionally as an anticonvulsant or as a preanesthetic agent.
	Oral barbiturates are well absorbed from the gastro-intestinal tract, and food delays but does not decrease this absorption. Sodium salts are well absorbed from intramuscular sites of injection.
	After metabolism by hepatic microsomes, metabolites are excreted in the urine. Long-term administration of barbiturates has significant effects on the hepatic metabolism of numerous drugs; however, these drugs are seldom administered to children for long periods of time.
	Concurrent administration of barbiturates with anti-histamines, psychotropics, or other central nervous system depressants increases the depressant effects of both agents.
	Barbiturates may produce drowsiness, ataxia, lethargy, and, in some children, paradoxical restlessness and excitement.
	Nausea, vomiting, and hypersensitivity (allergic) reactions are rare.

Table 8-3   Sedative-Hypnotics (*Continued*)

Drug and Dose	Comments and Nursing Actions
	Children receiving barbiturates should be assessed frequently for unsteady gait, decrease in mental alertness, and lethargy. They must be protected from injuries and prevented from games and activities which present a risk of injury (e.g., skate-boarding, roller-skating).
	Children with respiratory disorders must be encouraged to cough, deep-breathe, and change position frequently to prevent accumulation of secretions.
	Gastrointestinal distress and skin rashes should be communicated to the physician.
	Intravenous administration of barbiturates may produce apnea, severe coughing, laryngospasm, and other respiratory difficulties. Accidental injection into an artery results in spasm, intense ischemia, and occasionally gangrene (AMA Department of Drugs, 1977, p. 397).
NONBARBITURATES	
Chloral hydrate (Somnos, Noctec): Hypnotic pediatric dose: 50 mg/kg PO at bedtime, up to 1 g per dose Sedative pediatric dose: 8 mg/kg PO three times a day, up to 500 mg per dose	A nonbarbiturate sedative-hypnotic which is safe for infants and children who do not tolerate barbiturates.
	The drug is well absorbed from the gastrointestinal tract, and after being metabolized by the liver, metabolites are excreted in the urine. Children with hepatic or renal impairment require dosage reduction to prevent adverse reactions.
	Chloral hydrate increases the metabolism of oral anticoagulants, thereby decreasing their effects. In some patients, chloral hydrate displaces oral anticoagulants from albumin binding sites, thereby temporarily increasing their effects (AMA Department of Drugs, 1977, p. 399).
	Tolerance and addiction occur in adults; thus, the drug is included under the provisions of the Controlled Substances Act of 1970.
	The unpleasant taste of liquid oral dosage forms of chloral hydrate is particularly disagreeable to infants and young children.

Table 8-3   Sedative-Hypnotics (*Continued*)

Drug and Dose	Comments and Nursing Actions
	Nausea, vomiting, flatulence, and epigastric distress are not unusual.
	Hypersensitivity skin rashes occur occasionally.
	The drug may cause false-positive results for urinary glucose.
	Administration of liquid chloral hydrate in a chilled beverage decreases the unpleasant taste and minimizes gastric irritation.
Paraldehyde (Paral): Pediatric hypnotic dose: 0.3 ml/kg PO or IM per dose Pediatric sedative dose: 0.15 ml/kg PO or IM per dose	A nonbarbiturate used as a sedative-hypnotic, and occasionally to treat status epilepictus.
	The drug has some potential for abuse, particularly in adult alcoholics and narcotic addicts; thus, it is a controlled substance.
	There is no agreement about whether parenteral administration of paraldehyde is harmful; nevertheless, the drug is administered by the intramuscular and intravenous routes.
	Paraldehyde has a characteristic, unpleasant odor and taste which pediatric patients object to. After being metabolized in the liver, paraldehyde is excreted by both the kidney and lungs. Severe liver impairment results in accumulation of excessive concentrations unless dosage is reduced.
	Gastric and rectal irritation occur with oral and rectal administration, respectively.
	Intramuscular administration is associated with pain and sterile abscess formation.
	Intravenous administration of paraldehyde causes a high incidence of thrombophlebitis; severe cough, which may result in pulmonary hemorrhage, may also occur.
	Exposure of paraldehyde to air and light and contact of the drug with plastic syringes, measuring cups, or other plastic materials may result in decomposition of paraldehyde to toxic compounds. Administration of decomposed paraldehyde has resulted in serious poisoning and death.

Table 8-3   Sedative-Hypnotics (*Continued*)

Drug and Dose	Comments and Relevant Nursing Actions
	The drug should be stored in dark, tightly closed containers, which are opened freshly for each dose, after which unused drug is discarded. Plastics should not be used to measure or administer paraldehyde.
	Administration of oral paraldehyde in milk reduces gastric irritation.
	Intramuscular paraldehyde should be administered deep into the body of a large muscle mass.

Table 8-4   Anticholinergic Preanesthetic Drugs

Drug and Dose	Comments and Relevant Nursing Actions

Atropine sulfate
[the following preanesthetic doses to be administered IM, 45 to 60 min before anesthesia (AMA Department of Drugs, 1977, p. 304)]:
    Neonates: 0.1 mg
    Children 4 to 12 months: 0.2 mg
    Children 1 to 3 years: 0.3 mg
    Children 3 to 14 years: 0.4 mg
 	
(*United States Pharmacopeia XIX,* 1975, p. 40):
    Pediatric anticholinergic dose: 10 μg/kg SC four to six times a day
    Antidote to cholinesterase inhibitors: 1 mg IV or IM initially, followed by 500 μg to 1 mg every 10 to 15 min until signs of atropine toxicity appear
	A natural belladonna alkaloid, which exerts anticholinergic effects on the heart, bronchial musculature, salivary glands, gastrointestinal tract, biliary tract, urinary tract, and both pupil and ciliary body.
	
	The belladonna alkaloids are a large group of natural (e.g., scopolamine, belladonna tincture) and synthetic [e.g., adiphenine (Trasentine), propantheline (Pro-Banthine)] drugs which exert similar therapeutic and adverse effects. These drugs differ in potency and duration of action, and some have selective effects on specific systems.
	
	Atropine relaxes smooth muscle of the bronchi and bronchioles as well as decreasing bronchial secretions. Saliva and perspiration are decreased. While gastrointestinal tract tone and motility are significantly reduced, that of the biliary and urinary tracts is somewhat reduced.
	
	Vagal impulses which slow the heart are abolished by atropine.
	
	The drug also relaxes the ciliary muscle and dilates the pupil.
	
	Atropine is utilized in combination with a sedative or narcotic, as a preanesthetic agent. The drug dries bronchial secretions, reduces airway resistance, decreases saliva, reduces laryngospasm, and protects the heart from excessive vagal impulses which produce hypotension, bradycardia, and cardiac arrest.
	
	It is applied topically to the conjunctiva for examination of the eye.
	
	Atropine is also used to reduce hypermotility of gastrointestinal tract.
	
	In biliary colic atropine may be used with an analgesic to relieve pain and spasm.
	
	Large doses of atropine are also administered for treatment of poisoning with anticholinesterase

Table 8-4   Anticholinergic Preanesthetic Drugs *(Continued)*

Drug and Dose	Comments and Relevant Nursing Actions
	drugs [e.g., edrophonium (Tensilon), ambenonium (Mytelase)].
	In adults atropine is used to treat bradycardia associated with heart block and myocardial infarction.
	Atropine must be utilized with utmost caution in children with fever. The drug inhibits heat loss by suppressing sweating; thus, children with fever may develop hyperpyrexia.
	Adverse reactions may result from ingestion of the drug in over-the-counter sleep preparations or after ingestion of plants containing belladonna.
	Infants and young children are particularly susceptible to atropine poisoning, and many instances of such poisoning has followed systemic absorption of eye solutions.
	Fever, dry mouth, thirst, flushed, dry skin, and rash occur early in atropine poisoning. The pupil is fixed and dilated, and vision is blurred. Weak pulse, tachycardia in older children, and elevated blood pressure also occur. Difficulty voiding, constipation, abdominal distention, and drying of bronchial secretions are part of the picture. Hallucination, mania, and convulsions are not unusual.
	The condition is treated by administration of physostigmine (Eserine), an anticholinesterase, which reverses the anticholinergic effects of atropine and other belladonna alkaloids. Control of seizures by diazepam (Valium) and cool baths to reduce fever are also part of the treatment.
Scopolamine hydrobromide [the following preanesthetic doses to be administered IM 45 to 60 min before anesthesia (AMA Department of Drugs, 1977, p. 304)]:	A natural alkaloid of the belladonna group which shares the therapeutic and adverse effects of the group. The drug exerts anticholinergic effects on the heart, bronchial muscle, salivary glands, gastrointestinal tract, biliary tract, urinary tract, and on the pupil and ciliary muscle.

Table 8-4   Anticholinergic Preanesthetic Drugs (*Continued*)

Drug and Dose	Comments and Relevant Nursing Actions
Children 4 to 7 months: 0.1 mg Children 7 months to 3 years: 0.15 mg Children 3 to 8 years: 0.2 mg Pediatric anticholinergic dose: 6 μg/kg as single dose	Scopolamine also relaxes smooth muscle of bronchi and produces more drying of bronchial secretions and saliva than atropine. The drug produces stronger action on the pupil and ciliary muscle (i.e., dilation of pupil and paralysis of accommodation); however, action on the heart, gastrointestinal tract, and bronchial muscle are less potent and of shorter duration than that of atropine. The drug produces depression of the central nervous system; thus, drowsiness, euphoria, amnesia, and fatigue occur with usual doses. Scopolamine is utilized with a narcotic or barbiturate as a preanesthetic drug. It produces more drying of bronchial secretions and saliva than atropine; however, it does not provide as much protection against hypotension, brady-cardia, and cardiac arrest. The drug produces excellent sedation, which makes induction smooth; its antiemetic action reduces postanesthetic vomiting; however, delayed awakening and dizziness are common. Scopolamine also causes excitement, rest-lessness, and hallucinations in the presence of severe pain. The drug is also applied topically to the con-junctiva for eye examination, particularly for children who do not tolerate atropine. Adverse reactions associated with scopolamine are essentially those of atropine.

GENERAL ANESTHETICS
Indications

Regional anesthesia (e.g., topical, infiltration) is used for minor surgical and diagnostic procedures in children old enough to tolerate such anesthesia. Most infants and young children are unable to cooperate during procedures performed under local anesthesia; thus, most such procedures are performed under general anesthesia.

Anesthetic Agents

General anesthesia, the reversible state of insensitivity with loss of consciousness, is produced by inhalation and parenteral drugs. Inhalation anesthetics used for pediatric patients include nitrous oxide, cyclopropane, and halothane (Fluothane). These agents diffuse across respiratory tract membranes into the bloodstream, after which they rapidly penetrate the blood-brain barrier. Ketamine (Ketaject, Ketalar) is administered by the intramuscular and intravenous routes.

Use of Several Agents

During most surgical procedures more than one general anesthetic is utilized, to produce the advantages and avoid the disadvantages of each separate agent. The ease with which the child is anesthetized is related to the amount and type of preanesthetic medication, as well as to the general anesthetic used for induction. During the surgical procedure neuromuscular blocking agents (muscular relaxants) are also administered to relax skeletal muscle, thereby reducing the amount of general anesthetic required.

Pediatric Anesthesia

Children are usually brought to the operating room drowsy enough to permit induction of anesthesia without their awakening. The child may initially receive an inhalation anesthetic (e.g., cyclopropane with nitrous oxide) over the face by gravity flow until consciousness is lost. Once the child is asleep, the face mask can be applied, and the anesthetic continued by this route of administration.

Depth of General Anesthesia

Since several drugs are used to produce general anesthesia, estimation of signs or stages of anesthesia are extremely complex. Guedel used muscular function, respirations, eye motion, pupil size, and certain reflexes to identify signs or stages of general anesthesia. In the light of present-day use of multiple anesthetics, Guedel's classical signs of general anesthesia are reliable only for ether alone or in combination with nitrous oxide (AMA Department of Drugs, 1977, p. 286). Present-day efforts to estimate depth of general anesthesia generally focus on the purposes of anesthesia, e.g., sensory block, mental quiet, motor block, and reduction of adverse reflex responses (Goodman and Gilman, 1975, p. 61).

Table 8-5   General Anesthetics

Drug	Route of Administration and Comments
Halothane (Fluothane)	Halothane is a volatile liquid, which has the advantage of being nonexplosive and nonflammable. The drug has a pleasant smell, and can be administered by inhalation alone or in combination with nitrous oxide and muscle relaxants.
	The drug is an important general anesthetic for infants and children, and dosage requirements diminish as the child grows, i.e., infants require proportionately more halothane than do older children (Goudsouzian and Ryan, 1976, p. 345).
	Since there is minimal respiratory tract irritation, dilation of bronchioles, reduction of bronchial secretions, and decrease in laryngeal reflexes, the drug is safe for asthmatic children.
	While repeated administration of halothane has produced liver damage in adults, this reaction has not been reported in children.
	Temporary decrease in urine output has also occurred after halothane anesthesia.
	Parenteral administration of gentamicin (Garamycin), streptomycin, or other aminoglycoside antibiotic during halothane anesthesia may produce respiratory depression (*Evaluations of Drug Interactions,* 1976, p. 70).
	Recovery from anesthesia is usually rapid and uneventful.
Nitrous oxide	Nitrous oxide, a gas, is administered by inhalation; however, the drug lacks potency to provide adequate anesthesia for major surgical procedures. The drug is usually combined with a more potent inhalation agent (e.g., halothane) to provide surgical anesthesia. Neuromuscular blocking agents are also administered to relax skeletal muscle.
	While nitrous oxide does not irritate the respiratory tract, the drug may produce hypoxia with prolonged administration.
	The drug does not usually produce serious adverse reactions of the kidney or heart; however, repeated administration has resulted in bone marrow depression and death.
	Recovery from anesthesia is rapid and without unpleasant effects.
Cyclopropane	Cyclopropane is a flammable, highly explosive gas which is administered by inhalation. The drug is a potent anesthetic,

Table 8-5   General Anesthetics (*Continued*)

Drug	Route of Administration and Comments
	and it also produces muscular relaxation adequate for major surgical procedures.
	While cyclopropane causes minimal respiratory tract irritation, it does constrict bronchial musculature.
	Blood flow to the skin is increased, and increased bleeding of the operative wound may occur.
	Hepatic damage, decreased urinary output, and cardiac arrhythmias may also occur.
	Recovery is rapid; however, nausea and vomiting are more frequent than after other general anesthetics. Severe post-anesthetic headache, delirium, and hypotension occur occasionally.
Ketamine (Ketaject, Ketalar)	Ketamine, a sterile solution, is administered by the intravenous and intramuscular routes. The drug is often administered in combination with another general anesthetic and a neuro-muscular blocking agent.
	The drug produces a catatonic state in which the child appears to be awake, but is dissociated from his or her surroundings and does not respond to pain.
	Excessive salivation, aspiration, and laryngeal spasm have occurred during ketamine anesthesia. Response of infants is unpredictable; apnea and opisthotonic spasms have occurred in this age group.
	Skin rashes are common, and the incidence of epileptic convulsions in children seems to increase after ketamine anesthesia (Goudsouzian and Ryan, 1976, p. 349).
	Recovery is prolonged, and adults may have hallucinations, unpleasant dreams, and delirium. These psychic disturbances have recurred for days or weeks after recovery, and in adults with previous psychiatric problems have lead to serious disturbances. These psychic reactions are not common in children, presumably because they do not complain about nightmares, monsters, and other unpleasant dreams.
	Psychic disturbances can be reduced by providing a quiet environment during the recovery period. Minimal external stimulation and coordination of nursing care activities will provide an environment conducive to a smooth recovery.

Table 8-6   Neuromuscular Blocking Agents

Drug	Comments
Succinylcholine (Sux-Cert, etc.)	Succinylcholine produces flaccid paralysis of skeletal muscles which is of short duration. The drug depolarizes the postsynaptic membrane, thereby rendering the endplate refractory to acetylcholine.
	Infants require a proportionately larger dose of succinylcholine than do older children. Children with neuromuscular disorders or fluid and electrolyte disturbances may show abnormal responses to the drug.
	Cardiac arrhythmias, postoperative apnea, regurgitation, and muscular stiffness have occurred. Pain and stiffness usually involve muscles of the shoulder, back, and subcostal groups.
Tubocurarine (Tubarine)	Tubocurarine is a nondepolarizing agent which competes with acetylcholine for cholinergic receptor sites on the postjunctional membrane. Since the transmitter action of acetylcholine is blocked by the presence of tubocurarine at the endplate, the muscle is temporarily paralyzed. The duration of action is comparatively long; however, its action can be antagonized by neostigmine (Prostigmin) or other anticholinesterase.
	Neonates are particularly sensitive to the effects of the drug, and they require smaller doses per unit of body weight than older children.
	The effects of tubocurarine are increased by concurrent administration of gentamicin (Garamycin) or related antibiotics.

ANTICONVULSANTS

Epilepsy

Epilepsy, a condition characterized by episodes of brain dysfunction, is frequently associated with alterations of consciousness. The International Classification of Epileptic Seizures identifies two major categories of such seizures; however, many epileptic children have more than one type of seizure. The following epileptic seizures are seen in epileptic children.

Partial Seizures

- *Psychomotor:* Associated with confused behavior, and frequent impairment of consciousness. Also known as *temporal lobe epilepsy.*

- *Focal:* Motor (e.g., Jacksonian), sensory, or autonomic symptoms.

Generalized Seizures

- *Tonic-clonic:* Formerly grand mal, characterized by loss of consciousness, and alternating muscular contraction and relaxation.

- *Absences:* Formerly petit mal, characterized by loss of consciousness for brief periods. Rare before 3 years of age.

- *Infantile spasms:* Characterized by muscular spasms, loss of consciousness, and mental deterioration.

- *Akinetic:* Associated with loss of consciousness and complete relaxation of musculature.

- *Status epilepticus:* A serious emergency during which one generalized tonic-clonic (grand mal) seizure follows the other with little or no intermission.

Anticonvulsant Therapy

Regardless of the predominant seizure type, anticonvulsant therapy attempts to control seizures with minimal impairment of central nervous system function. Most anticonvulsants are not effective for all types of seizures; thus, a child may require more than one drug.

Age and Anticonvulsant Therapy

Children require a larger anticonvulsant dose per unit of body weight than do adults. Trauma (e.g., surgical procedures) and stress may increase the dose required to control seizures. The anticonvulsants have been characterized pharmacokinetically in infants and children, and serum anticonvulsant concentrations are utilized to adjust dosage, to assess compliance, and to avoid adverse reactions.

Table 8-7   Anticonvulsants

Drug and Dose	Comments and Relevant Nursing Actions
Phenobarbital, sodium (Luminal): Anticonvulsant pediatric dose: 15 to 50 mg PO two or three times a day; 3 to 5 mg/kg IM or IV; Sedative pediatric dose: 2 mg/kg PO, IM, or IV three times a day	Phenobarbital, a long-acting barbiturate, has anticonvulsant effects which are distinct from its sedative-hypnotic effects. In addition to being a relatively safe and a highly effective anticonvulsant, the drug is also inexpensive.

It is a primary agent for the long-term control of all types of epileptic seizures in pediatric patients. The drug is also administered for prevention of febrile convulsions in children, and is utilized to terminate status epilepticus.

In neonates phenobarbital is used to reduce serum bilirubin concentrations (see Chap. 1).

The drug is metabolized by hepatic microsomal enzymes, after which metabolites are excreted in the urine. While the half-life in adults averages 2 to 6 days, in children it is shorter (36 to 72 h) and more variable.

Phenobarbital produces significant effects on the metabolism of several drugs by virtue of its ability to induce the activity of hepatic microsomal enzymes.

The drug increases the metabolism of other barbiturates, phenytoin (Dilantin), digitoxin, chloramphenicol (Chloromycetin), oral anticoagulants, and adrenocorticosteroids (e.g., prednisone). These interactions reduce effectiveness of the second drug, and thus may necessitate dosage adjustment.

Concurrent administration of phenobarbital with another central nervous system depressant increases the central nervous system depression of both drugs.

The presence of acute intermittent porphyria is a contraindication to administration of phenobarbital and other barbiturates.

Since phenobarbital is a barbiturate, tolerance and dependence may occur with long- |

Table 8-7   Anticonvulsants (*Continued*)

Drug and Dose	Comments and Relevant Nursing Actions
	term use; however, this is unusual with the doses prescribed for seizure control. Abrupt withdrawal of phenobarbital may cause seizures in epileptic children who have received the drug for prolonged periods.
	At the start of phenobarbital therapy drowsiness, ataxia (loss of muscular coordination), and nystagmus (rhythmical oscillation of the eyeballs) may occur. These reactions often disappear with continued administration of the drug.
	Gastrointestinal upset, skin rashes, and paradoxical restlessness occur occasionally.
	Megaloblastic anemia due to folic acid deficiency and osteomalacia (rickets) due to vitamin D deficiency occur rarely with long term phenobarbital administration.
	Intravenous administration of the sodium salt may produce laryngospasm, severe cough, and respiratory depression, particularly if administration is too rapid.
	Accidental injection into an artery results in severe spasm and ischemia, which may result in gangrene (AMA Department of Drugs, 1977, p. 397).
Phenytoin, sodium (Dilantin, etc.): Pediatric anticonvulsant dose: 1.5 to 4 mg/kg PO two times daily, not to exceed 300 mg daily 0.5 to 4 mg/kg IV two times daily	Phenytoin, a member of the hydantoin anticonvulsant group, is a primary drug for the control of generalized tonic-clonic (grand mal) and most other seizures in older children. The drug is not only ineffective for absences (petit mal) but also may exacerbate such seizures. For long-term control of seizures phenytoin may be combined with phenobarbital. Intravenous phenytoin is also administered for treatment of status epilepticus in children maintained on the drug.
	In adults the drug is also used for treatment of cardiac arrhythmias, trigeminal neuralgias, and other related neuralgias.

Table 8-7   Anticonvulsants (*Continued*)

Drug and Dose	Comments and Relevant Nursing Actions
	Oral absorption of phenytoin is slow, erratic, and highly variable. While individual variations in phenytoin absorption do exist, oral suspensions and solid oral dosage forms produced by some manufacturers are subject to particularly poor absorption.
	Phenytoin is slowly and incompletely absorbed after intramuscular administration, and local inflammatory reactions are common.
	The drug is metabolized primarily by hepatic microsomes, and the rate at which the drug is metabolized is genetically determined. After metabolization, the drug is excreted in the urine. In adults the half-life averages 24 h; however, it is shorter in children. As phenytoin concentrations increase, plasma half-life increases, and urinary excretion decreases. This dose-dependent elimination is due to the limited capacity of the phenytoin drug metabolizing systems (i.e., hepatic microsomal enzymes) or to their inhibition by metabolites.
	Chloramphenicol (Chloromycetin), isoniazid (INH), and oral anticoagulants decrease phenytoin metabolism, thereby increasing its effects.
	While phenobarbital may decrease phenytoin absorption, the barbiturate can also increase metabolism of phenytoin, thereby decreasing its effects. Phenobarbital can also decrease phenytoin metabolism by competing for hepatic microsomal enzymes (Goodman and Gilman, 1975, p. 208).
	Drowsiness, ataxia (loss of muscular coordination), and visual disturbances (e.g., double vision, oscillation of the eyeballs) occur early in therapy if doses are large. Gastrointestinal upsets also occur.

Table 8-7   Anticonvulsants (*Continued*)

Drug and Dose	Comments and Relevant Nursing Actions
	Hirsutism in young girls, painless hypertrophy of the gums, and skin eruptions also occur. Scrupulous oral hygiene minimizes enlargement of the gums.
	Peripheral neuropathy, megaloblastic anemia, and rickets may occur with prolonged administration of phenytoin.
	Liver damage, bone marrow depression, and a systemic lupus erythematosus syndrome are rare reactions.
	Intravenous administration of phenytoin at rapid rates may result in central nervous system and cardiovascular system toxicity.
Primidone (Mysoline): Usual pediatric dose: 5 to 20 mg/kg PO daily [therapy started at lower dosage and increased gradually (Goodman and Gilman, 1975, p. 211)]	Primidone, a nonbarbiturate anticonvulsant, is chemically related to the barbiturates. In the body fluids the drug is partially metabolized to phenobarbital, and its action is due to the parent drug as well as to this metabolite. The drug is indicated for children who do not tolerate phenobarbital. Adverse reactions are essentially those of the barbiturates; however, the drug produces significant sedation, which can be minimized by gradual increase of the dosage.

Carbamazine (Tegretol):
  Children under 6 years: 100 mg PO daily
  Children 6 to 12 years: 100 mg PO twice daily
  Adolescents:
    400 mg PO in two divided doses the first day; dose is gradually increased in daily increments of 200 mg, given 3 or 4 times daily; usual maintenance for adolescents is 800 mg to 1.2 g daily
	Carbamazine is an alternative anticonvulsant for treatment of generalized tonic-clonic (grand mal) and psychomotor seizures which do not respond to phenytoin (Dilantin) or phenobarbital.
	
	The drug is a tricyclic compound which is closely related to the antidepressants, and is reported to have a psychotropic effect which increases mental alertness and elevates the mood. In adults the drug is used for the treatment of trigeminal neuralgia.
	
	Concurrent administration of phenytoin

Table 8-7   Anticonvulsants *(Continued)*

Drug and Dose	Comments and Relevant Nursing Actions
	(Dilantin) with carbamazine may result in decrease of phenytoin effects.
	Reversible drowsiness, ataxia (loss of muscular coordination), and double vision (diplopia) occur with large doses.
	Nausea, anorexia, and edema occur occasionally.
	Aplastic anemia, leukopenia (decrease in white blood cells), and a lupus erythematosus syndrome are rare adverse reactions to the drug.
Ethosuximide (Zarontin): Children under 6 years: 250 mg PO once daily Children over 6 years: 250 mg PO twice daily initially, increased as necessary every 4 to 7 days in increments of 250 mg	Ethosuximide, the drug of choice for absence seizures (petit mal), is also effective for myoclonic and akinetic seizures. The drug is also combined with phenytoin (Dilantin) or phenobarbital for treatment of generalized tonic-clonic (grand mal) seizures.
	In children the plasma half-life of ethosuximide averages 30 h.
	Hiccups, nausea, and vomiting are common with large doses.
	Euphoria, behavior changes, drowsiness, lethargy, and rash also may occur with large doses.
	Aplastic anemia, eosinophilia (decrease in eosinophils), and a lupus erythematosus syndrome occur rarely.
Clonazepam (Clonopin): Infants and children up to 10 years: 0.01 to 0.03 (maximum 0.05) mg/kg in two or three divided doses; total daily dose may be increased by increments of 0.25 to 0.5 mg every third day until a maximum of 0.1 to 0.2 mg/kg per day has been	Clonazepam, a drug which is closely related to diazepam (Valium), is an alternative drug for absence seizures (petit mal) not controlled by ethosuximide (Zarontin).
	Tolerance to its anticonvulsant effects develops after prolonged use, and dependence with withdrawal symptoms may also occur.
	Administration of other central nervous system depressants concurrently with

Table 8-7   Anticonvulsants (*Continued*)

Drug and Dose	Comments and Relevant Nursing Actions
reached (AMA Department of Drugs, 1977, p. 468)	clonazepam increases the central nervous system depression of both drugs.
	Drowsiness, ataxia, personality changes, dizziness, confusion, and abnormal eye movements are common with clonazepam therapy.
	Increase in respiratory tract secretions and depression of respirations also occur.
	Skin rashes, gastrointestinal tract distress, and anemia have also occurred.
	Children receiving the drug should be encouraged to cough and take deep breaths at regular intervals. Measures to remove secretions (e.g., suctioning, frequent turning,) must be utilized to prevent pulmonary complications.
Diazepam (Valium): Pediatric sedative dose: 40 to 200 μg/kg IM or IV; dose may be repeated in 2 to 4 h	Intravenous diazepam is the drug of choice for the treatment of status epilepticus. Effectiveness of the drug for long-term seizure control has yet to be determined.
	Diazepam is also used as a preanesthetic medication, as an antianxiety agent, and as a skeletal muscle relaxant.
	The drug has potential for abuse; thus, it is considered a controlled substance.
	Parenteral diazepam is supplied in a non-aqueous vehicle, and the drug should never be diluted, mixed with other drugs, or added to intravenous fluids.
	Absorption of intramuscular diazepam is slow and often incomplete (Greenblatt and Koch-Weser, 1976, pp. 542, 544).
	The sodium benzoate solvent used in parenteral diazepam may precipitate hyperbilirubinemia in newborn infants (see Chap. 1).

Table 8-7   Anticonvulsants (*Continued*)

Drug and Dose	Comments and Relevant Nursing Actions
	Concurrent administration of diazepam with phenytoin (Dilantin) and phenobarbital may increase the effects of the anticonvulsant and the barbiturate. Diazepam enhances the effects of other central nervous system depressants.
	Administration of intravenous diazepam must be very slow to prevent apnea, hypotension, and cardiac arrest. Intravenous administration of the drug frequently produces pain and thrombophlebitis, particularly if it is administered into small veins.
	Oral administration of the drug causes dizziness, ataxia, and, in some individuals, excitement.
	Diazepam increases saliva and bronchial secretions; thus, it must be used cautiously in children with respiratory tract disorders.

Table 8-8   Central Nervous System Drugs Used for Hyperkinesia

Drug and Dose	Comments and Relevant Nursing Actions
Dextroamphetamine (Dexedrine): Hyperkinetic children 3 to 5 years: 2.5 mg PO once a day, increased by 2.5 mg at weekly intervals Hyperkinetic children 6 years and older: 5 mg PO one or two times daily, increased by 5 mg at weekly intervals	Dextroamphetamine, methylphenidate, and pemoline are used as adjuncts in treatment of hyperkinetic children. The *hyperkinetic syndrome,* which is characterized by behavior and learning problems, is also termed *minimal brain dysfunction.* Use of these drugs for this condition is controversial; some authorities suggest that the hyperkinetic syndrome is overdiagnosed and that many children are medicated without justification. Parents and community groups consider these drugs a source of future abuse. Central nervous system stimulants are ideally used along with parental counseling and behavior modification techniques.
Methylphenidate (Ritalin): Hyperkinetic children over 6 years: 5 mg PO twice daily, increased by 5 to 10 mg at weekly intervals	Since these drugs have potential for abuse, they are included under the Controlled Substances Act. In children usual doses of central nervous system stimulants do not appear to produce euphoria or pleasurable effects (Cohen and Cohen, 1974, p. 97). It is not known whether or not long-term use of these drugs increases the incidence of their subsequent abuse.
Pemoline (Cylert): Hyperkinetic children over 6 years: 37.5 mg PO daily in a single dose in the morning; dose increased by weekly increments of 18.75 mg until desired response observed	The mechanism by which these drugs calm hyperkinetic children may be related to their effects on neurotransmitters, and this calming effect is apparently paradoxical. In children receiving the drugs, restlessness and impulsive behavior are decreased, while attention span and learning ability are increased. Withdrawal of drug leads to relapse; thus, long-term administration is necessary. These drugs produce insomnia, periods of excessive crying, gastrointestinal upsets, and anorexia. Retardation of weight gain and linear growth due to appetite suppression are frequent with prolonged administration of these drugs.

Table 8-8   Central Nervous System Drugs Used for Hyperkinesia (*Continued*)

Drug and Dose	Comments and Relevant Nursing Actions
	Central nervous system stimulants may decrease the effectiveness of some antihypertensive drugs, i.e., guanethidine (Ismelin) and methyldopa (Aldomet). During therapy with these drugs the nurse must keep accurate growth records to determine retardation of growth and development. Parents should be instructed to note the child's food intake and to provide nutritionally sound meals and snacks.

Table 8-9   Central Nervous System Drugs Used for Enuresis

Drug and Dose	Comments and Relevant Nursing Actions
Imipramine hydrochloride (Tofranil): Enuretic children 6 years and over: 25 mg PO 1 h before bedtime initially; if necessary, increase to 50 mg in children under 12 years or 75 mg in children over 12 years; in early bedwetters, divide into two doses, afternoon and bedtime; reduce dose gradually (Vaughn and McKay, 1975, p. 1779)	The tricyclic antidepressants are used for the short-term treatment of selected enuretic children and adolescents. They are generally utilized for children over 6 years of age, and their use is not recommended for a period longer than 8 weeks (Vaughn and McKay, 1975, p. 1256). While imipramine is the drug of choice for enuretic children, amitriptyline and nortriptyline are alternative drugs. The mechanism by which these drugs relieve enuresis is not understood; however, their metabolism by the liver is susceptible to genetic variations.
Amitriptyline (Elavil): Enuretic children 5 to 14 years: 23 mg PO daily at bedtime (AMA Department of Drugs, 1977, p. 480)	Tricyclic antidepressants increase the effects central nervous system depressants and of adrenergic drugs, while they decrease the antihypertensive effects of guanethidine (Ismelin).
Nortriplytine (Aventyl): Enuretic children 5 to 14 years: 25 mg PO once daily at bedtime (AMA Department of Drugs, 1977, p. 480)	They may cause insomnia, nervousness, mild gastrointestinal upsets, emotional disorders, and syncope in enuretic children (Vaughn and McKay, 1975, p. 1780).

BIBLIOGRAPHY

AMA Department of Drugs: *AMA Drug Evaluations,* 3d ed., Publishing Sciences Group, Littleton, Mass., 1977.

Bruga, M. A., and R. H. Bollin: "Epilepsy: A Controllable Disease," *American Journal of Nursing,* vol. 76, no. 3, 1976, pp. 388–397.

Cohen, S. N., and J. L. Cohen: "Pharmacotherapeutics: Review and Commentary," *Pediatric Clinics of North America,* vol. 21, no. 1, 1974, pp. 95–105.

Conners, C. K.: "Managing the Minimal Brain Dysfunction Child and His Family," *Patient Care,* vol. 8, no. 11, 1974, pp. 124–141.

"Drugs for Epilepsy," *The Medical Letter,* vol. 18, no. 6, March 12, 1976, pp. 25–28.

Engelhardt, D. M.: "Pharmacologic Basis For Use of Psychotrophic Drugs: An Overview," *New York State Journal of Medicine,* vol. 74, no. 2, 1974, pp. 360–366.

Evaluations of Drug Interactions, 2d ed., American Pharmaceutical Association, Washington, D.C., 1976.

Goodman, L. S., and A. Gilman: *The Pharmacological Basis of Therapeutics,* 5th ed., Macmillan, New York, 1975.

Goudsouzian, N. G., and J. F. Ryan: "Recent Advances in Pediatric Anesthesia," *Pediatric Clinics of North America,* vol. 23, no. 2, 1976, pp. 345–360.

Greenblatt, D. J., and J. Koch-Weser: "Intramuscular Injection of Drugs," *New England Journal of Medicine,* vol. 295, no. 10, 1976, pp. 542–546.

Maroz, L. A.: "Increased Blood Fibrinolytic Activity after Aspirin Ingestion," *New England Journal of Medicine,* vol. 296, no. 10, 1977, pp. 525–529.

McCaffrey, M., and L. L. Hart: "Undertreatment of Acute Pain with Narcotics," *American Journal of Nursing,* vol. 76, no. 10, 1976, pp. 1587–1591.

Mielke, H. C., et al.: "Hemostasis, Antipyretics and Mild Analgesics: Acetaminophen Versus Aspirin," *Journal of the*

American Medical Association, vol. 235, no. 6, 1976, pp. 613–616.

"Phenytoin," *The Medical Letter,* vol. 18, no. 5, February 27, 1976, pp. 23–24.

Smith, B. J.: "After Anesthesia," *Nursing 1974,* vol. 4, no. 12, 1974, pp. 28–32.

"Sodium Valproate: A New Anticonvulsant," *The Medical Letter* vol. 19, no. 23, November 18, 1977, pp. 93–94.

Vaughn, V. C., and J. R. McKay: *Textbook of Pediatrics,* 10th ed., Saunders, Philadelphia, 1975.

Zelechowski, G. P.: "Helping Your Patient Sleep: Planning Instead of Pills," *Nursing 77,* vol. 7, no. 5, 1977, pp. 63–65.

Drugs Which Affect the Blood

HEMATINIC AGENTS (See Table 9-1)

Drugs which increase the formation of red blood cells or the concentration of hemoglobin are termed *hematinic agents*. The most important such drugs are iron, folic acid (Folvite), and vitamin B_{12} (Rubramin, Berubigen).

While the red marrow of most bones produces red blood cells until adolescence, after this period of the growth cycle the marrow of long bones decreases erythrocyte formation. Once the change in long bone marrow occurs, red blood cell production takes place primarily in the marrow of vertebrae, sternum, and ribs.

After formation in the marrow, red blood cells undergo a series of maturational changes and acquire hemoglobin before entering the bloodstream.

Formation and maturation of red blood cells requires the presence of folic acid and vitamin B_{12}, two vitamins which function interdependently. Iron is essential not only for red blood cell formation but also for synthesis of hemoglobin.

SYSTEMIC HEMOSTATIC AGENTS (See Table 9-2)

Normal clotting consists of a complex series of events and requires several substances normally present in the blood and other body tissues. These clotting factors are now designated by a uniform numbering system, and several clotting factors are available for intravenous administration.

Hemostatic agents in current use include vitamin K, fibrinogen (Parenogen), and antihemophilic factor (Humafac, Hemofil).

BLOOD VOLUME EXPANDERS (See Table 9-3)

The plasma proteins by virtue of the colloid osmotic pressure which they exert prevent plasma from leaking out of the blood vessels into the interstitial spaces. Albumin, one of the plasma proteins, exerts approximately 70 percent of the total colloid osmotic pressure, and thus plays the dominant role in the maintenance of this pressure.

In selected instances of plasma compartment depletion (e.g., shock, burns) the blood volume can be temporarily expanded by administration of serum albumin or dextran. Although these preparations are conveniently stored and require no typing or cross-matching, their benefits are short-lived; thus, they are not substitutes for whole blood.

Table 9-1   Hematinic Agents

Drug and Dose	Comments and Relevant Nursing Actions

Ferrous sulfate (Feosol, Fer-In-Sol)
Prophylactic doses:
  Children 2 to 6 years:
  37.5 mg PO once daily
  Children over 6 years:
  75 mg PO once daily
Therapeutic doses:
  Children 2 to 6 years:
  150 mg PO 3 times daily
  Children over 6 years:
  300 mg PO 3 times daily
	An inexpensive, highly effective compound which is the drug of choice for treatment of iron-deficiency anemia. The standard against which other oral iron preparations are compared, ferrous sulfate is the most widely utilized iron preparation.
	
	Iron is necessary for formation of red blood cells and hemoglobin, and dietary sources may be inadequate during the growth years. Although iron-fortified foods are widely available, infants, growing children, adolescent girls, and low-income children are often likely to receive diets deficient in iron.
	
	The American Academy of Pediatrics recommends that term and premature infants receive iron supplementation from 4 and 2 months of age, respectively, until at least the end of the first year of life (American Academy of Pediatrics, 1976, p. 767).
	
	Oral iron preparations are indicated only for treatment of iron deficiency anemias associated with blood loss, inadequate absorption of dietary iron, or inadequate intake of dietary iron.
	
	Ferrous sulfate is supplied as syrup, elixir, tablets, enteric-coated tablets, and as sustained-release spansules.
	
	As with other ferrous salts, the drug is well absorbed after oral administration. While absorption is better when the stomach is empty, administration before meals increases the incidence of gastric irritation.
	
	While the more expensive enteric-coated and sustained-release iron preparations are promoted for their superior absorption, these dosage forms are often excreted unabsorbed in the feces.
	
	Ingestion of large amounts of milk may drastically decrease iron absorption; thus, limiting milk intake to 1 pt or less per day is recommended (Vaughn and McKay, 1975, p. 1118).

Table 9-1   Hematinic Agents (*Continued*)

Drug and Dose	Comments and Relevant Nursing Actions
	Concurrent ingestion of tetracyclines, some antacids, and cholestyramine (Questran) will also decrease absorption of oral iron.
	These preparations (i.e., oral iron dosage forms) should not be administered to children receiving parenteral iron or to those receiving repeated blood transfusions.
	Infants and children seem to tolerate therapeutic doses better than older patients; however, gastrointestinal irritative reactions, constipation, diarrhea, unpleasant taste, altered taste, epigastric distress, and nausea do occur. Reducing the dose by one-third or one-half tends to eliminate or to minimize these reactions. Administering the drug just after meals also tends to minimize gastric irritation; however, it also decreases absorption of the drug. In some children these irritative reactions subside as the iron preparation is continued.
	Administration of ferrous sulfate and other iron preparations also tends to aggravate ulcerative colitis, regional enteritis, and other gastrointestinal disorders.
	Long-term administration of large doses to infants may interfere with phosphorus assimilation and produce rickets (Goodman and Gilman, 1975, p. 1317).
	The drug colors the feces black and produces false-positive guaic results for occult stool blood.
	Accidental ingestion of iron, producing one kind of poisoning in children, is manifested by rapid onset of nausea, vomiting, green loose stools, hematemesis, shock, and coma. The risk of accidental iron poisoning is reduced if parents limit the amount of drug purchased at one time.
	Ferrous sulfate and other oral iron preparations should be administered either 3 h after or 2 h before tetracyclines, antacids, and choles-

Table 9-1 Hematinic Agents (*Continued*)

Drug and Dose	Comments and Relevant Nursing Actions
	tyramine (Questran) to promote maximum absorption of the iron.
	Children who have gastrointestinal upsets should receive iron immediately after meals to minimize gastric distress.
	Parents of ambulatory children should be alerted to expect black, tarry stools. It is also advisable to teach parents not to purchase more than a 1-month supply of iron and to keep all iron preparations well out of the reach of children to prevent accidental poisoning.
Iron dextran injection (Imferon) Infants weighing under 4.5 kg: up to 25 mg IM daily Children weighing under 9 kg: up to 50 mg IM daily Children weighing over 50 kg: up to 100 mg IM daily	A sterile colloidal solution of iron with low-molecular-weight dextrose; iron dextran injection contains 50 mg elemental iron per milliliter of drug.
	This preparation is not used for routine iron-deficiency anemia, but is reserved for children who are unable or unwilling to take oral dosage forms, and for those with iron losses too great to be corrected with oral iron.
	Dosage is carefully individualized according to the severity of the anemia and the child's response to the drug.
	The drug is most frequently administered intramuscularly; however, the intravenous route is also used occasionally.
	Administration of iron dextran injection should be preceded by administration of a small test dose to assess hypersensitivity (AMA Department of Drugs, 1977, p. 102)
	To avoid accumulation of excessive iron concentrations the child should not receive oral iron while iron dextran injection is administered.
	Intramuscular injection of the drug may cause pain, local inflammation, and tender inguinal node enlargement. Leakage of the drug from

Table 9-1   Hematinic Agents (*Continued*)

Drug and Dose	Comments and Relevant Nursing Actions
	muscular injection site into subcutaneous tissue will stain the skin brown for 1 to 2 years.
	Nausea, vomiting, headache, arthralgia, and rarely anaphylactic reactions have occurred after administration of the drug.
	Iron dextran injection should be administered by Z technique to avoid staining and local inflammatory reactions (see Table 2-3).
	A small test dose should be administered before the therapeutic dose is given and emergency drugs and equipment should be nearby.
	The child should be closely evaluated for difficulty in breathing, urticaria, circulatory alterations, or other evidence of hypersensitivity.
Folic acid (Folvite) Maintenance dose: 100 to 250 μg PO or IM once daily Therapeutic dose: 250 μg to 1 mg PO or IM once daily	A member of the vitamin B complex group, folic acid is necessary for normal hematopoiesis.
	The drug is available as tablets for oral administration and as sterile solution for parenteral injection.
	Folic acid is indicated for folate-deficiency anemias associated with hemolytic conditions (e.g., Cooley's and sickle-cell anemia), inadequate intake (e.g., in infancy), and malabsorption states (e.g., celiac disease, tropical sprue).
	After oral administration folic acid is well absorbed, converted to several metabolically active folate forms, and is ultimately excreted in the urine.
	Administration of large doses of folic acid to correct the folic acid deficiency associated with long-term phenytoin (Dilantin) therapy may increase the incidence of seizure activity. It has been postulated that folic acid may increase the metabolism of the anticonvulsant (*Evaluations of Drug Interactions,* 1976, pp. 197–198).
	Folic acid causes no adverse reactions in humans.

Table 9-1   Hematinic Agents (*Continued*)

Drug and Dose	Comments and Relevant Nursing Actions
Vitamin B_{12} cyanocobalamin (Rubramin, Berubigen) Maintenance dose: 100 μg IM monthly or every other month Therapeutic dose: 100 μg IM once or twice weekly	Cyanocobalamin (vitamin B_{12}) is a cobalt-containing compound which belongs to the vitamin B complex group. It is essential not only for normal hematopoeisis but also for cell reproduction, growth, and function. Although the vitamin is found in organ meats (e.g., liver), clams, oysters, egg yolk, some cheeses, and some fish, absorption from dietary sources requires a secretion of the gastric mucosa (intrinsic factor). Lack of this intrinsic factor can result in vitamin B_{12} deficiency in spite of adequate dietary intake. Vitamin B_{12} is available as a sterile solution for intramuscular injection, the dosage form of choice. Oral dosage forms are not only expensive and erratically absorbed, but many patients become refractory to them after continued administration. The drug is indicated only for anemias associated with vitamin B_{12} deficiency; e.g., juvenile pernicious anemia, celiac disease, tropical sprue, and anemia of infancy. After parenteral administration the drug is rapidly transported to the liver and other organs. There is no evidence that cyanocobalamin is metabolized, and it has been theorized that the drug is excreted by way of the bile. Aminosalicylic acid (PAS, Parasal) and neomycin (Neobiotic, Mycifradin) may decrease absorption of dietary vitamin B_{12}; and children receiving chloramphenicol (Chloromycetin) may respond poorly to vitamin B_{12} administration (*Evaluations of Drug Interactions,* 1976, p. 450). Although there have been occasional hypersensitivity reactions to preservatives contained in vitamin B_{12} preparations, serious adverse reactions have not been reported.

Table 9-1   Hematinic Agents (*Continued*)

Drug and Dose	Comments and Relevant Nursing Actions
	Parents of children who have juvenile pernicious anemia or malabsorption conditions should be informed that the child will need life-long administration of parenteral vitamin B_{12} to prevent nervous system damage.

Table 9-2   Systemic Hemostatic Agents

Drug and Dose	Comments and Relevant Nursing Actions

Vitamin K, phytonadione (Aquamephyton, Konakion)
Neonatal hemorrhagic disease:
  Prophylactic dose: 500 μg to 1 mg IM
  Therapeutic dose: 1 mg IM or SC
Other prothrombin deficiencies:
  Infants: 2 mg IM or SC
  Older infants and children: 5 to 10 mg IM or SC
	Phytonadione (vitamin K_1), a fat-soluble vitamin, is obtained from foods, while vitamin K_2 is synthesized by gastrointestinal tract bacteria. Menadione sodium bisulfite (vitamin K_3), a water-soluble drug, is produced synthetically.
	
	Vitamin K is necessary for the formation of prothrombin, and also for factor VII (proconvertin), factor IX (Christmas factor), and factor X (Stuart factor), all of which are necessary for blood clotting.
	
	The drug is available in tablets for oral administration, sterile preparations for intramuscular administration, and sterile preparations for intravenous administration. Oral dosage forms of menadione are absorbed in the absence of bile; however, other oral vitamin K preparations are fat soluble; and thus require bile for adequate absorption.
	
	Vitamin K is indicated immediately after birth to correct neonatal deficiency and to prevent bleeding caused by drop in neonatal plasma prothrombin concentration (Vaughn and McKay, 1975, p. 336).
	
	It is also indicated to prevent or treat bleeding associated with vitamin K malabsorption (e.g., cystic fibrosis, ulcerative colitis, regional enteritis, and prolonged administration of antibiotics) or as an antidote for excessive administration of warfarin (Coumadin).
	
	During vitamin K administration the dosage is kept as low as possible and the prothrombin time is monitored to assess the child's vitamin K status.
	
	In the newborn large doses of vitamin K may displace bilirubin from albumin binding sites, thereby precipitating kernicterus (see Chap. 1).
	
	Hemolytic anemia may result from administration of vitamin K to susceptible infants and children.

Table 9-2   Systemic Hemostatic Agents (*Continued*)

Drug and Dose	Comments and Relevant Nursing Actions
	Intramuscular administration may produce pain and delayed nodule formation. Intravenous administration has resulted in anaphylacticlike reactions with flushing, chest constriction, shock, and cardiovascular collapse.
	Parenteral solutions must be protected from light to promote retention of maximum potency. The package insert must be consulted concerning dilution, administration route, and whether unused, diluted solutions can be stored.
	Intravenous preparations must be given slowly and the child must be closely assessed during and after administration for evidence of hypersensitivity.
Human fibrinogen (Parenogen) Dose determined by careful monitoring of plasma fibrinogen levels and blood coagulation and clinical evaluation of hemostasis	Fibrinogen is a sterile preparation of factor I, a normal clotting factor produced by the liver and necessary for blood clotting. The drug is obtained from human plasma and is supplied as a sterile powder with distilled water for reconstitution.
	It is indicated for congenital low fibrinogen states, and for severe bleeding associated with deficiency states, e.g., during extensive surgical procedures. Fibrinogen is not a substitute for administration of whole blood; but it will produce insoluble fibrin.
	Viral hepatitis, cyanosis, tachycardia, and intravascular fibrin deposits may occur.
	Before reconstitution fibrinogen should be stored at a temperature of 2 to 8°C; reconstituted solutions must be administered within 1 h of preparation.
	The drug should be administered slowly and the child carefully evaluated before and after administration for cyanosis and tachycardia.
Human antihemophilic factor (Humafac, Hemofil)	A sterile, freeze-dried concentrate of factor VIII (antihemophilic factor) prepared from venous

Table 9-2   Systemic Hemostatic Agents *(Continued)*

Drug and Dose	Comments and Relevant Nursing Actions
Dosage individualized according to the severity of the condition, the severity of bleeding, and the clinical response to the drug	plasma, human antihemophilic factor is supplied as a sterile powder with sterile water for reconstitution. The drug accelerates the slow clotting time of hemophiliac and factor VIII–deficient children, thereby preventing serious hemorrhage. Antihemophilic factor is used for spontaneous or traumatic bleeding, as well as for bleeding which occurs during dental extraction, surgery, or diagnostic procedures. Administration of the drug may result in viral hepatitis, chills, or fever. Before reconstitution the drug should be stored at a temperature of from 2 to 8°C; reconstituted solutions, on the other hand, should not be refrigerated. While the drug can be administered rapidly without adverse effects, the child must be monitored for chills and fever.
Aminocaproic acid (Amicar) Initial dose: 100 mg/kg PO or IV Maintainence dose: one-third of initial dose hourly, to achieve plasma level of 13 mg/dl (Vaughn and McKay, 1975, p. 1772)	Aminocaproic acid, a synthetic compound, prevents the breakdown of fibrin (fibrinolysis) presumably by inhibiting both plasminogen activators and antiplasmin activity. The drug is supplied as tablets and syrup for oral administration, and as sterile solution for intravenous injection. It is indicated for serious hemorrhage associated with excessive fibrinolysis and for serious hematuria; to control bleeding during cardiovascular surgery; and to prevent bleeding during tooth extraction. After oral administration aminocaproic acid is well absorbed, and then is rapidly excreted unchanged by the kidney. With extensive use the drug is distributed to body fluids and cells, and may remain in extravascular clots, thereby preventing their dissolution.

Table 9-2   Systemic Hemostatic Agents (*Continued*)

Drug and Dose	Comments and Relevant Nursing Actions
	Aminocaproic acid is used only in the presence of hyperfibrinolytic conditions, and the child must be carefully assessed for evidence of thrombus formation during its administration.
	Hypotension, rash, nasal congestion, conjunctival erythema, and gastrointestinal upset (i.e., nausea, diarrhea, and dyspepsia) may occur during administration.
	Intravenous preparations should be diluted according to the directions of the package insert and should be infused slowly.
	The child should be evaluated carefully for thrombus formation, drop in blood pressure, and rash.

Table 9-3   Blood Volume Expanders

Drug and Dose	Comments and Relevant Nursing Actions
Normal human serum albumin (Buminate, Albumisol) Pediatric dose: 2 ml/kg IV (Vaughn and McKay, 1975, p. 1754)	This sterile preparation of plasma protein is obtained from donor plasma, and 96 percent of its total plasma protein is albumin. The drug is supplied as a solution in 5 and 25% strengths. Normal serum albumin elevates the plasma protein level, thereby restoring normal colloidal osmotic pressure of the blood. It is indicated for treatment of shock, severe bleeding, dehydration, prematurity, and other low-plasma-protein conditions which result in shock. The drug is also used after exchange transfusion in neonates with hemolytic disease, and for children with nephrosis. Serum albumin is contraindicated in the presence of congestive heart failure, and must be administered cautiously in children with severe anemia or with normal serum albumin levels. Chills, fever, urticaria, and alterations of blood pressure, pulse, and respirations may occur after administration of serum albumin. Hypervolemia with congestive heart failure may occur, particularly after rapid administration of the drug or in children with no albumin deficiency. Serum albumin should not be administered if the solution is turbid or contains sediment. It must be administered immediately after being opened.
Dextran 40 (LMWD, Rheomacrodex) Dextran 70 (Macrodex) Dextran 75 (Gentran-75) Children: 10 to 20 ml/kg of a 10% solution IV, total daily dose not to exceed 20 ml/kg (AMA Department of Drugs, 1977, p. 133)	Dextran is a sterile, colloidal, hypertonic solution biosynthesized from sucrose, and supplied in several molecular weights. Low-molecular-weight dextran (dextran 40) weighs approximately 40,000; while dextran 70 and dextran 75 weigh 70,000 and 75,000 respectively. Since these preparations are hypertonic, they produce rapid, short-lived expansion of the

Table 9-3   Blood Volume Expanders (*Continued*)

Drug and Dose	Comments and Relevant Nursing Actions
	plasma volume. The blood pressure, cardiac output, and central venous pressure are also increased with administration of the drug.
	Dextran preparations are used as priming solutions for pump oxygenators during extracorporeal circulation, and for temporary treatment of shock (e.g., due to blood loss, burns). It is important to state that they are not substitutes for whole blood and other protein volume expanders (e.g., serum albumin).
	Hypervolemia, congestive heart failure, renal failure, hypersensitivity, and severe bleeding are contraindications to the administration of dextran solutions.
	Nasal congestion, rash, dyspnea, and anaphylactic reactions are seen occasionally after administration of these preparations. These hypersensitivity reactions generally occur shortly after administration of the drug, and are more likely to occur with the higher molecular weight preparations (i.e., dextran 70, dextran 75), though they have also occurred after administration of dextran 40.
	Nausea, vomiting, and fever have also been reported.
	Children who have received dextran may have increased bleeding time; there may also be interference with tests of liver and kidney function as well as difficulty with typing and cross-matching.
	Specimens for type and cross-match should be obtained before starting the dextran infusion.
	During administration of the preparation the child must be assessed for evidence of hypersensitivity reactions, and emergency drugs and equipment must be close at hand. The infusion should be terminated and the physician notified at the first evidence of hypersensitivity.

Table 9-3   Blood Volume Expanders (*Continued*)

Drug and Dose	Comments and Relevant Nursing Actions
	Blood pressure should be monitored. Increase in blood pressure and manifestations of hypersensitivity are reasons to terminate the dextran infusion and to notify the physician.
	Since dextran is supplied in glass bottles, it can be stored at room temperatures; however, solutions which have been stored for prolonged periods or which have been subjected to variations of temperature may crystallize. Solutions which have undergone such crystallization may be safely warmed to promote dissolution.

BIBLIOGRAPHY

American Academy of Pediatrics: "Iron Supplementation for Infants," *Pediatrics*, vol. 58, no. 5, 1976, pp. 765–767.

AMA Department of Drugs: *AMA Drug Evaluations*, 3d ed., Publishing Sciences Group, Littleton, Mass., 1977.

Evaluations of Drug Interactions, 2d ed., American Pharmaceutical Association, Washington, D.C., 1976.

Goodman, L. S., and A. Gilman: *The Pharmacological Basis of Therapeutics*, 5th ed., Macmillan, New York, 1975.

Hoover, J. E., et al. (eds.): *Remington's Pharmaceutical Sciences*, 15th ed., Mack Publishing Co., Easton, Pa., 1975.

Vaughn, V. C., and R. J. McKay: *Textbook of Pediatrics*, 10th ed., Saunders, Philadelphia, 1975.

Drugs Which Affect the Gastrointestinal Tract

LAXATIVES (See Table 10-1)

Since adequate fluid intake and sufficient dietary roughage provide normal bowel elimination in most children, the routine administration of laxatives is not necessary. Children with megacolon or other disorders of the gastrointestinal tract require an individualized regimen of bowel therapy. Occasionally a child who does not heed the urge to defecate will have difficulty with constipation; and during illness, hospitalization, and other crises normal bowel routines will be deranged. Use of mild laxatives or stool softeners for short periods of time are not harmful; however, habitual use of these agents for children may result in dependence, loss of rectal reflex, hyperactive bowel syndrome, diarrhea, dehydration, electrolyte disturbances, or congestive heart failure.

ANTIDIARRHEAL DRUGS (See Table 10-2)

Diarrhea is a serious disorder in infants and young children, and although antidiarrheal drugs are utilized in some disorders, they are secondary to correction of fluid and electrolyte deficiencies, treatment of offending microorganisms, and other modalities of therapy.

MISCELLANEOUS GASTROINTESTINAL TRACT DRUGS (See Table 10-3)

Drugs for treatment of gastrointestinal hypermotility are used with limited success in pediatric patients; moreover, some such drugs have adverse reactions which make them unsuitable for use in children.

While antiemetics are quite effective, it is important to bear in mind that these drugs might mask vomiting associated with infection or central nervous system disorders.

Table 10-1 Laxatives

Drug and Dose	Comments and Relevant Nursing Actions

Bisacodyl, tablets and suppositories (Dulcolax, Biscolax):
  Suppository dose:
    Children under 2 years: 5 mg rectally
    Children over 2 years: 10 mg rectally
  Oral dose:
    Usual pediatric dose: 300 μg/kg PO
	Bisacodyl, a stimulant laxative, upon contact with the colonic mucosa stimulates peristalsis by its action on myoneural synaptic junctions.
	
	Evacuation occurs within 15 to 60 min after rectal insertion and within 6 h after oral ingestion. The stool is usually copious, soft or formed, and cleansing is adequate for rectal diagnostic tests (e.g., sigmoidoscopy), surgery, and other measures for which such cleansing is a prerequisite.
	
	The drug is supplied as enteric-coated tablets for oral administration and as rectal suppositories. The tablets cause gastric irritation if they are chewed; thus, they are not suitable for children too young to swallow them without chewing. They should not be administered within 1 h after ingestion of milk or an antacid, to prevent dissolution in the stomach with gastric irritation.
	
	Although bisacodyl produces no systemic adverse effects, mild rectal burning, tenesmus, and rectal irritation may occur with repeated use of the suppositories.
	
	Abdominal cramping, severe diarrhea, and fluid and electrolyte disturbances are associated with frequent use.

Castor oil
Castor oil, emulsified (Neoloid)
  Infants: 1 to 5 ml PO
  Children: 5 to 15 ml PO
	Castor oil, a potent stimulant laxative, produces increased peristalsis by its action the small intestine.
	
	While the drug is not recommended for routine constipation, it is suitable for use when prompt, thorough cleansing of the bowel is necessary (e.g., before x-ray diagnostic tests).
	
	Within 2 to 6 h castor oil usually produces one or two copious, semiliquid stools, accompanied by flatus.
	
	The drug is more effective if it can be administered on an empty stomach. Since its action is

Table 10-1 Laxatives (*Continued*)

Drug and Dose	Comments and Relevant Nursing Actions
	comparatively prompt, castor oil should not be administered at the child's bedtime. Castor oil emulsion (Neoloid) contains flavoring agents and may be more acceptable to some children; however, chilling the drug and following administration with carbonated drinks or fruit juices may also make it more agreeable. Intestinal cramping, griping, and excessive fluid loss occur frequently with therapeutic castor oil doses.
Milk of magnesia, magnesia magma Pediatric cathartic dose: 0.5 ml/kg PO	Milk of magnesia is an aqueous suspension of magnesium hydroxide, which may contain volatile oils for flavoring purposes and citric acid to minimize interaction of the drug with glass containers. While the drug is used primarily for its laxative effects, it also has antacid properties. The laxative effects make milk of magnesia unsuitable for use as a single antacid in treatment of peptic ulcer. As a saline laxative, the drug draws fluid into the intestine, thereby stimulating stretch receptors and increasing peristalsis. Evacuation, which usually occurs within 3 to 6 h after ingestion of milk of magnesia, consists of a fluid or semifluid stool. The drug generally provides adequate bowel cleansing to make it suitable for use before surgery or routine x-ray diagnostic procedures. Milk of magnesia is most effective if taken on an empty stomach with as much water as the child can drink. It is important to state that the drug must be well shaken before pouring to ensure adequate dispersion of insoluble particles. Concurrent administration of milk of magnesia with tetracyclines and oral anticoagulants (i.e., dicumerol, warfarin) may result in decreased absorption of the antibiotic and the anticoagu-

Table 10-1 Laxatives (*Continued*)

Drug and Dose	Comments and Relevant Nursing Actions
	lant (*Evaluations of Drug Interactions,* 1976, pp. 227, 266). To avoid such interaction affecting drug absorption, milk of magnesia should be administered at least 3 h before or after these drugs.
	Since any magnesium ions which have been absorbed are excreted in the urine, the drug is contraindicated in the presence of renal impairment to avoid hypermagnesemia.
	Excessive use may result in abdominal cramping, significant fluid loss with dehydration and electrolyte disturbances, and alkalinization of urine with decreased excretion of basic drugs (e.g., quinidine).

Dioctyl sodium sulfosuccinate (DSS, Colace)
  Usual pediatric dose: 1.25 mg/kg PO four times a day
 	
Dioctyl calcium sulfosuccinate (Surfak, Doxidan)
  Children under 2 years: 25 mg PO daily
  Children 2 to 12 years: 50 to 150 mg PO daily
	The sodium and calcium salts of dioctyl sulfosuccinate are wetting agents which lower fecal surface tension, thereby permitting entry of water and fats. They may also promote secretion of both water and electrolytes within the lumen of the large intestine.

	While these stool softeners do not increase peristalsis, they produce a stool which is evacuated without straining or rectal discomfort.
	These agents generally require 24 to 48 h to exert their maximum effect, and they should be administered with as much water as the child can drink.
	They are indicated for relief of constipation when propulsive action is not required to evacuate the bowel.
	The sodium salt (Colace, DSS) is available as capsules, tablets, and liquid (drops or syrup), while the calcium salt (Surfak, Doxidan) is supplied only as capsules. There are, apparently, no differences in pharmacological action, effects, and indications.

Table 10-1   Laxatives (*Continued*)

Drug and Dose	Comments and Relevant Nursing Actions
	Since both drugs increase absorption of mineral oil, they should not be administered with mineral oil.
	Drops and syrup should be administered with fruit juice, milk, or formula to disguise their bitter taste.
	While neither drug produces any known systemic reactions of a serious nature, rash and diarrhea have occurred after administration of both. Mild, intermittent cramping pains have occurred after ingestion of the calcium salt (Surfak, Doxidan).

Sodium phosphate and sodium biphosphate, oral solution (Fleet Phospho-Soda)
  Children 5 to 10 years: 2.5 to 5 ml PO
  Children over 10 years: 5 to 10 ml PO
 	
Sodium phosphate and sodium biphosphate, enema
  Children 2 years and over: 60 ml rectally
	This saline laxative is a solution of sodium phosphate with sodium biphosphate–purified water. As a saline laxative, it osmotically draws fluid into the intestine, thereby stimulating stretch receptors and increasing peristalsis.

	The drug produces a fluid or semifluid stool, usually within 1 h if taken before a meal or overnight when taken at bedtime. Bowel evacuation usually occurs within 2 to 5 min of administration of an enema.
	Effectiveness of the drug is promoted by administering oral solutions on an empty stomach with as much water as the child can drink.
	Bowel evacuation may be adequate for x-ray diagnostic procedures, and the fluid stool can be used for laboratory examination of parasites.
	The oral solution is available with flavoring agents, and the enema is supplied in a ready-to-administer plastic squeeze bottle. A special pediatric-size enema and a pediatric dosage level indicator on the regular-size enema unit are available.
	To avoid congestive heart failure and electrolyte disturbances this laxative is not used in

Table 10-1 Laxatives (*Continued*)

Drug and Dose	Comments and Relevant Nursing Actions
	children with cardiac disorders or renal impairment. Use in children with megacolon may cause osmotic dehydration, and thus should be avoided.
	Overuse may result in abdominal cramping, dehydration, and dependency.

Table 10-2 Antidiarrheal Drugs

Drug and Dose	Comments and Relevant Nursing Actions
Cholestyramine resin (Questran, Cuemid) Children over 6 years: 80 mg/kg PO three times daily	Cholestyramine, an ion-exchange resin, absorbs and combines with bile salts in the intestine, forming an insoluble complex which is excreted in the feces. This removal of bile salts prevents their reabsorption, thereby decreasing blood cholesterol and lipoprotein levels. In pediatric patients cholestyramine is indicated for diarrheas caused by increased bile salts in the intestine. It is used to relieve pruritis associated with partial biliary tract obstruction, and, in adults, to lower elevated blood cholesterol and lipoprotein levels. The drug is contraindicated for use in children with complete biliary tract obstruction. Cholestyramine is supplied as a dry, grainy powder, and to avoid esophageal irritation and blockage, it should not be taken in the dry form. Most children accept the drug if the powder is well mixed with flavored soups, cooked cereal, mashed banana, jello, crushed pineapple, applesauce, or other fruit with adequate pulpy consistency and high water content. Older children may prefer to have the drug mixed with milk, water, fruit juice, or carbonated beverages; however, to ensure a uniform suspension and to avoid lumping or excessive foaming (i.e., with carbonated beverages) the drug must be prepared according to directions of the package insert. Concurrent administration of cholestyramine with several other drugs results in formation of an insoluble complex, and thus decreases their absorption. Cholestyramine decreases absorption of thyroid hormone, digitalis derivatives, oral anticoagulants, and weak organic acids such as aspirin, phenobarbital, tetracycline, and chlorothiazide (Diuril) (*Evaluations of Drug Interactions*, 1976, p. 432). To avoid these interactions of drug absorption cholestyramine should be administered at least 4 h after other drugs (AMA Department of Drugs, 1977, p. 1065).

Table 10-2 Antidiarrheal Drugs (*Continued*)

Drug and Dose	Comments and Relevant Nursing Actions
	Since chronic administration of the drug may decrease absorption of fat-soluble drugs, parenteral supplementation of vitamins K, A, and D might be indicated.
	Constipation, fecal impaction, flatulence, abdominal distention, and perianal irritation are common after administration of the drug.
Diphenoxylate hydrochloride and atropine sulfate (Lomotil) Children 2 to 5 years: 4 ml PO three times a day Children 5 to 8 years: 4 ml PO four times a day Children 8 to 12 years: 4 ml PO five times a day The solution usually available contains 2.5 mg of diphenoxylate hydrochloride and 25 μg of atropine per 5 ml	Lomotil is an antiperistaltic drug which contains diphenoxylate, a derivative of meperidine (Demerol, Dolosal), and is subject to the provisions of the Controlled Substances Act. The drug does not produce euphoria or dependence at recommended doses, and its poor solubility in aqueous solutions make parenteral abuse impractical. A small amount of atropine is added to the synthetic narcotic contained in Lomotil to discourage use by drug abusers.
	The drug decreases peristalsis by inhibiting intestinal mucosal receptors, an action which abolishes mucosal peristaltic reflexes.
	While the drug is used frequently for nonbacterial diarrheas, it is contraindicated for use in children with hepatic impairment or acute inflammatory disorders of the colon.
	Lomotil is supplied as oral tablets and as oral solution.
	Since the drug will potentiate the effects of sedatives and other central nervous system depressants, children receiving such drugs concurrently with Lomotil must be carefully evaluated for evidence of central nervous system depression.
	Concurrent administration of Lomotil with the antimicrobial furazolidone (Furoxone) might be expected to precipitate a hypertensive crisis (*Evaluations of Drug Interactions,* 1976, p. 10).
	While adverse reactions are not common, it is important to remember that children are sensi-

Table 10-2   Antidiarrheal Drugs (*Continued*)

Drug and Dose	Comments and Relevant Nursing Actions
	tive to atropine toxicity. Atropine poisoning is more likely to occur in children with Down's syndrome, and is characterized by fever, flushing, dilated pupils, urinary retention, abdominal distention, tachycardia, and mental confusion.
	Rash, drowsiness, and intestinal obstruction occur rarely with administration of Lomotil.

Kaolin mixture with pectin (Kaopectate, Pargel)
 	
No dosage recommendations are available; the following are suggested dosages to be taken after each evacuation (AMA Department of Drugs, 1977, p. 1068):
    Children 3 to 6 years: 15 to 30 ml PO
    Children 6 to 12 years: 30 to 60 ml PO
    Children over 12 years: 60 ml PO
	This antidiarrheal agent combines kaolin, an aluminum silicate, with pectin, a purified carbohydrate obtained from fruits. The kaolin component of the mixture reportedly attracts and holds (adsorbs) irritants, as well as forming a protective coating on the gastric and intestinal mucosa. Pectin is said to consolidate the stool, increase its bulk, and decrease its fluidity.

	Although this drug is a popular over-the-counter product, adequately controlled studies supporting its effectiveness are lacking at this time.
	The drug is available as a sweetened, flavored oral suspension.
	Its use in children under 3 years of age or in children with intestinal obstructive conditions is contraindicated (AMA Department of Drugs, 1977, p. 1068).
	Concurrent administration of this drug with clindamycin (Cleocin) or lincomycin (Lincocin) decreases absorption of the antibiotic (*Evaluations of Drug Interactions,* 1976, p. 135). Administering the antidiarrheal agent at least 3 h before the antibiotic will prevent this interaction.
	Chronic use of the drug may result in constipation or fecal impaction.

Table 10-3   Miscellaneous Gastrointestinal Tract Drugs

Drug and Dose	Comments and Relevant Nursing Actions
Dicyclomine hydrochloride (Bentyl, Dyspas) Infants: 5 mg PO three or four times daily Children: 10 mg PO three or four times daily	Dicyclomine is a synthetic antispasmotic which relaxes gastrointestinal tract smooth muscle by exerting a nonspecific, direct action on muscle fiber. While the drug decreases smooth-muscle spasm and motility of the gastrointestinal tract, it has minimal effect on gastric secretion and reportedly has little atropinelike activity. Effectiveness of dicyclomine varies from patient to patient; thus, dosage must be carefully individualized. The drug is used for disorders characterized by spasm and hypermotility of the gastrointestinal tract, e.g., infant colic, mild diarrhea, and abdominal cramping not complicated by obstruction, and in adults as an adjunct for peptic ulcer. There is no agreement regarding its use for treatment of hypermotility due to ulcerative colitis and regional enteritis. The drug is available as tablets, capsules, and syrup for oral administration; and as a sterile solution for parenteral administration. Dicyclomine is contraindicated for use in children with gastrointestinal obstructive conditions (e.g., pyloric stenosis), or with toxic megacolon (Hirschsprung's disease), or with myasthenia gravis. Since the drug delays gastric emptying, drugs administered concurrently remain in contact with gastric mucosa for a longer period of time, and are thus more completely absorbed. Increased absorption of slow-dissolving digoxin tablets will result in elevation of serum digoxin concentrations and possibly in digoxin toxicity (*Evaluations of Drug Interactions,* 1976, p. 65). This interaction can be prevented by administering digoxin liquid dosage form (i.e., elixir), or by administering digoxin tablets which dissolve rapidly by United States Pharmacopeia standards (*Evaluations of Drug Interactions,* 1976, p. 65).

Table 10-3 Miscellaneous Gastrointestinal Tract Drugs (*Continued*)

Drug and Dose	Comments and Relevant Nursing Actions
	Adverse reactions associated with administration of dicyclomine include constipation, diarrhea, paralytic ileus, urinary retention, drowsiness, hypotension, and, rarely, rash.
Diphenidol hydrochloride (Vontrol) Children at least 6 months of age, or weighing 12 kg or more (Vaughn and McKay, 1975, p. 1748): Not to exceed 5 mg/kg in 24 h, PO or rectal, divided into six doses Intramuscular dose 60 percent of the oral-rectal dose	Diphenidol, an effective antiemetic drug, not only controls nausea and vomiting by inhibiting the chemoreceptor trigger zone but also controls vertigo by antivertigo effects on the vestibular apparatus. There is some evidence that the drug also exerts weak peripheral anticholinergic effects. The drug is indicated for prevention and treatment of nausea and vomiting due to radiation sickness, antineoplastic drugs, infections, malignancies, and general anesthetics. While diphenidol is effective for control of vertigo associated with motion sickness and vestibular apparatus disorders (Ménière's syndrome, labyrinthitis) in adults, its use for control of vertigo in children has not been studied. Anuria, hypotension, and gastrointestinal obstruction (pyloric stenosis, etc.) are contraindications to use of the drug. Auditory and visual hallucinations may occur with recommended doses of this drug, and for this reason the drug should be used only for children who are under close nursing or parental supervision. In the event that hallucinations occur, the drug should be immediately withheld, the physician should be notified, and the child protected from injury and given supportive reassurance. Dry mouth, dizziness, fatigue, and, rarely, blurred vision, mild hypotension, nausea, and rash might also occur during administration of the drug.
Ipecac syrup Children under 1 year: 5 to	Ipecac is an alkaloid, used primarily for its emetic action, which not only acts directly on

Table 10-3 Miscellaneous Gastrointestinal Tract Drugs (*Continued*)

Drug and Dose	Comments and Relevant Nursing Actions
10 ml PO Children over 1 year: 10 to 30 ml PO The above dose may be repeated in 20 min if emesis does not occur. Dosage should be recovered by lavage if emesis does not occur after second dose.	the chemoreceptor trigger zone of the medulla, but also exerts indirect stimulation of the gastrointestinal tract. Vomiting generally occurs within 30 min of ingesting the drug, and both stomach and upper intestine are emptied. Administering the drug with water increases its effectiveness. Syrup of ipecac is used to induce vomiting after ingestion of some poisons; however, its use is contraindicated after poisoning with petroleum distillates (gasoline, kerosene), corrosives (lye, strong acids), and strychnine. It should never be administered to an unconscious child. The drug is also administered, in either emetic or subemetic doses, to break the laryngeal spasm associated with infectious and spastic croup. Although it is a component of some over-the-counter cough preparations, its effectiveness as an expectorant or antitussive is yet to be demonstrated. The drug is available for over-the-counter purchase in small (30 ml maximum), clearly labeled containers. Failure to remove ipecac syrup by emesis or lavage results in systemic absorption of the drug, and cardiac adverse reactions. These cardiotoxic reactions may include conduction disturbances, atrial fibrillation, or fatal myocarditis (AMA Department of Drugs, 1977, p. 1189).
Pancreatin (Panteric, Viokase) Children: Initially 300 to 600 mg with each meal; dosage may be increased if stools contain fat (AMA Department of Drugs, 1977, p. 1086)	Pancreatin, a mixture of several pancreatic hormones, is derived from hog or cattle pancreas, and aids digestion in children with pancreatic enzyme deficiency. Children with cystic fibrosis require life-long administration of pancreatin, while those with deficiencies associated with other causes (e.g., malignancy) will require the drug for the duration of the deficiency state.

Table 10-3   Miscellaneous Gastrointestinal Tract Drugs (*Continued*)

Drug and Dose	Comments and Relevant Nursing Actions
	The drug is available as tablets, capsules, and granules for oral administration, and dosage is individualized according to the child's clinical response (i.e., laboratory determination of fat content of stools).
	It is important that the child take the drug not only with regular meals but with all snacks as well.
	Adverse reactions to pancreatin are not common; however, nausea, vomiting, and diarrhea may occur with large doses.
	A beef preparation is available for use in children who are hypersensitive to the pork product, or for those to whom pork products are unacceptable.
Trimethobenzamide hydrochloride (Tigan) Children: 15 mg/kg per day PO or rectally, divided into three or four doses; rectal route not recommended for neonates (Vaughn and McKay, 1975, p. 1748)	Trimethobenzamide is an antiemetic which controls nausea and vomiting by inhibiting vomiting impulses to the chemoreceptor trigger zone of the medulla oblongata. The drug is moderately effective and its duration of action is approximately 4 to 6 h.
	It is indicated for control of vomiting associated with antineoplastic drugs, radiation sickness, infections, and malignancies.
	The drug is supplied as capsules and pediatric suppositories, and, although the intramuscular route is not recommended for children, as sterile parenteral solution.
	Rectal irritation following suppository administration is common; drowsiness, rash, and exaggeration of preexisting nausea might also occur. There have also been reports of extrapyramidal reactions: muscular rigidity, tremor, and propulsive gait.

BIBLIOGRAPHY

AMA Department of Drugs: *AMA Drug Evaluations*, 3d ed., Publishing Sciences Group, Littleton, Mass., 1977.

Bertholf, C. B.: "Protocol: Acute Diarrhea," *Nurse Practitioner,* vol. 3, no. 3, 1978, pp. 16–20.

Black, C. D.: "Drug Interactions in the GI Tract," *American Journal of Nursing,* vol. 77, no. 9, 1977, pp. 1426–1429.

Cormon, M. L., et al.: "Cathartics," *American Journal of Nursing,* vol. 75, no. 2, 1975, pp. 273–279.

Evaluations of Drug Interactions, 2d ed., American Pharmaceutical Association, Washington, D.C., 1976.

Goodman, L. S., and A. Gilman: *The Pharmacological Basis of Therapeutics,* 5th ed., Macmillan, New York, 1975.

Habeeb, M. C., and M. D. Kallstrom: "Bowel Program for Institutionalized Adults," *American Journal of Nursing,* vol. 76, no. 4, 1976, pp. 606–688.

Vaughn, V. C., and J. R. McKay: *Textbook of Pediatrics,* 10th ed., Saunders, Philadelphia, 1975.

Drugs Used to Treat Neoplasms

GENERAL CONSIDERATIONS

Chemotherapy, an integral part of the treatment of childhood malignancies, is utilized with surgical excision, radiation, and supportive drugs [e.g., allopurinol (Zyloprim), antinausea drugs] to prolong life.

Antineoplastic drugs may be used alone for malignancies of the blood-forming system (leukemia, Hodgkin's disease), or with surgery and radiation for pediatric solid malignancies. In spite of their cytotoxic effects on normal tissues, these drugs are credited with producing an impressive percentage of remissions and cures and prolongations of life expectancy in several childhood cancers.

Retinoblastoma, neuroblastoma, rhabdomyosarcoma, Wilms's tumor, and acute lymphoblastic leukemias which are seen in infants and children, are responsive to antineoplastic drugs. Osteogenic sarcoma, Ewing's sarcoma, and Hodgkin's disease, which usually occur in adolescents, have been treated with these drugs also. Vaginal adenocarcinoma, seen in girls who were exposed to diethylstilbestrol or other synthetic estrogens during gestation, has not been treated with chemotherapy.

Most antineoplastic agents attack malignant cells at a precise phase of the cell division process (also termed the *cell cycle*). Such agents are referred to as *cell-cycle specific*, and are effective only against actively dividing cells. Nondividing cells are resistant to cell-cycle specific agents; however, some antineoplastic agents kill cells during all phases of the cycle. Natural and acquired resistance to antineoplastic drugs, a poorly understood phenomenon, occurs with all antineoplastic agents in present use, and cross-resistance to chemically related or chemically dissimilar agents is also not uncommon.

Malignancies which proliferate rapidly (e.g., leukemia) are more responsive to the cytotoxic effects of antineoplastic drugs than malignancies which proliferate slowly (e.g., tumors of lung). Unfortunately the drugs also attack normal cells, and rapidly dividing normal cells (e.g., of bone marrow, hair follicles, intestinal mucosa) are more susceptible to this attack than slowly dividing normal cells (e.g., of liver and kidney). Common toxic reactions to these drugs include the following: depression of normal bone marrow function, ulceration of gastrointestinal mucosa, and cutaneous eruptions. With highly skilled nursing care, careful monitoring of adverse reactions, and availability of diagnostic and preventive facilities it is possible to administer antineoplastic drugs with reasonable safety.

ANTINEOPLASTIC DRUGS

Classification

Antineoplastic drugs may be divided as follows.

The *alkylating agents* [e.g., cyclophosphamide (Cytoxan), dacarbazine (DTIC), and mechlorethamine (Mustargen)] effect cell kill by interfering with cell growth and function. Alkylating agents contain alkyl groups, which combine with nucleic acids, thereby disrupting DNA synthesis during all phases of the cell cycle. Since their effects were once compared with that of ionizing radiation (radiation), alkylating agents were once termed *radiomimetic*.

Antimetabolites [cytarabine (Cytosar), mercaptopurine (Purinethol), and methotrexate (Amethopterin)] prevent biosynthesis of purine or pyrimidine bases by inhibiting production of DNA constituents or by entering into DNA as fraudulent precursors. They are primarily cell-cycle specific, i.e., cell kill occurs usually during the phase that DNA is synthesized.

Miscellaneous antineoplastic agents include the plant alkaloid vincristine (Oncovin), the antibiotics [dactinomycin (Cosmegen), bleomycin (Blenoxane), and doxorubicin (Adriamycin)], and procarbazine (Matulane). Vincristine, a cell-cycle agent, disrupts mitosis and produces metaphase rest. The antineoplastic antibiotics do not exert antimicrobial effects but prevent synthesis of RNA, DNA, and protein. Procarbazine, a drug which is not related to other antineoplastic agents, also inhibits RNA, DNA, and protein synthesis.

Combination Regimens

Single antineoplastic drugs are reasonably successful in producing remissions in several childhood malignancies [e.g., vincristine (Oncovin) and dactinomycin (Cosmegen) for rhabdomyosarcoma]; however, single drugs are much less effective than drug combinations and are more likely to produce drug resistance.

Combination regimens of two or more drugs with different mechanisms of action but without overlapping adverse reactions produce additive cell kill throughout the cell division process. Administration of these drugs in rational sequence prevents potentiation of adverse reactions and permits recovery of bone marrow, intestinal mucosa, hair follicles, and skin.

Such combinations in present use include COAP [cyclophosphamide (Cytoxan), vincristine (Oncovin), cytarabine (Cytosar), and prednisone (Deltasone)] and

(*Text continued on page 324.*)

Table 11-1 Adverse Reactions Associated with Administration of Antineoplastic Drugs

Adverse Reaction	Drug(s) Implicated	Pertinent Diagnostic Studies
Bone marrow depression	All antineoplastic drugs may cause this reaction.	Serial blood counts (WBC, differential, RBC, hemoglobin, hematocrit, platelet) at frequent intervals. Reports should be recorded on flow charts to provide comparison with baseline and subsequent counts. Bone marrow studies may also be necessary.

Note: Most adverse reactions are dose-related. There may also be individual variation in severity, in duration, and in time between drug administration and appearance of the reaction.

Clinical Manifestations	Nursing Actions Which Prevent or Minimize Reaction, and Usual Medical Treatment
Anemia—pallor, cold extremities, fatigue, and dyspnea.	Provide frequent naps or other rest periods. Maintain body heat.
Thrombocytopenia—bleeding from body orifices, gums, and mucous membranes. Epistaxis, hematuria, melena, and subcutaneous bleeding.	Avoid aspirin. Protect from injury. Use soft toothbrush. Assess frequently for subcutaneous and intracavitary bleeding.
	Avoid intramuscular injections; use only small-bore needles (number 23 or 25) if such injections are necessary.
	Multiple platelet transfusions may be necessary. Assess for transfusion reaction.
Leukopenia—highly susceptible to infection. Fungal and gram-negative strains from body flora may cause infection.	Assess frequently for evidence of urinary tract, respiratory tract, gastrointestinal tract, and cutaneous infection. Culture all suspicious lesions.
	Provide aseptic care to all open wounds, catheters, tubes, and venipuncture sites.
	Take frequent temperature readings. (Bear in mind that prednisone will "mask" signs of infection.)
	Keep child's nails short and clean, teach correct cleansing technique, and thorough hand-washing after using toilet. Provide supervision for children unable to observe these measures without assistance.
	Provide hygienic environment. All nursing personnel coming into contact with child should be free of infections. Hands must be thoroughly washed before touching child. Children with infections should be denied contact with

Table 11-1 Adverse Reactions Associated with Administration of Antineoplastic Drugs (*Continued*)

Adverse Reaction	Drug(s) Implicated	Pertinent Diagnostic Studies
Immunosuppression	All antineoplastic drugs have been implicated; however, cytarabine (Cytosar), cyclophosphamide (Cytoxan), mechlorethamine (Mustargen), and methotrexate (Purinethol) exert potent immunosuppressive effects.	
Ulceration of mucous membranes of mouth, gastrointestinal tract, and rectum	Methotrexate (Amethopterin), dactinoymcin (Cosmegen), doxorubicin (Adriamycin), mercaptopurine (Purinethol), and cyclophosphamide (Cytoxan) are associated	

Clinical Manifestations	Nursing Actions Which Prevent or Minimize Reaction, and Usual Medical Treatment
	those receiving antineoplastic drugs. Protective isolation might be indicated (e.g., with sharp drop in WBC).
	Infections are treated with appropriate antibiotics.
Destruction of lymphocytes, decrease in antibody production, and suppression of other immune mechanisms. Child is highly susceptible to viral infections. Body is unable to produce antibodies in response to live virus vaccines.	
Varicella (chickenpox) in younger child and herpes zoster (shingles) are serious infections.	Avoid exposing child to individuals with varicella or herpes zoster.
	Assess for pain, tenderness, and vesicular lesions along course of a spinal nerve (herpes zoster), and vesicular lesions of skin and mucous membrane (chickenpox).
Reactivation of latent viral infections can produce serious consequences.	
Administration of live virus vaccines results in active disease.	Administration of live virus vaccines (smallpox, measles, polio) is avoided.
	Laminar flow room may be indicated for total immunosuppression.
* Mild stomatitis with inflammation of mouth (lips, gums, and tongue), fissures, and soreness (might indicate intestinal involvement).	Inspect oral cavity daily for evidence of involvement. Assess moisture content, swallowing ability, and changes in voice. Culture suspicious lesions.
	Administer oral hygiene (gently cleansing with soft toothbrush to remove debris) using a normal saline—hydro-

* Withhold drug and communicate reaction to physician.

Adverse Reaction	Drug(s) Implicated	Pertinent Diagnostic Studies
	with high risks of this reaction.	
Anorexia, nausea, vomiting, and diarrhea (non-bloody)	Severity, onset, and duration vary from drug to drug. Mechlorethamine (Mustargen) and	

Clinical Manifestations	Nursing Actions Which Prevent or Minimize Reaction, and Usual Medical Treatment
	gen peroxide mixture or other acceptable effective solution. Every 4 h is usually adequate.
	Nystatin (Mycostatin) oral suspension or another antifungal drug may be prescribed for prevention.
	Provide nonirritating, easily chewed foods, and cool, soothing liquids.
* Severe stomatitis with ulcerations of oral cavity, bleeding, severe pain, difficulty chewing and swallowing, dryness, and sore throat.	Continue preventive measures. Administer oral hygiene every 2 to 3 h around the clock.
Gastrointestinal tract ulceration, bleeding, infection and perforation may accompany this reaction. Abdominal cramps, diarrhea, rectal ulcerations, and severe pain may also occur.	Local anesthetic [e.g. lidocaine (Xylocaine) gel] or systemic analgesic [e.g., acetaminophen (Tylenol) elixir] are prescribed for pain.
	Inspect rectum frequently for evidence of ulceration.
	To prevent rectal perforation, oral or axillary temperatures are taken.
	Keep rectal area clean and dry. Apply soothing, protective ointments (e.g., A and D Ointment) as indicated.
	Measure diarrhea, inspect visually, and test (e.g., using guaic) for occult blood if no frank blood is present.
	Assess fluid and electrolyte status. Intravenous fluids, electrolytes, and vitamins are prescribed. Systemic antimicrobial agents are also prescribed.
	Administer antiemetics before drug is administered (suppository or parenteral dosage forms may be indicated). Place emesis basin and tissues within

* Withhold drug and communicate reaction to physician.

Table 11-1   Adverse Reactions Associated with Administration of Antineoplastic Drugs (*Continued*)

Adverse Reaction	Drug(s) Implicated	Pertinent Diagnostic Studies
	dacarbazine (DTIC) produce severe nausea and vomiting, while vincristine (Oncovin) seldom produces these reactions.	
Toxicity involving hair follicles, skin, and nails	Most antineoplastic agents can produce these reactions, particularly after radiation.	
Local irritation; phlebitis or cellulitis at injection site; severe pain,	Vincristine (Oncovin), mechlorethamine (Mustargen), dacarbazine	

Clinical Manifestations	Nursing Actions Which Prevent or Minimize Reaction, and Usual Medical Treatment
	reach, without suggesting that vomiting is inevitable.
	Inspect vomitus for unabsorbed drug (discuss alternate administration route if indicated), measure amount, and assess fluid and electrolyte status.
	Administer oral hygiene after each emesis.
	Intravenous fluids and electrolytes may be prescribed for severe fluid and electrolyte depletion.
Partial or complete loss of scalp, axillary, and pubic hair.	Before starting chemotherapy child and parent should understand that reversible alopecia often occurs. They should also know that regrowth may differ in color and texture. Caps, turbans, or wigs can be purchased in advance.
	Application of a scalp tourniquet during intravenous drug administration is painful, frightening, and not always successful in preventing hair loss (Bingham, 1978, p. 1205).
Hyperpigmentation; often involving nail beds, and dermal creases.	
Eruptions, desquamation (peeling), erythema, and pruritis.	Antihistamines, local antipruritic drugs. Keep nails short and clean to prevent infection. Encourage frequent handwashing.
Potentiation of radiation-associated skin reaction.	Change position frequently to prevent breakdown of skin.
Exaggerated sunburn.	
Transverse ridging of nails.	
Induration, pain, or redness along the course of the vein.	These drugs are injected into the tubing of a running intravenous infusion. This reduces the risk of infiltration and

Adverse Reaction	Drug(s) Implicated	Pertinent Diagnostic Studies
necrosis, and tissue slough if drug infiltrates subcutaneous tissues	(DTIC), doxorubicin (Adriamycin), and dactinomycin (Cosmegen) produce this reaction.	
	Doxorubicin (Adriamycin) and mechlorethamine (Mustargen) are highly irritative to skin and eyes of patient and others.	
Hyperuricemia with uric acid crystallization in urinary tract	Mercaptopurine (Purinethol), mechlorethamine (Mustargen), and methotrexate (Amethopterin) are most likely to produce this reaction. Children with leukemia or Hodgkin's disease tend to have hyperuricemia regardless of medication regimens.	Serial serum uric acid determinations may be used to adjust allopurinol dose.
Cystitis	Cyclophosphamide (Cytoxan) causes sterile, hemorrhagic cystitis in approximately 20 percent of children.	Urine microscopic examination is useful in detecting early hematuria.
Liver damage with biliary stasis and cirrhosis	Most antineoplastic agents are capable of producing this reaction, and it is usually reversible.	Serum transaminase (SGOT, SGPT) is used to assess hepatic function.
	Cytarabine (Cytosar), methotrexate (Ametho-	

Clinical Manifestations	Nursing Actions Which Prevent or Minimize Reaction, and Usual Medical Treatment
	dilutes the drug before it comes into contact with the vein.
	Immobilize extremity to prevent infiltration. Discontinue infusion at first sign of pain or other evidence of infiltration.
Powder or solution produces rash, pruritis, and blistering of skin surfaces.	Wear surgical gloves to prepare and administer these drugs. If drug touches skin, wash well with soap and water. Protect eyes from powder and solutions.
	Force fluids to dilute uric acid and prevent crystallization. Measure urine output, and assess for evidence of hematuria.
	Allopurinol (Zyloprim) may be prescribed to reduce production of uric acid.
	Administration of sodium bicarbonate to alkalinize the urine may be indicated to reduce the risk of renal damage.
* Dysuria, frequency, and frank hematuria.	Push fluids to dilute metabolites which are excreted in the urine. Encourage voiding every 2 to 3 h and at bedtime. Measure urine output, and inspect for hematuria.
	Transfusion may be required.
Jaundice, pruritis.	

* Withhold drug and communicate reaction to physician.

Table 11-1 Adverse Reactions Associated with Administration of Antineoplastic Drugs (*Continued*)

Adverse Reaction	Drug(s) Implicated	Pertinent Diagnostic Studies
	pterin), dacarbazine (DTIC), and mercaptopurine (Purinethol) appear to have higher risk of producing hepatic dysfunction.	
Neurotoxicity	Vincristine (Oncovin) frequently produces neurotoxicity. While the reactions are reversible, they may persist for several months after the drug is discontinued. Procarbazine (Matulane) occasionally produces these reactions.	
	Mechlorethamine (Mustargen) occasionally produces central nervous system stimulation.	
Pulmonary toxicity	Bleomycin (Blenoxane) may cause nonreversible pulmonary toxicity, which may result in pulmonary fibrosis. Cyclophosphamide (Cytoxan) and high-dose methotrexate (Amethopterin) rarely cause this reaction.	Daily chest film and auscultation can detect these reactions.
Cardiac pathology	Doxorubicin (Adriamycin) may produce nonreversible cardiac pathology which may terminate in congestive heart failure.	Electrocardiograms can detect early signs of cardiac toxicity

Clinical Manifestations	Nursing Actions Which Prevent or Minimize Reaction, and Usual Medical Treatment
* Mental depression, agitation, and, rarely, convulsions.	Daily neurological assessment with evaluation of deep tendon reflexes.
Abnormal sensations in extremities, muscle weakness, difficulty walking, foot drop, loss of deep tendon reflexes.	Active and passive range-of-motion exercises to all joints. Maintain proper body alignment. Protect from falls and other injuries.
Severe constipation, colicky abdominal pain, paralytic ileus.	High-bulk diet, increased fluid intake. Stool softeners or mild laxatives as indicated.
Convulsions, muscle paralysis.	
* Dyspnea, cough, rales. Pulmonary infiltration.	Encourage coughing and deep breathing every 2 to 3 h. Assess pulmonary status at least twice daily. Encourage ambulation; change position every hour while on bed rest.
* Arrhythmias. Severe congestive heart failure.	Take apical and radial pulses twice daily. Assess for dyspnea, orthopnea, and edema of lower extremities.

* Withhold drug and communicate reaction to physician.

Table 11-1   Adverse Reactions Associated with Administration of Antineoplastic Drugs *(Continued)*

Adverse Reaction	Drug(s) Implicated	Pertinent Diagnostic Studies
Hypersensitivity	Hypersensitivity reactions with anaphylaxis occur in approximately 6 percent of individuals receiving bleomycin (Blenoxone). Dactinomycin (Cosmegen) and Doxorubicin (Adriamycin) also cause this reaction occasionally.	
Gonadal reactions	All antineoplastic drugs suppress gonadal function. The teratogenic potential of these drugs is quite high.	

POMP [vincristine (Oncovin), methotrexate (Amethopterin), mercaptopurine (Purinethol), and prednisone (Deltasone)], both of which are used for acute childhood leukemias. Others, MOPP [mechlorethamine (Mustargen), vincristine (Oncovin), procarbazine (Matulane), and prednisone (Deltasone)] and COP (cyclophosphamide (Cytoxan), vincristine (Oncovin), and prednisone (Deltasone)], are used for treatment of Hodgkin's disease. As resistance to drugs in these regimens emerges, newer combinations are being investigated and accepted (Vinciguerra, 1977, p. 33).

Dosage

Antineoplastic regimens, whether single or combination, are individualized so that each child receives the chemotherapy which achieves maximal antitumor ac-

Clinical Manifestations	Nursing Actions Which Prevent or Minimize Reaction, and Usual Medical Treatment
* Hypotension, rash, cardiorespiratory collapse.	Bleomycin therapy is initiated with one or two 1-U test doses. If there is no evidence of hypersensitivity, regular doses can be given. Assess child closely during and after administration of these drugs. Have emergency drugs, airways, oxygen, and tracheostomy sets on hand.
Delay in puberty (menarche may be 1 to 2 years late). Amenorrhea, sterility.	Child and parents should be informed of this reaction before chemotherapy is started.

* Withhold drug and communicate reaction to physician.

tivity with minimal adverse reactions. Selection of drugs, dose, and regimens is dependent upon the site of the neoplasm; the stage of the neoplasm; the physical condition of the child (nutritional, fluid, and growth and developmental status); the status of hepatic, renal, and hematological function; and on whether surgery, radiation, or previous chemotherapy has been received.

After careful evaluation of liver, kidney, and bone marrow function by laboratory methods, a regimen is selected for the individual child. During chemotherapy serial laboratory tests, chest films, and other studies are interpreted in the light of clinical manifestations to identify early adverse reactions. Close nursing assessment of clinical response can detect early adverse reactions, and skilled nursing care can prevent or minimize some adverse reactions. Reducing dosage or discontinuing the drug at appearance of early adverse reactions will usually prevent severe consequences. The nurse must know which reactions warrant immediate communication to the physician and withholding or interrupting of drug administration.

Parent and Child Preparation

Parents and children should understand both the benefits and the risks of drugs to be administered. Most parents ask questions regarding immediate and long-term effects on growth processes (linear growth, menarche in girls), school achievement, immunization schedules, and cosmetic effects. They should be given the opportunity to express fears, frustrations, and anger; and it is prudent to avoid raising false hopes. Many parents will require help in explaining chemotherapy and its effects to siblings, and they may also require advice on whether to inform the child's peers. Clear written instructions for clinic or office visits, drug administration, prevention of infection, and skin and mouth care and other concrete information should be given.

The child may have questions regarding school activities, participation in sports, and friends' reactions once chemotherapy is started. When child and parent are informed about the techniques of the drug regimen and how it will affect hair, skin, mouth, and bone marrow, it is usually wise to repeat the information several times. Children may express anxiety about changes in body image (e.g., hair loss, weight loss, skin eruptions), fear of death, and fear of injections, mutilation, and pain.

Child and parents require warmth, honesty, and supportive instruction before and during chemotherapy. There must also be provision for support of those parents whose religious beliefs do not permit cooperation in aggressive chemotherapy regimens. Parents are generally urged to permit near-normal activities for the child (e.g., attendance at nursery school, regular school, play) and to avoid permitting him or her to "manipulate" the family situation.

(*Text continued on page 332.*)

Table 11-2   Antineoplastic Drugs

Drugs, Indications, and Combination Therapy	Comments and Relevant Nursing Actions

BLEOMYCIN SULFATE (BLENOXANE)

In the combination below, it is indicated for advanced Hodgkin's disease and for MOPP-resistant Hodgkin's disease.	Bleomycin is an antibiotic which inhibits synthesis of RNA, DNA, and protein. As a single agent bleomycin is used to treat Hodgkin's disease.
Bleomycin sulfate (Blenoxane) *with* Doxorubicin (Adriamycin) Vincristine (Oncovin) Dacarbazine (DTIC)	Supplied as sterile powder, which is stable at room temperature for 2 years. After reconstitution solutions are stable for 7 days under refrigeration.
	The drug is administered by the intravenous, intramuscular, and subcutaneous routes.
	Adverse reactions include pulmonary toxicity, moderate bone marrow depression, cutaneous reactions, ulcerations of the mouth and gastrointestinal tract, and anaphylactic reactions (see Table 11-1). Pain of tumor sites is not uncommon during bleomycin administration.

CYCLOPHOSPHAMIDE (CYTOXAN)

In combination regimens cyclophosphamide is effective for disseminated Hodgkin's disease, acute lymphoblastic leukemia, neuroblastoma, rhabdomyosarcoma, and Ewing's sarcoma. It is a component of the COAP regimen, which is listed below.	Cyclophosphamide is derived from nitrogen mustards and is generally considered an alkylating agent. Its mechanism of action is unknown.
Cyclophosphamide (Cytoxan) *with* Vincristine (Oncovin) Cytarabine (Cytasar) Prednisone (Deltasone)	The drug is supplied as tablets for oral administration and as sterile powder for parenteral administration. After reconstitution drug solutions are stable for 6 days under refrigeration and for 24 h at room temperature.
	Administration of large doses of phenobarbital may increase the metabolism and leukopenic action of cyclophosphamide.

Note: Dosage of these drugs is dependent on whether they are used as single agents or as components of combination therapy. Previous treatment modalities, stage of the malignancy, and condition of the child are also factors in dosage determination.

Table 11-2 Antineoplastic Drugs (*Continued*)

Drugs	Comments and Relevant Nursing Actions
	Hemorrhagic cystitis, bone marrow depression, alopecia, gastrointestinal upsets, skin reactions, and hyperpigmentation may occur (see Table 11-1).

CYTARABINE (CYTOSAR)

Used in combination regimens for acute lymphoblastic leukemia. The COAP regimen is listed below.

  Cytarabine (Cytosar)
     with
  Cyclophosphamide (Cytoxan)
  Vincristine (Oncovin)
  Prednisone (Deltasone)

Cytarabine is an antimetabolite which inhibits both DNA polymerase and RNA function.

The drug is supplied as a freeze-dried powder which should be stored under refrigeration. After reconstitution drug solutions are stable for 48 h at room temperature. Solutions which develop slight haze should be discarded.

Cytarabine is administered by the subcutaneous and intravenous (injected into the tubing of a running infusion) routes.

Local inflammation, severe bone marrow depression, ulceration of gastrointestinal tract, renal toxicity, and liver damage may occur (see Table 11-1).

DACARBAZINE (DTIC)

Utilized in the following combination for MOPP-resistant Hodgkin's disease.

  Dacarbazine (DTIC)
     with
  Doxorubicin (Adriamycin)
  Bleomycin (Blenoxane)
  Vincristine (Oncovin)

Dacarbazine is a potent alkylating agent which disrupts synthesis of DNA.

Supplied as sterile powder for reconstitution, the drug must be protected from light. After it has been reconstituted, dacarbazine is stable for 72 h under refrigeration. It is administered by injection into the tubing of a running intravenous infusion.

Severe gastrointestinal upsets, significant bone marrow depression, facial flushing, alopecia, and liver toxicity may occur (see Table 11-1).

Table 11-2 Antineoplastic Drugs (*Continued*)

Drugs	Comments and Relevant Nursing Actions

DACTINOMYCIN (COSMEGEN)

In combination with other drugs and radiation, dactinomycin is effective for treatment of Wilms's tumor, neuroblastoma, rhabdo-myosarcoma, and Ewing's sarcoma. The following combination is used with radiation to treat childhood malignancies.

   Dactinomycin (Cosmegen)
     with
   Vincristine (Oncovin)
   Cyclophosphamide (Cytoxan)

Dactinomycin is an antibiotic which exerts potent cytotoxic activity by inhibiting DNA synthesis.

Supplied as powder, it must be protected from light and excessive heat. Unused reconstituted solutions should be discarded.

Dactinomycin is injected into the tubing of a running intravenous infusion to prevent venous irritative reactions.

Severe bone marrow depression, ulceration of the gastrointestinal tract, alopecia, cutaneous reactions, phlebitis, and, rarely, hypersensitivity reactions may occur (see Table 11-1).

DOXORUBICIN SULFATE (ADRIAMYCIN)

Effective in combination for Wilms's tumor, Hodgkin's disease, and leukemia. The following combination is used for osteogenic sarcoma.

   Doxorubicin sulfate (Adriamycin)
     with
   Cyclophosphamide (Cytoxan)
   Vincristine (Oncovin)
   Methotrexate (Amethopterin)

Doxorubicin is a highly toxic antibiotic which apparently inhibits synthesis of nucleic acids.

The drug is supplied as a sterile powder which is stable at room temperature. After reconstitution the solution is stable for 48 h if refrigerated and protected from light. Doxorubicin powder and solution is a vesicant, and thus should not come into contact with the skin (see Table 11-1). To avoid phlebitis and tissue damage the drug is injected into the tubing of a running intravenous infusion.

The drug colors the urine red, and this does not indicate hematuria.

Cardiac toxicity, severe bone marrow depression, ulceration of the gastrointestinal tract, phlebitis and tissue damage, complete alopecia, skin reactions, and, rarely, hypersensitivity reactions may occur (Table 11-1).

Table 11-2 Antineoplastic Drugs (*Continued*)

Drugs	Comments and Relevant Nursing Actions

MECHLORETHAMINE (NITROGEN MUSTARD, MUSTARGEN)

Used in the MOPP regimen listed below for advanced Hodgkin's disease.

   Mechlorethamine (Mustargen)
       with
   Vincristine (Oncovin)
   Procarbazine (Matulane)
   Prednisone (Deltasone)

Mechlorethamine is an effective alkylating agent which disturbs the fundamental mechanism of cell reproduction, growth, and function.

The drug is supplied as a powder with accompanying diluent. After reconstitution solutions must be used immediately, and unused drug should be discarded. To prevent phlebitis and infiltration, mechlorethamine is injected into the tubing of a running intravenous infusion. Since the drug is a vesicant, the skin and eyes must be protected from contact with the powder or solution (see Table 11-1).

Administration of the drug may be accompanied by severe bone marrow depression, phlebitis and local tissue damage, hyperuricemia, alopecia, and, rarely, convulsions (see Table 11-1).

MERCAPTOPURINE (PURINETHOL)

Used in combination regimens for treatment of acute lymphoblastic leukemia. The POMP regimen is listed below.

   Mercaptopurine (Purinethol)
       with
   Methotrexate (Amethopterin)
   Vincristine (Oncovin)
   Prednisone (Deltasone)

Mercaptopurine is an antimetabolite which prevents the synthesis of nucleic acids.

The drug is supplied as oral tablets, and, if tolerated, can be administered as a single daily dose.

Concurrent administration of allopurinol (Zyloprim) may inhibit metabolism of mercaptopurine, thereby increasing its effects. When the two drugs are administered together the mercaptopurine dose is usually reduced by one-third to one-fourth (*Evaluations of Drug Interactions,* 1976, p. 148).

Delayed bone marrow depression, ulceration of gastrointestinal tract, hyperuricemia, liver damage, gastrointestinal upsets, and minor skin reactions may occur (see Table 11-1).

Table 11-2   Antineoplastic Drugs (*Continued*)

Drugs	Comments and Relevant Nursing Actions

METHOTREXATE (AMETHOPTERIN)

Effective for acute leukemia, Hodgkin's disease, and osteogenic sarcoma. The following combination is used for osteogenic sarcoma.

Methotrexate (Amethopterin) in high doses
with
Leucovorin (folinic acid) "rescue"
Cyclophosphamide (Cytoxan)
Doxorubicin (Adriamycin)

Methotrexate is an antimetabolite which inhibits biosynthesis of folate reductase.

The drug is dispensed as oral tablets and parenteral dosage form for intravenous, intrathecal, and intramuscular administration.

Concurrent administration of sulfonamides, aspirin, and phenytoin (Dilantin) may displace methotrexate from albumin binding sites thereby increasing its effects (*Evaluations of Drug Interactions,* 1976, pp. 156, 195).

Administration of intramuscular leucovorin within 6 h after high-dose methotrexate administration may reverse methotrexate-induced inhibition of folic acid antagonism, thereby preventing damage to normal cells. This interaction is termed "rescue" (*Evaluations of Drug Interactions,* 1976, p. 155).

Methotrexate administration may be accompanied by ulceration of the gastrointestinal tract, hyperuricemia, liver damage, and pulmonary infiltrations (see Table 11-1).

PROCARBAZINE HYDROCHLORIDE (MATULANE)

Effective as a component of the MOPP regimen listed below, which is used for advanced Hodgkin's disease.

Procarbazine (Matulane)
with
Mechlorethamine (Mustargen)
Vincristine (Oncovin)
Prednisone (Deltasone)

Procarbazine is not related to other antineoplastic agents, and while its mechanism of action is not clearly understood, there is evidence that the drug might inhibit synthesis of DNA and RNA.

The drug is supplied as capsules for oral administration.

Concurrent administration with adrenergic drugs (e.g., epinephrine) or tyramine-rich foods (e.g., Chianti wine, cheddar cheese) produces hypertensive crisis.

Table 11-2 Antineoplastic Drugs (*Continued*)

Drugs	Comments and Relevant Nursing Actions
	Procarbazine potentiates the central nervous system—depressant action of narcotics and sedatives.
	Ingestion of alcohol results in a syndrome characterized by headache, abdominal pain, nausea, and vomiting (Antabuse-like reaction).
	The drug may produce central nervous system toxicity, cutaneous reactions, gastrointestinal tract ulceration, gastrointestinal tract upsets, bone marrow depression, and, rarely, hemolysis with anemia (see Table 11-1).
VINCRISTINE SULFATE (ONCOVIN)	
Used in several combination regimens for treatment of Wilms's tumor, leukemia, Ewing's sarcoma, retinoblastoma, neuroblastoma, and rhabdomyosarcoma. The COAP regimen for leukemia is listed below.	Vincristine is a plant alkaloid derived from a flowering herb which disrupts mitosis and produces metaphase rest.
	The drug is supplied as sterile powder for reconstitution. To avoid phlebitis the drug is injected into the tubing of a running intravenous infusion (see Table 11-1).
Vincristine (Oncovin) *with* Cytarabine(Cytosar) Cyclophosphamide (Cytoxan) Prednisone (Deltasone)	The drug frequently causes long-lasting neurotoxicity, alopecia, phlebitis, and local tissue damage (see Table 11-1).

Administration

Mercaptopurine (Purinethol), cyclophosphamide (Cytoxan), and methotrexate (Amethopterin) are administered by the oral route; this route of administration does not increase the incidence of intestinal ulceration or gastrointestinal distress.

Bleomycin (Blenoxane) may be administered subcutaneously; while methotrexate (Amethopterin), and cytarabine (Cytosar) may be administered by the intramuscular route.

Some drugs can be administered by the intravenous route at a flowrate which can be adjusted according to the child's response. Highly irritating antineoplastic drugs [doxorubicin (Adriamycin), dactinomycin (Cosmegen)] are injected into the tubing of a running intravenous infusion. This method of administration decreases vein-drug contact time, thereby reducing the risk of thrombophlebitis and other local inflammatory reactions. It may be advisable to administer antineoplastic drugs which cause gastrointestinal upsets (anorexia, nausea, and vomiting) as a single intravenous injection, rather than as several small-dose infusions. Such administration produces an episode of nausea and vomiting, but it prevents the inconvenience and discomfort of repeated episodes.

Some antineoplastics are administered directly into the femoral or hepatic vein, and methotrexate (Amethopterin) is administered intrathecally for central nervous system leukemia.

Oral administration is usually the responsibility of the nurse; however, intravenous administration is usually performed by the physician. It is important that parenteral drugs be prepared, administered, and stored according to the recommendations of the manufacturer.

BIBLIOGRAPHY

AMA Department of Drugs: *AMA Drug Evaluations*, 3d ed., Publishing Sciences Group, Littleton, Mass., 1977.

Bingham, C. A.: The Cell Cycle and Cancer Chemotherapy," *American Journal of Nursing*, vol. 78, no. 7, 1978, pp. 1201–1205.

Bruya, M. A., and N. P. Madeira: "Stomatitis after Chemotherapy," *American Journal of Nursing*, vol. 75, no. 8, 1975, pp. 1349–1352.

Burns, N. B.: "Cancer Chemotherapy: A Systemic Approach," *Nursing '78*, February 1978, pp. 57–63.

"Cancer Chemotherapy," *The Medical Letter*, vol. 18, no. 26 December 17, 1976.

Evaluations of Drug Interactions, 2d ed., American Pharmaceutical Association, Washington, D.C., 1976.

Nirenberg, A.: "High-Dose Methotrexate for the patient with Osteogenic Sarcoma," *American Journal of Nursing*, vol. 76, no. 11, 1976, pp. 1776–1780.

Showfety, M. P.: "The Ordeal of Hodgkin's Disease," *American Journal of Nursing*, vol. 74, no. 11, 1974, pp. 1987–1991.

Vinciguerra, V., et al.: "A New Combination for Resistant Hodgkin Disease," *Journal of the American Medical Association*, vol. 237, no. 1, 1977, pp. 33–35.

12

Hormones

INSULIN

Insulin, a hormone secreted by pancreatic beta cells (islets of Langerhans), consists of two connected amino acid chains. The secretion and function of the hormone are interrelated with those of several other hormones (e.g., thyroid hormone, growth hormone, epinephrine, glucocorticoids). Functions of insulin include facilitation of glucose utilization, synthesis of protein, and both formation and storage of fats.

By virtue of its action on cell membranes, insulin promotes glucose entry into cells, where it provides a major source of energy. Insulin promotes protein synthesis from amino acids and also prevents protein catabolism. These actions combined with the protein-sparing effect of increased carbohydrate metabolism promote growth. Insulin also facilitates release of hepatic glucose and causes increase in hepatic glucose metabolism, two actions which decrease hepatic glycogen stores. The hormone prevents the mobilization of lipids (free fatty acids, cholesterol, triglycerides) from adipose tissue deposits.

Diabetes

Diabetes, a metabolic disorder in which there is a significant decrease in pancreatic production, requires administration of exogenous insulin, dietary modification, and life-long medical supervision.

In addition to hyperglycemia and glycosuria, in untreated diabetic children there is also accelerated protein catabolism and decreased protein synthesis (negative nitrogen balance). Untreated or poorly controlled diabetic children fail to thrive, and therefore are below average size.

Parent and Child Teaching   Parents and diabetic children must be taught all aspects of diabetic care including aseptic administration of insulin into deep subcutaneous fat, rotation of injection sites, recognition and prevention of insulin overdose, storage and preparation of insulin, storage of disposable needles and syringes, and sterilization and care of reusable needles and syringes (glass). The parents should understand that the child should carry a card or wear an identification bracelet identifying the child as a diabetic, and giving home address and clinic or physician's address. Teachers, scouting leaders, and other supervising adults should know the child is diabetic and that as such may require special attention in the event of changes in glucose levels. Orange juice, lump sugar, honey, or comparable glucose should always be readily available to the diabetic child. Parents should be taught how to administer intramuscular glucagon in the event of hypoglycemia.

Commercial Insulins (See Tables 12-1 and 12-2)

Insulin of common usage is a mixture of beef and pork extracts; however, single-beef or single-pork insulin are available on special order for children who require them. Pork insulin bears a closer similarity to the human hormone and also produces fewer hypersensitivity (allergic) reactions than does its beef counterpart.

Dosage of insulin is expressed in *United States Pharmacopeia* units rather than in milligrams, and the hormone is supplied in three concentrations: U-40 (40

Table 12-1 Rapid-Acting Insulins

Insulin	Time of Administration	Onset	Maximum Action	Duration	Comments and Relevant Nursing Actions
Insulin injection (regular, crystalline zinc)	15 to 30 min before meals	30 min	2 to 4 h	6 to 8 h	Regular and crystalline zinc insulin contain no modifying protein, and are used interchangeably for management of unstable diabetes, to "cover" glycosuria, and for emergency treatment of hypoglycemia or ketoacidosis.
					They are the only insulins which can be administered intravenously. Both preparations can be mixed with intermediate-acting insulins to supplement rapid action with intermediate action.
					These insulins should be stored in a refrigerator, and should not be administered unless they are water-clear.
Prompt insulin zinc suspension (Semilente)	30 to 45 min before meals	30 min	2 to 4 h	12 to 16 h	Prompt insulin zinc contains no modifying protein. Its small particles are rapidly absorbed; however, its duration of action is short.
					This preparation can be mixed only with other Lente insulins (Lente, Ultralente). It should not be injected into the vein, and it is not suitable for treatment of emergencies (hypoglycemia, ketoacidosis).
					It should be stored in the refrigerator, protected from freezing and light, and well dispersed (by gently rotating the vial) throughout the suspending fluid before withdrawal of the dose.
					Do not use if there is evidence of granular deposits, clumping, or solid particles adhering to sides of the vial.

Table 12-2 Intermediate-Acting Insulins

Insulin	Administration Time	Onset	Maximum Action	Duration	Comments and Relevant Nursing Actions
Isophane insulin suspension(NPH)	1 h before breakfast	2 h	8 to 10 h	28 to 30 h	Isophane insulin contains protamine, a modifying protein. It is compatible only with regular and crystalline zinc insulins, and it should not be injected into the bloodstream. NPH insulin is not used for emergencies. It is indicated for long-term control of stabilized diabetic children. While many children can be maintained on NPH insulin, hypoglycemic reactions may occur in mid to late afternoon. The drug should be refrigerated, and it must be protected from freezing. To ensure correct dosage NPH insulin must be well dispersed (by gently rotating vial) before withdrawal of the dose.
Insulin zinc suspension (Lente)	1 h before breakfast	2 to 4 h	8 to 12 h	20 to 26 h	Lente insulin contains no modifying protein; however, the drug can not be administered by the intravenous route. It is not used for emergency situations, and it can be mixed only with other Lente insulins. It is sometimes used interchangeably with NPH insulin. Hypoglycemia may occur in mid to late afternoon. The drug should be stored in the refrigerator, and must be protected from freezing and from light. To ensure accurate dosage the suspension must be well dispersed in the suspending fluid (by gently rotating vial) before withdrawing the dose.

Table 12-3   Glucagon

Drug and Dose	Comments and Relevant Nursing Actions
Glucagon for injection Usual pediatric dose: 25 μg/kg SC, IM, or IV; repeated in 20 min if necessary	A polypeptide hormone secreted by alpha pancreatic cells which elevates blood glucose by converting liver glycogen to glucose.
	The drug is administered parenterally (intravenously, intramuscularly, or subcutaneously) for emergency treatment of severe hypoglycemia in children unable to take oral carbohydrate (because of stupor confusion), or when intravenous dextrose can not be given.
	It is important that parents be taught the importance of having glucagon available, and that they be taught to prepare and administer the drug (Krupp, 1976, p. 738).
	While children are generally less responsive to glucagon than adult diabetics, response in children requires 15 to 20 min (Gutherie, 1977, p. 54). Failure of the child to respond indicates complete depletion of hepatic glycogen, and intravenous dextrose must be administered to avoid permanent brain damage. Since the effects of glucagon are short-lived, the child should receive oral carbohydrate (orange juice, sugar cube) as soon as she or he is able to swallow.
	Nausea and vomiting may occur after administration of glucagon to juvenile diabetics.
	The drug is supplied as a sterile powder with a special diluent and after reconstitution is stable for 3 months under refrigeration.

U/ml), U-80 (80 U/ml), and U-100 (100 U/ml). A special U-500 (500 U/ml) insulin is available, but it is seldom used for pediatric patients. The U-100 insulins were introduced in 1973 to eliminate the dosage errors arising from patient confusion by U-40 and U-80 calibrations on insulin syringes, to reduce injection volumes, and to acknowledge movement toward adoption of the metric system (Moss, 1977, 1823). After withdrawal of U-80 and U-40 insulins from the market, all insulin syringes and insulin preparations will be standardized at 100 U/ml.

Insulins are classified according to their onset and duration of action into the rapid-acting [regular, crystalline zinc, prompt insulin zinc suspension (Semilente)], the intermediate-acting (Lente, NPH), and the long-acting (PZI, Ultralente). Many pediatric patients receive rapid-acting and intermediate-acting insulins; however, the long-acting preparations tend to produce hypoglycemia during sleep and are seldom used for children.

Actual onset and duration of insulin activity varies according to the volume of the injection, concentration of the drug, and location and blood supply of the injection site.

Insulin Dosage

Dosage of insulin is carefully individualized by blood glucose determination, serial urine glucose determination, and clinical evaluation of the child. The severity of the diabetes, growth and developmental requirements, exercise, and diet are factors which affect dosage.

Mixing Insulins

Some children receive both a rapid-acting (regular insulin) and an intermediate-acting insulin at the same time. Such a combination produces a rapid onset and an intermediate duration of action. Not only are these insulin mixtures unstable, requiring preparation by the nurse or the parents, but the sequence in which the insulins are combined has a direct effect on the dose actually administered (Moss, 1977, 1823). A volume of air equal to the amount of insulin to be administered should be injected into each vial before withdrawing either insulin. The regular insulin should be withdrawn first, and after withdrawing the intermediate insulin, no attempt should be made to mix the two insulins within the syringe (Krupp, 1976, p. 734).

Errors in Dosage

Errors in dosage and errors in the proportion of each kind of insulin actually administered have been attributed to the space between the needle tip and syringe hub (dead space). The amount of dead space, which varies with manufacture of the needle from 0 to 10 units, may be particularly crucial when small dosages of insulin are administered or when two insulins are combined in the same syringe (Shainfeld, 1975, p. 302). Diabetics stabilized on one brand of syringe may have derangement of blood glucose levels when another brand of syringe is used in hospital or clinic settings. Moss reports that administration of rapid-acting and intermediate-acting insulin mixtures to healthy subjects produced little difference in serum insulin levels even when given under conditions reproducing dead space errors (Moss, 1977, p. 1824).

Storage

Insulin is stored in the refrigerator; however, it must be protected from freezing. Newer, highly purified insulins contain no foreign proteins which might precipitate; thus, these preparations can be supplied at neutral pH. These insulins can be mixed with other insulins, and they are said to cause fewer episodes of local inflammatory reactions, and fewer hypersensitivity (allergic) reactions.

Insulin suspensions contain insoluble particles which must be well dispersed to ensure accurate dosage. Gently rotating the vial avoids formation of froth and adequately mixes the suspension in the fluid.

Interactions

Concurrent ingestion of alcoholic beverages with insulin administration may result in severe hypoglycemia, coma, permanent central nervous system damage, and death (*Evaluations of Drug Interactions*, 1975, p. 242).

Children receiving glucocorticoids (e.g., prednisone) with insulin therapy may require an increase in insulin dosage (*Evaluations of Drug Interactions*, 1975, p. 39).

Adverse Reactions

Hypoglycemia, a common adverse reaction associated with insulin administration, may be due to delay or omission of meals, dosage error, or excessive physical exercise. The severity of this reaction is determined not only by the drop in blood glucose but also by the rate and duration of the drop.

Mild hypoglycemia is characterized by anxiety, abdominal pain, hunger, shortened attention span, and mood changes. Administration of orange juice, lump sugar, honey, or other readily absorbed dextrose is indicated for this reaction.

Severe hypoglycemia is evidenced by profuse perspiration, aggressive or combative behavior, headache, tremors, and confusion. Unless treated promptly the condition may terminate in coma, irreversible brain damage, or death. Oral dextrose should be given at first sign of severe hypoglycemia; however, it should never be poured into the mouth of an uncooperative or unresponsive child. Unconscious or uncooperative children should receive intramuscular glucagon, and when they have responded, oral dextrose should be administered (Vaughn and Mckay, 1975, p. 1267). After severe or prolonged hypoglycemia recovery of normal neurological function may require several hours or days.

Atrophy of subcutaneous fat (lipodystrophy) or hypertrophy of these tissues (lipohypertrophy) has been attributed to injection of highly acidic older insulins, injection of large volumes, and injection of insulins which contain impurities. While these areas generally return to normal over months or years, they are sources of great anxiety in older children and adolescents. The risk of these adverse reactions might be prevented by rotating injection sites so that no site is used more often than once every 3 weeks. Injection of a neutral, highly purified insulin into the affected tissues may restore the normal appearance (AMA Department of Drugs, 1977, p. 588).

Serious hypersensitivity reactions to insulin are uncommon; however, induration, pruritis, and erythema at the injection site occur occasionally. Use of pure pork insulin usually eliminates these reactions since the porcine hormone is chemically closer to human insulin and is thus less immunogenic.

After a period of chronic insulin administration, most diabetics develop antibodies to commercial insulins. Binding of these antibodies to insulin may result in decreased insulin effectiveness with an increase in insulin requirements. Decreased insulin binding at receptor sites may also explain some episodes of insulin resistance in obese diabetic children. Changing to insulin of a different species (e.g., pork or beef), gradual reduction of insulin dosage, or dividing the insulin dose may resolve this reaction.

ADRENOCORTICOSTEROIDS

The adrenal cortex produces glucocorticoids [hydrocortisone (cortisol), corticosterone], mineralocorticoids (aldosterone, desoxycorticosterone), and small amounts of testosteronelike androgenic hormones.

These corticosteroids permit the individual to cope with physiological, traumatic, psychological, and other types of stressors. Their functions are intricately interrelated with those of epinephrine, norepinephrine, and lipolytic hormones.

Glucocorticoids increase blood glucose concentrations and exert anti-inflammatory activity, while mineralocorticoids promote sodium retention and potassium excretion. Since most corticosteroids exert the activities of both groups, this division between glucocorticoids and mineralocorticoids is not well defined.

In addition to the above functions, glucocorticoids inhibit inflammatory responses, promote renal excretion of calcium, alter the protective barrier of the gastric mucous layer, increase collagen breakdown, modify hypersensitivity reactions, and limit bone growth and calcification.

Commercial Corticosteroids (See Tables 12-4 and 12-5)

Corticosteroids in clinical use include naturally occurring hormones and numerous synthetic preparations which are produced by altering the chemical structure of the parent drug. These drugs differ in anti-inflammatory activity, extent of sodium retention, and solubility. Hydrocortisone (cortisol), the most abundant naturally occurring glucocorticoid, is the standard against which naturally occurring and synthetically produced glucocorticoids are compared.

Glucocorticoids are administered by the oral, intramuscular, intravenous, and pulmonary routes (aerosol inhalation). They are also injected into joint spaces or lesions and administered rectally as retention enemas. (Topical application is discussed in Chap. 13.) Mineralocorticoids are administered intramuscularly, orally, and as slowly absorbed subcutaneous implants.

Indications Corticosteroids of both groups are indicated for replacement therapy in acute or chronic adrenal insufficiency (Addison's disease) and in adrenal insufficiency due to other disorders.

Administration of glucocorticoids is indicated for treatment of juvenile rheumatoid arthritis, rheumatic carditis, ulcerative colitis, and pemphigus vulgaris. They are also indicated for acute hypersensitivity reactions (serum sickness, angioedema, anaphylaxis), and for acute and chronic bronchial asthma which does not respond to other measures. These drugs are an important

Table 12-4   Corticosteroids Which Exert Primarily Mineralocorticoid Action

Drug	Comments and Relevant Nursing Actions
Fludrocortisone acetate (Florinef)	A hydrocortisone derivative which exerts potent salt-regulating (mineralocorticoid) action and moderate anti-inflammatory (glucocorticoid) action.
	The drug is supplied as tablets for oral administration.
	The adverse reactions associated with its salt-regulating actions (edema, hypertension, hypokalemia) limit its use to replacement therapy in Addison's disease and congenital adrenogenital syndromes.
Cortisone acetate (Cortone)	A naturally occurring corticosteroid, which exerts both salt-regulating (mineralocorticoid) action and anti-inflammatory action (glucocorticoid) action.
	Cortisone is supplied as tablets for oral administration, and as a sterile preparation for intramuscular injection.
	While it is used primarily for replacement therapy in adrenocortical deficiency states (Addison's disease, congenital adrenogenital syndromes), it is occasionally used for short-term treatment of inflammatory and allergic conditions.
	Edema, hypertension, and hypokalemia are not unusual during cortisone therapy.

part of the treatment of acute lymphocytic leukemia, Hodgkin's disease, and other malignancies. Their use in celiac sprue, nephrotic syndrome, and cerebral edema due to brain tumors is also warranted.

Cautions   Since these drugs lower the child's resistance to infection, they are not used in the presence of infection unless appropriate antibiotics are given or other measures are taken to control the infection. It is also important to point out that since they alter the inflammatory response, local and systemic indications of infection (fever, swelling, pain) do not occur even in the presence of severe infection.

Table 12-5 Corticosteroids Which Exert Primarily Glucocorticoid Action

Drug	Comments and Relevant Nursing Actions
Hydrocortisone-cortisol (Cortril, Solu-Cortef) Usual pediatric dose: 160 μg/kg to 1 mg/kg IM one or two times a day 140 μg/kg to 2 mg/kg PO four times a day	Hydrocortisone, the most abundant naturally occurring corticosteroid, is the standard against which the anti-inflammatory (glucocorticoid) and salt-regulating (mineralocorticoid) potency of other corticoids is compared. Its anti-inflammatory action is much less potent than that of newer synthetics [e.g., dexamethasone (Decadron)]; however, hydrocortisone exerts more potent salt-regulating action than do these newer drugs. Pituitary suppression produced by hydrocortisone is short-lived (Newton, 1977, p. 28). The drug is supplied as tablets for oral administration, solution for rectal administration (retention enema), and sterile preparations for intravenous, intramuscular, or intraarticular administration. Indications for use include replacement therapy in adrenal deficiency states and occasionally as short-term therapy for inflammatory disorders.
Prednisone (Meticorten, Deltasone) Usual pediatric dose: 35 to 500 μg/kg PO four times a day	A cortisone derivative which exerts more potent anti-inflammatory action and less potent salt-regulating action than does hydrocortisone. Prednisone may produce some edema and sodium retention with prolonged administration. The pituitary suppression produced by prednisone is of intermediate duration. The drug is supplied as tablets for oral administration. Prednisone is indicated for treatment of asthma, ulcerative colitis, nephrotic syndrome, juvenile rheumatoid arthritis, and neoplastic diseases (e.g., leukemias, Hodgkin's disease).
Prednisolone (Delta-Cortef, Hydeltrasol) Usual pediatric dose: 35 to 500 μg/kg PO four times a day 40 to 250 μg/kg IM or IV one or two times a day	A hydrocortisone derivative which exerts more potent anti-inflammatory and less potent salt-regulating action than does the parent compound. Since prednisolone differs from prednisone only in solubility, the two drugs are considered equivalents. The drug is available as tablets for oral administration and as a sterile preparation for intramuscular, intravenous, or intraarticular administration.

Table 12-5 **Corticosteroids Which Exert Primarily Glucocorticoid Action** (*Continued*)

Drug	Comments and Relevant Nursing Actions
Triamcinolone (Aristocort, Kenacort) Children over 6 years of age: 30 to 200 μg/kg IM, once daily to once weekly	A prednisolone derivative which exerts moderate anti-inflammatory action and minimal salt-regulating action. The pituitary suppression produced by triamcinolone is of intermediate duration. Triamcinolone is supplied as tablets and syrup for oral administration, and sterile preparations for intravenous, intramuscular, or intraarticular administration. The drug produces moderate edema in some children, and it is likely to cause muscular atrophy and osteoporosis (Newton, 1977, p. 33).
Dexamethasone (Decadron, Hexadrol) Usual pediatric dose: 6 to 85 μg/kg PO four times a day 6 to 40 μg/kg IM or IV one or two times a day	A prednisolone derivative which exerts remarkably potent anti-inflammatory and antihypersensitivity actions but very weak salt-regulating actions. Its pituitary suppression actions are of long-acting duration. Dexamethasone is available as tablets and elixir for oral administration, as solution for aerosol inhalation, and as preparations for intramuscular, intravenous, or intraarticular administration. The drug is used for treatment of inflammatory, hypersensitivity, and other disorders which respond to glucocorticoids (malignant disorders, cerebral edema). Parenteral administration of dexamethasone to a pregnant woman 24 to 72 h before delivery prevents respiratory distress syndrome in premature infants. The drug tends to increase appetite, and children gain weight as a result of this reaction. It is also likely to produce muscular wasting and osteoporosis (Newton, 1977, p. 33).

Corticosteroids suppress immune mechanisms; thus, administration of live vaccines (e.g., measles, mumps, rubella) or other immunizing agents [tetanus and diphtheria toxoids (Td)] is contraindicated during corticosteroid therapy.

Dosage   Dosage of corticosteroids is carefully individualized according to the severity of the disorder, clinical response to the drug, anticipated duration of drug therapy, and the potency of the drug. The child receives the smallest dose possible, and elimination of all signs and symptoms of the disorder is seldom possible. Close medical and nursing surveillance for early evidence of adverse reactions is essential for all children receiving corticosteroid therapy. Many children on long-term corticosteroid therapy receive the drug on alternate days, and after completion of therapy the drug dose is gradually reduced over 1 or more weeks to permit return of normal hormonal mechanisms.

Adverse Reactions   Adverse reactions are most likely to occur in children who receive large doses over a prolonged period of time. Daily administration of corticosteroids for approximately 1 week may suppress normal pituitary and adrenal function and leave the child unable to produce natural corticosteroids during stressful situations (infection, trauma, pain, etc.). Suppression of pituitary and adrenal function can be minimized by administering an intermediate-acting corticosteroid (e.g., prednisone) on alternate days, at a time of day when hydrocortisone levels are normally at their maximum (6 to 8 A.M.).

Children receiving corticosteroid therapy are highly susceptible to infections, and reactivation of dormant tuberculosis is not uncommon. Frequent evaluation of the child for bacterial, viral, and fungal infection is essential throughout the duration of the therapy. It is not unusual for children on long-term corticosteroid therapy to receive preventive therapy for tuberculosis.

While alternate-day administration of corticosteroids

may minimize suppression of growth, children on these drugs should always have accurate growth charts to assess their growth patterns.

Administration of corticosteroids may also result in elevated blood glucose levels and glycosuria. To avoid this reaction the urine is often tested for glucose and acetone (although ketosis does not usually occur) before meals and before bedtime.

Edema, hypertension, and hypokalemia secondary to sodium retention and potassium excretion by the kidney may occur, particularly with natural corticosteroids. Low-sodium diet, potassium supplementation, monitoring of blood pressure, and daily weighing may be required to assess the child for these reactions.

Negative nitrogen balance with muscle wasting may occur with long-term therapy. Administration of a high-protein diet, careful assessment of muscular function, and a program of muscle exercises may minimize this reaction.

Restlessness, euphoria, reversible psychosis, and convulsions have also occurred in children.

Peptic ulcer may result from administration of the corticosteroids; thus, careful assessment of the child for melena, hematemesis, and anemia are essential. This reaction can be prevented by administering an antacid just before and between corticosteroid doses (Newton, 1977, p. 32).

Osteoporosis secondary to urinary excretion of calcium occurs occasionally in nephrotic children who have received large corticosteroid doses for prolonged periods. Daily ambulation will decrease the risk of this reaction; however, the child must be assessed carefully for evidence of pathological fractures.

After completion of corticosteroid therapy children have developed increased intracranial pressure during gradual reduction of drug dose. Cataracts have also occurred in children who have received these drugs over a prolonged period of time.

Acne, thinning of skin, striae, hirsutism, menstrual disorders, and maldistribution of fat deposits (e.g., "buffalo hump") may also occur during administration of corticosteroids.

Interactions   Concurrent administration of phenobarbital or other barbiturate or phenytoin (Dilantin) may increase corticosteroid metabolism, thereby decreasing the drugs' effects. Administration of a potassium-losing diuretic [e.g., chlorthalidone (Hygroton)] may result in excessive potassium loss (Hansten, 1976, p. 149).

During long-term corticosteroid therapy the child should carry a card or other means of identifying him or her as a corticosteroid-dependent individual.

THYROID HORMONES

The thyroid gland produces thyroxine (T_4) and liothyronine (T_3), two hormones which promote metabolism of vitamins, proteins, carbohydrates, and fats. Since these hormones also promote protein anabolism, they are necessary for normal growth and development. The thyroid gland also produces calcitonin, a hormone which appears to lower serum calcium concentrations during periods of hypercalcemia.

Blood concentrations of thyroxine and liothyronine are controlled by hypothalamic and pituitary hormones, which stimulate the thyroid to produce thyroxine and liothyronine when concentrations of T_4 and T_3 decrease, and which suppress production of these hormones when their concentrations increase.

Thyroid Drugs (See Table 12-6)

Drugs used for thyroid-deficiency states include animal thyroid preparations (e.g., thyroid tablets), synthetic derivatives of thyroid hormones [e.g., liothyronine (Cytomel)], and mixtures of animal thyroid hormones with synthetically derived products [liotrix (Euthroid)].

While the various thyroid preparations differ in potency, price, and speed of onset, they exert identical metabolic and clinical actions.

Table 12-6 Thyroid Drugs

Drug and Dose	Comments and Relevant Nursing Actions

Thyroid tablets (Thyrocrine, Thy-span)
 	
  Usual pediatric dose: 4 mg/kg PO once daily
  In cretinism infants under 1 year of age should not receive less than 60 mg daily
	Thyroid hormone, obtained from animals slaughtered for food, consists of dried, cleaned, and powdered thyroid glands. The preparation contains not only thyroid hormones (T_3, T_4), which account for its therapeutic actions, but also other organic materials.
	
	It may be considered a crude, poorly standardized preparation; however, it is inexpensive, widely used, and generally well accepted by patients.
	
	The drug has a slow onset of therapeutic effects, and full effects might not be achieved for 1 to 2 weeks after initiation of thyroid hormone therapy. Since these effects are cumulative, they might persist for 1 or 2 months after cessation of administration.
	
	Thyroid hormone is supplied as tablets, enteric-coated tablets, and capsules for oral administration.
	
	The drug is administered once daily; however, since effects are cumulative, administration time can be individualized according to the child's daily schedule.

Liothyronine sodium tablets (Cytomel)
  Initial dose:
    Children weighing under 7 kg: 2.5 μg PO once daily
    Children weighing over 7 kg: 5 μg PO once daily increased in increments of 5 μg at weekly intervals until desired effect is obtained
  Maintenance dose: 15 to 20 μg PO once daily
	A synthetic preparation derived from a naturally occurring thyroid hormone (thyronine, T_3) which is highly purified and possesses the properties of the parent drug.
	
	It is the most rapid acting of the thyroid drugs, and has both a rapid onset of action and a short duration of activity.
	
	Liothyronine is useful in severe hypothyroid conditions when immediate effects are desired. The drug is also used in diagnosing thyroid disease (T_3 suppression tests).
	
	Rare allergic skin reactions have occurred. It is important to begin therapy with small doses and to increase dosage slowly to prevent overdosing the child.

Table 12-6 Thyroid Drugs (*Continued*)

Drug and Dose	Comments and Relevant Nursing Actions
	The drug is supplied as oral tablets, and once-a-day administration is recommended.
Levothyroxine sodium tablets (Letter, Synthroid) Usual pediatric dose: 6 μg/kg PO once daily Infants with cretinism should not receive less than 100 μg once daily	A synthetic thyroid preparation which is derived from thyroxine (T_4), a naturally occurring thyroid hormone. The drug is purified and maintains constant biologic activity, and therefore its effects may be more predictable than those of other thyroid drugs.
	The drug is variably and incompletely absorbed from the gastrointestinal tract, and as much as 30 to 40 percent may be excreted in the feces. Its onset of action is slower than that of liothyronine (Cytomel); however, its duration of action is longer.
	Levothyroxine is supplied as oral tablets, and once-a-day administration, preferably before breakfast, is recommended.
Liotrix (Euthroid, Thyrolar) Initial pediatric dose: Therapy is started with small doses and increased at intervals of every 2 weeks, according to clinical response and thyroid function tests Maintenance pediatric dose: Final maintenance dose determined by response to therapy	A mixture of two purified, synthetic thyroid hormones which consists of four parts T_4 (levothyroxine) to one part T_3 (liothyroxine). This constant ratio represents the normal secretion of the thyroid gland; thus, this drug is said to approximate normal thyroid function.
	During liotrix therapy results of thyroid function tests [T_3, T_4, protein-bound iodine (PBI)] are consistent with clinical response, and such tests can be used to assess effectiveness of the drug.
	The drug is supplied as oral tablets for once-a-day administration.

Dosage Dosage of these drugs must be carefully individualized according to the severity and duration of hypothyroid state, potency of the drug, and the child's clinical response. Since the hypothyroid child is very sensitive to thyroid preparations, therapy is started with a relatively small dose, and dosage is slowly increased until a maintenance dose is reached. Dosage is carefully assessed by clinical response (growth rate, changes in skin, etc.) and by laboratory determination of T_4 concentration.

Indications   Thyroid preparations are indicated for replacement therapy in hypothyroid states due to congenital hypothyroidism, juvenile acquired hypothyroidism, autoimmune thyroiditis, or other causes. Since permanent mental retardation results from prolonged hypothyroid states in infants and young children, early diagnosis and treatment are essential.

Effects   Administration of thyroid drugs promotes full mental and physical development of the hypothyroid child. Proper functioning of all organ systems, proper teething, and increase in metabolic rate occur with replacement therapy. The skin and hair return to normal, the child is alert, constipation is resolved, and the child's sleep patterns improve.

Drug therapy with thyroid preparations is contraindicated in the presence of untreated adrenal insufficiency.

Adverse Reactions   Overdose of thyroid drugs produces nervousness, insomnia, heat intolerance, fever, tremor, headache, vomiting, and diarrhea in children.

Interactions   Administration of thyroid hormone with cholestyramine resin (Questran) decreases absorption of the hormone. To avoid this interaction the two drugs should be administered 5 h apart (*Evaluations of Drug Interactions,* 1976, p. 239).

Thyroid drugs enhance the action of oral anticoagulants [e.g., warfarin (Coumadin)], and to prevent hemorrhage the prothrombin time must be closely monitored, and the dosage of the anticoagulant reduced if so indicated (*Evaluations of Drug Interactions,* 1976, p. 302).

BIBLIOGRAPHY

AMA Department of Drugs: *AMA Drug Evaluations,* 3d ed., Publishing Sciences Group, Littleton, Mass., 1977.

Evaluations of Drug Interactions, 2d ed., American Pharmaceutical Association, Washington, D.C., 1976.

Fonville, A. M.: "Teaching Patients to Rotate Injection Sites," *American Journal of Nursing,* vol. 78, no. 4, 1978, pp. 880–883.

Goodman, L. S., and A. Gilman: *The Pharmacological Basis of Therapeutics,* 5th ed., Macmillan, New York, 1975.

Gutherie, D. W.: "Exercise, Diets, and Insulin for Children with Diabetes," *Nursing '77,* February 1977, pp. 48–54.

Hallal, J. C.: "Thyroid Disorders," *American Journal of Nursing,* vol. 77, no. 3, 1977, pp. 418–432.

Hansten, P. D.: *Drug Interactions,* 3d ed., Lea & Febiger, Philadelphia, 1976.

Krupp, M. A., and M. J. Chatton: *Current Medical Diagnosis and Treatment,* Lange Medical Publications, Los Altos, Calif., 1976.

Moss, J. M.: "Commentary: U-100 Insulin, a Progress Report," *Journal of the American Medical Association,* vol. 238, no. 17, 1977, pp. 1823–1824.

Newton, D. W., et al.: "You Can Minimize the Hazards of Corticosteroids," *Nursing '77,* June 1977, pp. 26–33.

Shainfeld, F. J.: "Errors in Insulin Doses Due to the Design of Insulin Syringes," *Pediatrics,* vol. 56, no. 2, 1975, pp. 302–303.

Wolfe, L.: "Insulin: Paving the Way to a New Life," *Nursing '77,* November 1977, pp. 38–41.

Vaughn, V. C., and J. R. McKay: *Textbook of Pediatrics,* 10th ed., Saunders, Philadelphia, 1975.

13

Topical Agents

COMMON PEDIATRIC SKIN DISORDERS

Skin disorders in pediatric patients vary according to age, whether the child is toilet trained, and the hygienic practices of the mother. Sensitive, easily irritated skin, which may predispose the child to some skin disorders, will generally respond to changes in hygiene or to over-the-counter preparations. Replacing harsh laundry soaps or bath soaps with mild soaps (e.g., Ivory) and thorough rinsing of diapers and clothing may resolve the problem. Bathing the child with a nonsoap cleanser (e.g., Alpha-Keri), or a neutralized soap (e.g., Basis) may also reduce the risk of irritative skin disorders. Application of soothing creams will not only lubricate dry skin but also promote retention of natural moisture. Uncomplicated excoriation of the diaper area will usually respond to prompt changing of wet or soiled diapers; gentle, thorough cleansing of the skin; application of a protecting ointment (e.g., petroleum jelly); and elimination of plastic pants.

In infants and young children the most common skin disorders requiring topical agents include diaper dermatitis, atopic dermatitis (eczema), seborrheic dermatitis (e.g., cradle cap, dandruff), contact dermatitis, and fungal infections of mouth and skin folds (moniliasis).

Dermatologic disorders in older children include psoriasis, fungal infections [tinea capitis (scalp ringworm), tinea corporis (body ringworm), tinea pedis (athlete's foot)], and parasitic infections [pediculosis (lice infestation), scabies]. Adolescents also might have acne of varying severity.

Stages

These conditions vary in severity, duration, and the amount of discomfort and inconvenience they pose for the child. Acute conditions are characterized by oozing, swollen lesions which often burn and produce intense itching. While subacute dermatoses are less swollen and uncomfortable, there is some oozing and pruritis. Chronic conditions produce thickened, scaly lesions, which often are characterized by encrustations and fissures.

DRUGS FOR TOPICAL APPLICATION (See Table 13-1)

Topical agents consist of one or more active ingredients incorporated in a suitable vehicle. While the vehicle is usually inert, it may determine how effectively the drug remains in contact with the lesions and how effectively the drug is released. Many topical agents also include preservatives, emulsifiers, dispersing agents, and emollients which facilitate application to the skin. These drugs may be used alone, in combination with another topical agent, or with another treatment modality. Administration of systemic antibiotics, corticosteroids, and antihistamines has replaced use of topical agents for many acute and chronic skin disorders.

Topical preparations are used to relieve inflammation, to preserve moisture, to relieve itching, to promote shedding of hypertrophied skin layers, to protect and soothe irritated skin, and to eliminate infection and infestation.

(Text continued on page 363.)

Table 13-1   Drugs For Topical Application

Drug and Application	Comments and Relevant Nursing Actions
Hexachlorophene detergent lotion, Hexachlorophenl liquid soap, (pHisoHex, Soy-Dome cleanser): Applied topically to the skin as the sole detergent, followed by *thorough rinsing*	Hexachlorophene, a phenol derivative, is bacteriostatic for coagulase-positive *Staphylococcus,* most other gram-positive bacteria, and some fungi. Since the drug has been implicated in causation of fatal neurotoxicity in newborns and older children with burns, it has limited indications for use in pediatric patients. Although hexachlorophene exerts highly effective antibacterial activity against susceptible microorganisms, maximal action requires a relatively long period of time. After 2 to 4 days of repeated applications (i.e., two or more applications), a residual hexachlorophene film develops, and bacterial flora is reduced by as much as 95 to 99 percent. Application of alcohol or use of a nonhexachlorophene cleansing agent removes this residual film; consequently, growth of skin bacteria resumes rapidly. To avoid the risk of neurotoxicity, routine bathing of newborns with hexachlorophene is not recommended (Vaughn and McKay, 1975, p. 335; American Academy of Pediatrics, 1974, pp. 682–683). In the event of a newborn nursery staphylococcal outbreak, a total of two whole body baths with hexachlorophene 3% followed by a thorough rinse is indicated for full-term infants (American Academy of Pediatrics, 1974, p. 683). Since acne is often caused by gram-negative and anaerobic strains, use of hexachlorophene for this condition is no longer tenable. Hexachlorophene hand scrubs are used for nursery and other pediatric health workers to minimize risk of spreading contamination from the hands. The drug should not be applied to burn areas, denuded skin, or to mucous membranes. There are two official hexachlorophene preparations: detergent lotion with 3% hexachlorophene in an aqueous vehicle, and a liquid soap with 0.25% hexachlorophene in a potassium soap. An emulsion with 3% hexachlorophene and other compounds (pHisoHex) may be more effective than the same concentration of hexachlorophene in a soap solution (AMA Department of Drugs, 1977, p. 893).

Table 13-1 Drugs For Topical Application (*Continued*)

Drug and Application	Comments and Relevant Nursing Actions
	Over-the-counter products are no longer permitted to incorporate hexachlorophene; preparations which contain the drug require a prescription.
	Hexachlorophene is rapidly absorbed through intact skin; however, enhanced permeability of premature infants' skin results in increased absorption. Excessive absorption also is associated with application to burn areas, mucous membranes, and broken skin in patients of all age groups.
	The drug is apparently albumin bound, stored in body fat, and excreted in stool and urine. Estimated blood half-life is 10; however, laboratory blood concentrations do not necessarily reflect tissue hexachlorophene concentrations (Chilcote, 1977, p. 459).
	Although there is no agreement on concentrations or on the total number of applications which cause brain injury, it is agreed that excessive hexachlorophene blood concentrations have caused fatal encephalopathy in premature infants and children with burns. In premature infants the risk is related to birth weight, concentration of the drug, number of baths received, and thoroughness of the rinse (Shuman, 1974, p. 691).
	Hexachlorophene-associated neurotoxicity is characterized by irritability, lethargy, twitching, confusion, convulsions, respiratory arrest, and death.
	Allergic reactions are not common; however, dermatitis, photosensitivity (sensitivity to sunlight and ultraviolet lighting), and mild scaling may occur.
	Accidental ingestion of hexachlorophene is associated with nausea, vomiting, abdominal cramps, electrolyte disturbances, collapse, coma, and death. To avoid hexachlorophene ingestion, the drug should never be poured into cups or drinking glasses, or left within reach of children.
Povidone-iodine (Betadine, Isodine): Apply topically to skin or mucous	This topical antimicrobial preparation is a complex of organic iodine with a solubilizing agent, the former of which slowly releases free iodine in solution. Since the antibacterial activity is due to free iodine, the

Table 13-1   Drugs For Topical Application (*Continued*)

Drug and Application	Comments and Relevant Nursing Actions
membranes as the equivalent of a 0.75 to 1% solution of iodine	efficacy of the drug is directly related to the availability of such free iodine. While it is less irritating than aqueous and alcoholic solutions of iodine, it is not more effective against pathogens than the aqueous and alcoholic solutions.
	Povidone-iodine is a rapid-acting bacteriocide which is effective against bacteria, viruses, yeasts, and protozoa. The duration of its antimicrobial activity is approximately 6 to 8 h.
	The drug is used to prevent and treat infections of the skin, scalp, pharynx, vagina, and other mucous membranes. It can be applied directly to burns, abrasions, and lacerations, as well as to wounds. Shampoos for scalp applications and vaginal douches and gels for direct application are also utilized.
	Povidone-iodine is also used to remove skin microorganisms before injections, before aspiration of body cavities (e.g., paracentesis), and for routine skin care of venipuncture or hyperalimentation sites.
	It is also utilized to cleanse the skin before operative procedures.
	The drug is available in a variety of concentrations (0.05 to 10%), and the available iodine equivalent is less than the iodine concentration. Available iodine equivalent of a povidone-iodine preparation can be calculated by dividing the preparation's iodine concentration by 10 (Osol, 1975, p. 1098).
	A variety of aerosol sprays, ointments, shampoos, vaginal douches, vaginal gels, and other liquid forms are available.
	Application of povidone-iodine is not only less irritating than elemental iodine preparations but it is also nonsensitizing.
	Children who are hypersensitive to iodine might manifest fever, blistering, and crusting of application sites. Accidental ingestion causes nausea, vomiting, diarrhea, and, rarely, coma and respiratory arrest.

Table 13-1 Drugs For Topical Application (*Continued*)

Drug and Application	Comments and Relevant Nursing Actions
	Systemic absorption of povidone may be sufficient to produce alteration of laboratory tests for protein-bound iodine.
Zinc oxide ointment; Zinc oxide paste: Applied topically to skin as a 20 to 25% preparation	Zinc oxide is available as the official ointment and paste, and the drug is also included in numerous other topical preparations. These preparations include ointments, pastes, and powders, which use zinc oxide for its mild protective, astringent, and antiseptic action. Zinc oxide paste and ointment are applied to areas of diaper rash, and are used for treatment of eczema, impetigo, psoriasis, and ringworm. Addition of salicylic acid to the paste produces a product (Lassar's paste) which is effective for athlete's foot and other cutaneous fungal infections. Calamine lotion, Desitin ointment, and Caldesene ointment are commonly used preparations which include zinc oxide.
Gamma benzene hexachloride–lindane (Kwell, Gamene): Applied topically to the skin as a 10% preparation; may be repeated within 1 week if necessary	Lindane, a chlorinated hydrocarbon, is highly effective for treatment of scabies and pediculosis (lice). The 1% cream and lotion require a prescription; however, an over-the-counter spray for use on inanimate objects (e.g., linens, furniture, clothing, etc.) is also available. After application to the skin, the drug is slowly absorbed, and after a prolonged sojourn in the body, it is slowly excreted in the urine. Cutaneous absorption is greater in infants and young children; consequently, the drug might not be safe for this age group. Excessive or prolonged application of lindane has produced convulsions in children. Exposure to the drug as an insecticide spray or for treatment of pets has been associated with blood dyscrasis in humans ("Kwell and Other Drugs," 1977, p. 19). Contact dermatitis has occurred after repeated application of the drug. To ensure maximal effectiveness, lindane should be applied according to the manufacturer's recommendations.

Table 13-1   Drugs For Topical Application (*Continued*)

Drug and Application	Comments and Relevant Nursing Actions
Hydrocortisone acetate ointment (Cortef, Pramosone): Applied topically to the skin as a 0.5 to 2.5% ointment, one to four times a day	A relatively inexpensive steroid which exerts moderate topical anti-inflammatory activity with minimal systemic effects. While other more expensive and more potent topical corticosteroids are available, they do not offer any advantages over hydrocortisone. The drug is indicated for treatment of contact dermatitis, eczematous eruptions, psoriasis, diaper dermatitis, and selected seborrheic lesions. Hydrocortisone and other topical corticosteroids are contraindicated for use in children with viral skin disease, and for those with circulatory impairment. The effectiveness of the drug is increased by applying the preparation beneath a sheet of clear plastic; however, this also increases systemic absorption. Excessive absorption of hydrocortisone may result in suppression of adrenal function. Cutaneous bacterial or yeast infection may occur with long-term use of topical hydrocortisone. The child must be closely evaluated for signs of such infection, and any infection must be treated promptly. Preparations of hydrocortisone with antibacterial or antifungal agents might be prescribed for these infections. Local burning, skin atrophy, and irritation are rare with hydrocortisone application.
Clotrimazole cream or solution (Lotrimin): Apply cream or solution to affected areas twice daily, morning and evening (AMA Department of Drugs, 1977, p. 833)	A broad-spectrum antimicrobial drug which is active against fungi (tinea capitis, tinea corporis, tinea pedis) and several gram-positive bacteria. The drug is used to treat scalp ringworm, body ringworm, athlete's foot, and moniliasis. It also is used to treat mixed fungal and bacterial infections. Supplied as a 1% cream or solution, clotrimazole may produce blistering, peeling, edema, or stinging. The drug should be discontinued in the presence of these adverse reactions, and accidental application to the eyes must be avoided.
Coal tar (Zetar emulsion, Lavatar tar bath,	Coal tar, a by-product of bituminous coal distillation, exerts antipruritic, antiseptic, antiseborrheitic, and mild

Table 13-1   Drugs For Topical Application (*Continued*)

Drug and Application	Comments and Relevant Nursing Actions
Estar gel): Use as directed by the physican	irritative actions. The drug loosens and softens both crusts and scales and promotes return of normal keratinization.
	It is used alone to treat chronic atopic dermatitis, seborrhea, eczema, and other conditions associated with itching or epithelial proliferation. Coal tar is also used alone or with ultraviolet therapy to treat psoriasis.
	The drug is available in concentrations of 2 to 10%, as lotions, bath emulsions, gels, shampoos, ointments, and soaps.
	Coal tar preparations should not be applied to open or inflamed areas.
	The drug has a characteristic, unpleasant odor, and may stain hair and skin.
	Since the drug is phototoxic, exposure of treated areas to sunlight should be avoided unless otherwise prescribed by the physician.
	While local irritation after application is rare, the drug should be discontinued should this reaction occur.
	Some coal tar preparations for the bath may stain plastic or fiberglass bathtubs.
Sulfur and salicylic acid (Acne-Dome, Ex-zit, Fostex): Use according to directions of product	Numerous creams, lotions, cakes, cleansers, and shampoos containing 2% sulfur and 2% salicylic acid are used for treatment of acne and seborrhea.
	While the sulfur dries excess oil and promotes loosening of blackheads, the salicylic acid loosens cornified epithelium, peels away dead skin, and exerts a slight antiseptic action.
	These preparations should not be applied to inflamed, cystic, or nodular acne lesions, and they should be discontinued if excessive drying or irritation occurs.
Sulfur and benzoyl peroxide (Sulfoxyl, Epi-Clear, Vanoxide):	Lotions, creams, gels, and cleansing preparations containing benzoyl peroxide are used for acne vulgaris and acne rosacea.

Table 13-1 Drugs For Topical Application (*Continued*)

Drug and Application	Comments and Relevant Nursing Actions
Use according to directions of product	The benzoyl peroxide liberates active oxygen and exerts mild antimicrobial action against anaerobic strains. Its mild irritative action results in peeling of cornified epithelium and drying of excessive oils.
	While the first applications usually produce stinging or burning sensations, these usually decrease in intensity with continued use. The skin of the neck and circumoral areas is generally very sensitive to these preparations, and the eyes and mucosa should be avoided. These preparations should not be used concurrently with harsh, abrasive cleansers or on children.
	Local irritative reactions, bleaching of hair or fabrics, and excessive drying may accompany use of these preparations. All benzoyl peroxide–containing preparations should be stored in a cool place.

Vehicles

Vehicles in common use include wet compresses, creams, lotions, gels, pastes, and ointments. Selection of one vehicle over another is dependent upon the stage and severity of the skin condition, its location, and the physical and chemical characteristics of drug and vehicle. Some topical drugs are available in two or more vehicles.

During the acute stage of the skin disorder, open, wet compresses of sodium bicarbonate, colloidal oatmeal, magnesium sulfate, colloidal starch, or another ingredient can be applied to any body site several times a day. These compresses cleanse the lesions, help drain exudate, provide evaporative cooling, and relieve itching.

Creams (e.g., Lotrimin cream) are semisolid emulsions that can be applied to moist, hairy areas or to skin folds during the subacute stage. They not only provide lubrication for dry skin but also promote retention of moisture.

Lotions (e.g., Solfoxyl lotion) are liquid suspensions of dry drugs in a liquid vehicle. They are intended for external application to nonhairy skin surfaces during the acute phase. After evaporation of the liquid vehicle the active drug remains on the skin, where it provides protection or antipruritic action. To ensure adequate dispersion of solid particles throughout the liquid portion of the preparation, the lotion must be well shaken before each use.

Gels (e.g., Estar gel) are semisolid preparations consisting of a suspension within a liquid. They are suitable for use on both hairy and nonhairy areas, and some gels have a tendency to produce drying and burning.

Pastes (e.g., zinc oxide paste) are ointmentlike preparations which consist of a fine powder in an ointment base. Suitable for application to nonhairy areas during both subacute and chronic stages, pastes provide excellent protection.

Ointments (e.g., Cortef ointment) are semisolid preparations which are more greasy than both creams and pastes. During the chronic stage small amounts of ointments can be applied to all skin surfaces for lubrication and to promote retention of moisture.

Application

Drugs intended for application to skin surfaces should be kept away from the eyes, eyelids, and other sensitive areas. Since some of these preparations are irritants, they are not applied to mucous membrane surfaces or to the neck or lips. To avoid irritation and discomfort it is important that the drug be applied according to the directions of the package insert or the dispensing pharmacist. During topical therapy skin surfaces should be inspected frequently for excessive drying, peeling, and irritation. In the event that these reactions occur, the drug should be withheld and the physician notified.

Since the skin of the neonate does not present a barrier to absorption of topical drugs, newborns must be carefully assessed for systemic effects associated with topical therapy.

BIBLIOGRAPHY

American Academy of Pediatrics: "Skin Care of Newborns," *Pediatrics,* vol. 54, no. 6, 1974, pp. 682–683.

AMA Department of Drugs: *AMA Drug Evaluations,* 3d ed., Publishing Sciences Group, Littleton, Mass., 1977.

Chilcote, R., et al.: "Hexachlorophene Storage in a Burn Patient Associated with Encephalopathy," *Pediatrics,* vol. 59, no. 3, 1977, pp. 457–459.

Derbes, V. J.: "Rashes: Recognition and Management," *Nursing '78,* vol. 8, no. 3, 1978, pp. 54–59.

"Desoximetasone and Other Corticosteroids," *The Medical Letter,* vol. 19, no. 21, October 21, 1977, pp. 85–86.

Glass, G. K.: "Skin Rashes in Infants and Children," *American Journal of Nursing,* vol. 78, no. 6, 1978, pp. 1–32.

Goodman, L. S., and A. Gilman: *The Pharmacological Basis of Therapeutics,* 5th ed., New York, Macmillan, 1975.

"Kwell and Other Drugs for Treatment of Lice and Scabies," *The Medical Letter,* vol. 19, no. 4, February 25, 1977, pp. 18–20.

Matus, N. R.: "Topical Therapy: Choosing and Using the Proper Vehicle," *Nursing '77,* November 1977, pp. 8–10.

Osol, A., et al. (eds.): *Remington's Pharmaceutical Sciences,* 15th ed., Mack Publishing Co., Easton, Pa., 1975.

Shuman, R. M.: "Neurotoxicity of Hexachlorophene in the Human: I. A Clinicopathologic Study of 248 Children," *Pediatrics,* vol. 54, no. 6, 1974, pp. 689–694.

Vaughn, V. C., and J. R. McKay: *Textbook of Pediatrics,* 10th ed., Saunders, Philadelphia, 1975.

Index

Page numbers in *italic* indicate tables.